CRITICAL PRAISE FOR CAROL WHITE'S
CATSKILL PEAK EXPERIENCES

Anyone who has hiked in the Catskill Mountains can relate to the adventures chronicled in the book. … Besides being entertaining, this book is a good resource for hikers who would like to learn more about the Catskills. Even nonhikers will enjoy the tales of wilderness adventure in our "local" mountains. **TrailWalker**

The book serves as an excellent resource for hikers or anyone who wants to learn more about this beautiful mountain range. But even serious couch potatoes will enjoy the nonstop action and high drama of these tales of the ultimate wilderness adventure. **Hudson Valley magazine**

A 304-page collection of informative, entertaining, absorbing, and often incredible personal tales of triumph in local mountain climbing.
Hudson Valley Newspapers

Carol White covers 3500 Club history, strenuous marathons, misadventures, meeting wildlife, weather, winter, being lost and navigating in the wilderness. Having experienced bits of all of those scenarios, I recommend that you read this book as you begin or continue to hike the magnificent Catskills. The episodes and narration will save you the anguish that befell others that fortunately survived to hike another day.
Joe Gardner, Outings Chair, Sierra Club Hudson-Mohawk Group

The Catskills have provided and will continue to provide, as evidenced in the stories that White has assembled, a rare opportunity to explore the uncharted, to experience a true wilderness adventure, and to challenge one's abilities   Reading these stories will instill an appreciation for the many wilderness resource provides.
William (Bill) Rudge, Natural Resourc
New York State Department of Envir

D1557520

It is said: The shortest distance between two people is a story. As I read *Catskill Peak Experiences,* I connect with its many storytellers; I feel a special kinship among those who hike the Catskills. While I relish reading recounts of faraway Himalayan expeditions by Herzog, Viesturs, and Krakauer, it is these vignettes of Catskill climbers that are most real to me.
Skip Doyle, Conservation Chair, New York–North Jersey Chapter,
Appalachian Mountain Club

ADIRONDACK PEAK
E·X·P·E·R·I·E·N·C·E·S

MOUNTAINEERING ADVENTURES, MISADVENTURES, AND THE PURSUIT OF "THE 46"

Compiled and Edited by
Carol Stone White

BLACK·DOME

Published by

Black Dome Press Corp.
1011 Route 296, Hensonville, New York 12439
www.blackdomepress.com   Tel: (518) 734–6357

First Edition Paperback 2009

ISBN-13: 978-1-883789-63-3
ISBN-10: 1-883789-63-X

Library of Congress Cataloging-in-Publication Data

Adirondack peak experiences : mountaineering adventures, misadventures, and
the pursuit of the 46 / compiled and edited by Carol Stone White. — 1st ed.
paperback 2009.
    p. cm.
Includes bibliographical references.
ISBN 978-1-883789-63-3 (trade paper)
  1. Hiking—New York (State)—Adirondack Mountains—Anecdotes.
  2. Mountaineering—New York (State)—Adirondack Mountains—Anecdotes.
  3. Trails—New York (State)—Adirondack Mountains—Anecdotes. I. White, Carol, 1940–

GV199.42.N652A3427 2009
796.52'2097475—dc22
                        2009005853

Front cover: *Neil Luckhurst topping out on the Snowy Mountain Slide.*
  Photograph by Tom Haskins.
Adirondacks map: Ron Toelke
Design: Toelke Associates
Printed in the USA

10 9 8 7 6 5 4 3 2 1

CAUTION

Outdoor recreational activities are by their very nature potentially hazardous
and contain risk. All participants in such activities must assume the responsibility for their own actions and safety. No book can replace good judgment.
The outdoors is forever changing. The author and publisher cannot be held
responsible for inaccuracies, errors, or omissions, or for any changes in the
details of this publication, or for the consequences of any reliance on the information contained herein, or for the safety of people in the outdoors.

Rocky Peak in the Adirondack High Peaks. Photo by David White.

CONTENTS

GEOGRAPHICAL INDEX TO THE STORIES

BY STORY NUMBER

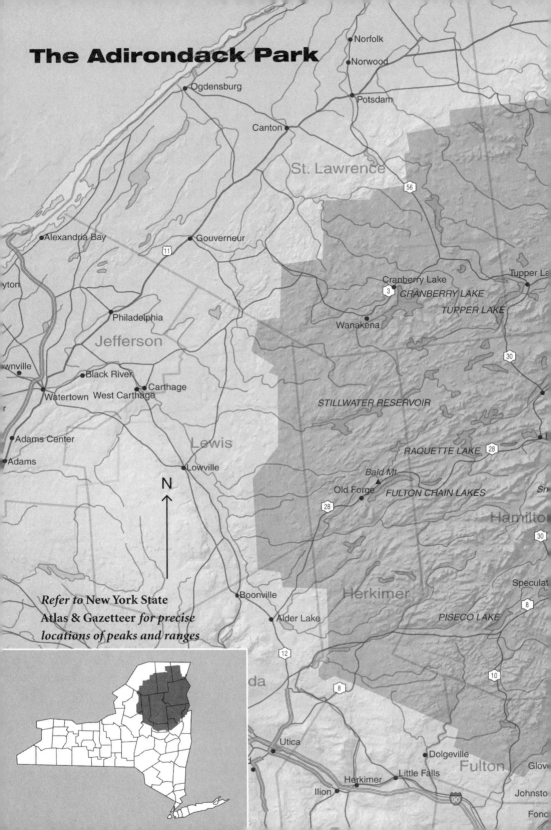

The Adirondack Park

Refer to New York State Atlas & Gazetteer for precise locations of peaks and ranges

Norfolk
Norwood
Ogdensburg
Potsdam
Canton
St. Lawrence
56
Alexandria Bay
Gouverneur
11
Cranberry Lake
Tupper L
3 CRANBERRY LAKE
TUPPER LAKE
Philadelphia
Wanakena
Jefferson
30
Black River
Carthage
Watertown West Carthage
STILLWATER RESERVOIR
Adams Center
Lewis
RAQUETTE LAKE 28
Adams
Lowville
Bald Mt.
Old Forge FULTON CHAIN LAKES
N
28
Hamilto
30
Boonville
Sp
Speculat
Alder Lake
Herkimer
PISECO LAKE 8
12
da
8
10
Utica
Dolgeville
Little Falls Fulton
Herkimer
Glov
Ilion 90
Johnsto
Fond

FOREWORD

Adirondack Peak Experiences is a wonderfully written and compiled anthology of hiking and mountaineering adventures in the Adirondacks, especially its peerless High Peaks region. Carol Stone White is the perfect person to assemble this remarkable collection of true stories. She is a very experienced mountaineer and hiking leader. She and her husband and constant hiking partner David care deeply about our Adirondack Mountains, preserved "forever wild" under our state constitution. They are long-time members and leaders of the Adirondack Mountain Club, have climbed all 46 Adirondack High Peaks and became members of the exclusive fraternity of Winter 46ers in 1997. Carol believes deeply that if people appreciate nature and wild places, they will use their voices, words and votes to protect those precious places. To appreciate nature, especially the mountains, you must embrace them. You must experience them in all of their glory, their dangers and moods.

This then is a book about men and women who venture out in all seasons and in all weathers to explore the mountains. This is a book of true accounts, of real adventures and yes, some misadventures. All the accounts are instructive. I have hiked and climbed in the Adirondacks and in the High Peaks for four decades. Many of the most experienced and knowledgeable people that I have met on the trails and summits tell their stories in this book. I found myself vividly reliving my own hikes and climbs as I read their accounts.

I recalled what it was like to be snowshoeing from Winter Camp in the Johns Brook Valley to the summit of Haystack in a party of five, breaking trail in nearly two feet of fresh powder, trying to persuade the indomitable leader to relinquish the lead so we would all get our turn for the glory and the warmth! I recall using the last of the water from my water bottle to begin to melt snow while winter camping on a 30 below weekend on the top of the Seward Range. I can picture the wide smile of my friend Alan Via as he munched cold pizza on a 100-mile visibility February day on the summit of Basin.

This book is an invitation, as the pages fly by; you cannot escape the growing desire to get out there, to be part of it. You will begin to think about maps and routes, about companions and destinations. Lace up your boots, load your pack and find a mountain to climb, for that is the subliminal message of this book. Even experienced hikers and mountaineers will learn from the true accounts that enliven and enrich this collection of adventures.

Newcomers to our sport will garner a treasure trove of valuable knowledge—hard-earned lessons from the actual field experiences of some of the most preeminent and well-travelled of the men and women that live to summit our Adirondack peaks and explore the region's magnificent forests and lakes. You gain their insight and mountain lore from the comfort and safety of your armchair. You will learn what it takes to make good decisions for yourself and your companions on mountainside and summit from the accumulated wisdom of this book.

Carol White skillfully plants the seed and lights the fire. She inspires us all to get on the trail. The men and women that populate these pages share a healthy, fulfilling shared pleasure. She knows that you will succumb to the lure of the mountains, their lovely grandeur in all weathers and in all seasons. She knows you will be drawn into the fellowship of the trail and the summit. She knows you will give back to the mountains by working on the trails, teaching a child a love of nature or raising your voice to protect wilderness.

Good climbing and see you on the trail, onward and upward to the summit.

Neil F. Woodworth
Executive Director and Counsel,
Adirondack Mountain Club
February 2009

ACKNOWLEDGMENTS

I am indebted to the many gifted writers whose tales of adventure and exploration in this book will, I hope, tempt readers to discover the exciting life of hiking and mountaineering. In these pursuits, not only do we experience the grandeur and perils of the wild world, but we also develop long-lasting friendships, discover delightful new qualities in our loved ones, and learn much about our own strengths and interdependence as we explore and challenge ourselves in new ways.

Great thanks to Neil Woodworth of the Adirondack Mountain Club (ADK) for devoting valuable time to reading *Adirondack Peak Experiences* and offering important commentary in his foreword to this anthology. His study and exploration of the Adirondack and Catskill Forest Preserves, combined with decades of advocacy and public education through ADK, have gone far to ensure that these areas shall "be forever kept as wild forest lands." I am honored that he is part of this work.

I also thank Tony Goodwin, editor of ADK's authoritative *Adirondack Trails: High Peaks Region* since 1984 and author of several ADK ski touring guides, and Russell Dunn, *Adirondack Waterfall Guide* author and coauthor of *Adirondack Trails With Tales*, for generously contributing their insights and commentary.

I would like to express my deep appreciation to Neil Luckhurst, (cofounder ADK Highpeaks Foundation, www.adkhighpeaks.com/forums) for providing a striking photograph for the front cover and for generously sharing many spectacular photographs to illustrate stories about the Adirondack Mountains in all seasons. I also thank Steve Boheim and Bill Ingersoll for sharing some of their extensive collection of enticing photographs.

For providing striking photos of the natural world and images of historical and human interest, thank you, also, to John Kettlewell of the Adirondack Mountain Club, Nancie Battaglia, Glen Bladholm, Ronnie Cusmano, Robert Goodwin, Ed Hale and the Watertown Daily Times, Brian Hoody, Dan Kriesberg, Al Laubinger, Paul Misko, Denise Mongillo, Adam Morrell, Spencer Morrissey, Jay O'Hern, Ira Orenstein, Heidi Rockwell, Richard Sederquist, Arlene Heer Stefanko, Anita Stewart, Belinda Spinner Taylor, David White, and Robert Wright.

Thanks to Andrea Masters of ADK for permission to reprint stories from Adirondac magazine, and to the executive committee of the Adirondack Forty-Sixers organization for permission to reprint stories from *Peeks* magazine. Deborah

Allen, owner and publisher of Black Dome Press, and editor Steve Hoare have offered great skills, conscientiousness, and reliable communication in making a manuscript into a beautiful book.

I appreciate the diligence of proofreaders Matina Billias and Natalie Mortensen. I thank Jack Freeman and Bruce Wadsworth for their overview of the history and programs of the Adirondack Mountain Club, Robert Ringlee for historical information, and Phil Corell for reviewing and adding information about the Adirondack Forty-Sixers organization.

Most of all I am grateful for my husband David's great good humor, patient encouragement and kindness on the trails to keep me stretching the boundaries of what I think possible, with innumerable rich rewards. Discovering new paths on this journey of life with Dave has been a true peak experience.

PREFACE

T his book is dedicated to those inspired lovers of the wild who write about the natural world. Through their insight and eloquence, we learn about the relationship between humanity and the greater web of life and, perhaps, we follow them and venture into the wilderness. Ralph Waldo Emerson wrote, "One comes out of the wrangle of the shop and office, and sees the sky and the woods, and is a man again ... he finds himself." John Muir observed, "Thousands of tired, nerve-shaken, over-civilized people are beginning to find out that going to the mountains is going home." Naturalist John Burroughs believed that regular retreat to the natural world is the catalyst for a return to simplicity and reverence. "Nature we have always with us, an inexhaustible storehouse of that which moves the heart, appeals to the mind, and fires the imagination—health to the body, a stimulus to the intellect, and a joy to the soul," he wrote. Poet William Blake experienced "Heaven in a wild flower, Eternity in an hour." Henry David Thoreau could hardly contain himself: "The indescribable innocence and beneficence of nature—of sun and wind and rain, of summer and winter—such health, such cheer, they afford forever!" Thoreau wrote that it was not until later, after the hike, that he really went over the mountain—reflecting on the experience.

In *Adirondack Peak Experiences*, lovers of the Adirondacks write about their adventures in gripping detail and attempt to explain why, in spite of myriad difficulties, they keep coming back for more. As they share a bit of their lives with us, many write about "being hooked" during a special day in the mountain wilderness and how these transforming experiences change much of what they do and value. This may be the meaning of Thoreau's enigmatic statement, "In wildness is the preservation of the world." Reading about adventuring may inspire us to leave the malls and walls and, as Emerson believed, gain greater understanding of nature and human nature in the wild world.

Many of these are cautionary tales, however, about Mother Nature's unforgiving side should we venture into her realm unprepared. *Adirondack Peak Experiences* is a book of true stories with some hard-earned advice, but it is not a guidebook. I strongly recommend the books to be found in "Suggestions for Further Reading" for their essential tips on wilderness safety. Experience is the best teacher, but secondhand experience through reading the accounts in this book can be almost as enlightening. Many tales have been written by some of the most experienced mountaineers in the Northeast yet, as you will soon see, they nonetheless became injured, suffered hypothermia or frostbite, ventured out in dangerous weather, underestimated the equipment and sustenance necessary to survive the unforeseen, got lost, and miscalculated the time required to hike difficult terrain. Hiking clubs such as the Adirondack Mountain Club, The Adirondack Forty-Sixers, the Sierra Club, the Appalachian Mountain Club, the Catskill 3500 Club, the Catskill Mountain Club, and Rip Van Winkle Hikers provide knowledge about hiking and, through their group hikes, the safety of numbers.

THE ADIRONDACKS

The Adirondack region features the only mountains in the eastern United States that are not geologically Appalachian; rather, they are the southern appendage of the vast, billion-year-old Canadian Shield. Precambrian igneous and metamorphic bedrock is exposed in the geologically young Adirondacks, which are slowly rising by a few millimeters per century. Yosemite's Half Dome and the Black Hills of South Dakota are other examples of upward doming, which results from a welling up of magma that, unlike volcanoes, does not reach the surface. The molten rock pushes upward into great bulges, and the magma hardens into rock. Then, the softer rock cover above the dome is gradually worn away by erosion. The Adirondack High Peaks, 15 percent of the Forest Preserve, consist of anorthosite rock—gray-blue plagioclase feldspar formed many miles below the Earth's surface. This rock, interestingly, closely resembles lunar rock.

The Adirondacks remained largely unexplored until the 1830s. Mount Marcy, the state's highest peak at 5,344 feet, was first climbed in 1837. By 1850 the vast forest was being harvested rapidly; New York led the nation in timber production. Following Verplanck Colvin's survey of the High Peaks in the 1870s, the New York State Legislature created the Adirondack and Catskill Forest Preserves in 1885, deeming that these areas shall "be forever kept as wild forest lands." The Adirondack State Park was created in 1892 by the legislature and comprises six million acres (as large as the State of Vermont) including both private and public land, delineated on maps with a blue line. In 1894, in response to continuing abuses of the "forever wild" law, the citizenry gave constitutional protection to its wild lands and remains the only state to do so. Article XIV mandates that the Forest Preserve lands in the Adirondacks and Catskills "shall not be leased, sold, or exchanged, or be taken by any corporation, public or private, nor shall timber thereon be sold, removed, or destroyed."

The "forever wild" Adirondack Forest Preserve—owned by the citizens of New York State—includes 2.5 million acres and constitutes about 40 percent of the Adirondack Park, the largest park in the lower forty-eight states. The Adirondacks include both the largely coniferous northern boreal forest and the southern deciduous forest with an attractive mix of many species. The High Peaks of the Adirondacks feature rare and fragile alpine plants and flowers usually found hundreds of miles to the north. The Adirondack arctic-alpine zone, marked by signs, is a unique natural region in New York State. Its rare flowers, mosses, lichens and grasses are virtually irreplaceable if trampled upon. Conditions above timberline are often near-arctic in winter, and true winter conditions can begin in early November and last until May. Summer temperatures in the High Peaks drop below freezing at night, and snow or ice is not uncommon most months of the year.

THE ADIRONDACK MOUNTAIN CLUB

by John P. Freeman and Bruce C. Wadsworth

History

In January 1921, Meade Dobson, secretary of the Palisades Interstate Park Conference, innocently but illegally caught a trout through the ice of a pond near Utica. He bragged about it to a friend who was the chief game protector for the New York State Conservation Commission. Partly in good humor, Dobson was hauled before Conservation Commissioner George Pratt, who assessed a small fine. Dobson took advantage of the occasion to discuss the inadequate recreational hiking system in the Adirondacks and suggested that a club be formed to organize a state trail system, as the Appalachian Mountain Club and the Green Mountain Club had done elsewhere. New York had appropriated land from lumber companies that had refused to pay taxes after logging the Adirondack forest, and Dobson said that their abandoned logging roads could be the basis of a recreational trail network.

Pratt asked his assistant, William G. Howard, to form a club with Dobson and, in December 1921, forty people met at the "Log Cabin" on the roof of Abercrombie & Fitch in New York City. On April 3, 1922, 208 charter members of the Adirondack Mountain Club (ADK) elected Pratt president and Dobson vice president, and the Certificate of Incorporation was signed on April 29. Former Governor of New York State Franklin Delano Roosevelt, Wilderness Society founder Bob Marshall, United States Supreme Court Justice William O. Douglas, and the first chief of the United States Forest Service, Gifford Pinchot, participated in founding the Adirondack Mountain Club.

Seven of the eight Objects of the Club focused on trails. By November, ADK had cut the 135-mile Northville-Placid Trail, formed the Albany Chapter, and had 583 members. The New York Chapter was organized in 1923, and the Glens Falls Chapter in 1928.

ADK was founded, in part, to help protect the "forever wild" Forest Preserve of the Adirondacks and the Catskills and to provide for responsible recreational use on them. The eighth objective of the Club dealt with conservation, and today the Club's 30,000 members in twenty-five chapters have expanded this mission to include other state parks and wild lands.

ADK Lodges

Conservation Commissioner Pratt wanted to encourage public recreational use of the Forest Preserve so that people would come to value the Preserve and wish to protect it. A destination for hikers in the Adirondack High Peaks was needed. In 1922 the commission's superintendent of forests, Clifford Pettis, approached the J & J Rogers Company concerning New York State's purchase of the company's land in Johns Brook Valley. When that land became Forest Preserve, it would no longer be possible legally to create a lodge there. The company offered ADK a small parcel prior to the state's purchase, and ADK's Johns Brook Lodge was constructed there in 1924. Its guests numbered 325 in its first year.

Adirondak Loj (originally spelled "Adirondack Lodge") is also owned and operated by ADK. It was built by Henry van Hoevenbergh in the early 1870s on what was then called Clear Lake. Van Hoevenbergh also built many trails, including the one up Mt. Marcy that bears his name. He renamed Clear Lake as "Heart Lake," and a small peak next to it "Mt. Jo" (for a former fiancée, Josephine Scofield). Van Hoevenbergh lost ownership of the lodge in 1899, but remained as innkeeper. The Lake Placid Club purchased it in 1900, but the great 1903 forest fire destroyed the lodge. Van Hoevenbergh barely escaped the flames with his life. In 1928 the Lake Placid Club built a less pretentious structure on the site. Following the phonetic dictates of the Lake Placid Club's Melville Dewey, Adirondack Lodge became Adirondak Loj. ADK's relationship with the Loj began in 1932 when ADK's Fred Kelsey leased the Heart Lake property and became sole stockholder in his Adirondak Loj Corporation. He opened the lodge for ADK members to use at a small charge, but took responsibility for all incurred expenses. When Kelsey died in 1957, the Lake Placid Club sold the property to ADK at a very reasonable price so that the property wouldn't have an owner who was only interested in commercial profits.

Programs

Conservation, education, and recreation were the three primary concerns of the ADK until a fourth was added years later—advocacy. A volunteer board of directors, fourteen advisory committees, and an executive committee govern ADK. Through the New York State Department of Environmental Conservation's (DEC) Adopt-a-Natural-Resource Program, ADK members have adopted 147 lean-tos and 55 trails in the Adirondacks and Catskills. ADK volunteers helped restore eight fire towers. ADK has become DEC's biggest partner in Forest Preserve trail maintenance; ADK's professional and volunteer trail crews build stone steps, harden trails, and improve trail drainage so that trails can sustain heavy usage with little environmental damage. The Forest Preserve is monitored by ADK in regard to illegal use or overuse, and many areas of New York State outside the Forest Preserve also benefit from trail maintenance or construction by ADK chapters or individuals.

Education

An Education Committee was formed by the ADK in 1929 to teach the public how best to use and protect the Forest Preserve. The committee presents educational information at its lodges, workshops, natural history areas, outings, and through Adirondac magazine and club pamphlets on such topics as black bears, hypothermia, and giardiasis (a common waterborne disease in humans in the United States caused by a parasite found on surfaces or in soil, food, or water). A naturalist and three summer interns augment a paid education director. The Summit Steward Program is a cooperative effort of the Adirondack Mountain Club, the Adirondack Chapter of the Nature Conservancy, the New York State Department of Environmental Conservation, and New York State Natural Heritage Program. The program is funded in part by the Forty-Sixer Conservation Trust and the Waterman Fund, and educates the public about the fragile summit alpine environment. The High Peaks Information Center was built in the 1970s on the Heart Lake property and features a weekly lecture series on Adirondack topics, educational exhibits and brochures, audio-visual presentations, and camping supplies and equipment. Trail conditions and weather forecasts are updated daily. ADK is New York's foremost training organization in Leave-No-Trace principles.

Conservation and Advocacy

The primarily volunteer Conservation Committee recommends conservation policies to ADK's board of directors. If approved, the policies become the basis for staff advocacy before state agencies, the state legislature, Congress, federal agencies, and even the Supreme Court when issues directly affect New York State's environmental interests. This committee is also active in the field; it led the "Carry It In, Carry It Out" campaign in the 1960s, which was responsible for removing trash dumps at lean-to sites and cleaning the littered summit of Mt. Marcy.

ADK members attend and testify at hearings on open space affairs throughout the state, and lobby for annual funding of the Environmental Protection Fund. The club advocates state purchase of land, lakes, and wild river corridors. It has formed a partnership with the New York–New Jersey Trail Conference to ensure greater protection of New York's downstate parks, Sterling Forest, and the Catskill Forest

Preserve. ADK assisted the International Paper Company in deciding which of its lands should have development and recreational easements with the state.

Publishing

ADK publishes books and maps, including eight Forest Preserve Series hiking guides, four guides to canoe routes, hiking samplers that offer day hikes and backpacking trips in the Forest Preserve, a rock-climbing guide, and a guide-book to all public-accessible fire towers in the Forest Preserve. It also publishes a bimonthly magazine, *Adirondac*. Eleanor Roosevelt wrote in the January/February 1961 issue of *Adirondac*: "I am pleased that our Club has observed the 75th anniversary of the establishment of the New York State Forest Preserve, because people need to be reminded of the great recreational and spiritual resource that they have in that region. Few people east of the Mississippi are so fortunate as to have a great wilderness area for camping, hiking, canoeing and general enjoyment of nature within a few hours of their home."

This history is based on Bruce Wadsworth's 1997 book, *With Wilderness at Heart: A Short History of The Adirondack Mountain Club*, and John P. Freeman's "The Adirondack Mountain Club: Its Programs and History," appearing in the *Adirondack Journal of Environmental Studies*, Vol. 12, No. 1, Spring/Summer 2005. This updated introduction was edited by Wadsworth and Freeman and is used with permission of the AJES publisher. For further information on the Adirondack Mountain Club, visit www.adk.org.

The Adirondack Forty-Sixers organization recognizes those who have climbed the 46 original peaks designated to be over 4,000 feet in elevation. The club's mission is to educate the public on responsible wilderness use and to encourage stewardship in the High Peaks region. Visit www.adk46r.org for membership procedures and organization benefits.

History

Robert and George Marshall and their friend and guide, Herbert Clark, identified 46 Adirondack mountains as being 4,000 feet in elevation or more and ascended them all between 1918 and 1925. In 1927 the publication of *Peaks and People of the Adirondacks* by Russell Carson inspired others to climb in the High Peaks.

A fifteen-year-old, Grace Leach, experienced a life-changing climb of Mt. Marcy in 1922, when she learned by experience what her father had counseled—"It doesn't matter if you reach the summit, but it does matter how you make the climb." She did achieve the summit on this three-day adventure—while some did not—and with "good grace!" When she married Ed Hudowalski, who had never climbed, she urged him to take his church school class to climb in the Great Range … "and the rest is history." Ed, with Ernest Ryder, the minister of Troy's Grace Methodist Church, completed climbing all 46 high peaks in 1936. They were the sixth and seventh persons to do so, and the following year Grace completed her climbs on Esther Mountain. A small group of these new "46ers" formed the Forty-Sixers of Troy to bring together mountain climbing enthusiasts. Grace was #9, the first woman to climb the 46. She wrote, "When we first went to climb, it had to be on Sunday—in the Great Depression we worked six days a week, and so we had our service on the mountains. The vespers we have at today's meetings date back to that custom."

By May 1948, with recorded 46ers now numbering fifty-four, the Adirondack Forty-Sixers was created. The organization decided to adhere to the forty-six original summits mentioned in Carson's book. Grace Hudowalski was the first president of the new organization and became its historian and beloved correspondent, a task she cherished for the next fifty years. She wrote more than a thousand individual letters a year on a typewriter, and urged people to describe in detail their adventures in the mountains. "These are very precious experiences," she said, "and if you don't write them down you won't remember." She donated thousands of Forty-Sixer letters and records to the New York State Archives, where they are available to the public. Adolph G. ("Ditt") Dittmar served fifty-three years as the first treasurer.

The Adirondack Forty-Sixers created a questionnaire for new 46ers and appointed a committee to mark true summits and to determine qualifying peaks; the criteria for a "peak" is that there be at least a 300-foot drop between it and the nearest peak, or it must be at least three-quarters of a mile away from the nearest peak. In 1950 canisters were placed on the summits of twenty peaks without marked and maintained trails. These contained registers for climbers to sign, date, and note the names of the three climbers who had immediately preceded them; these registers were then sent to Grace. In 2001 the canisters were removed to conform to new Department of Environmental Conservation (DEC) standards that seek to minimize the presence of non-natural objects and structures in the wilderness. The Forty-Sixers trail crew, with the approval of the DEC and sometimes the Adirondack Park Agency, determine the best paths to these summits, and these are officially termed Wilderness Paths. They contain no markings and, to date, not all trailless peaks have Wilderness Paths. "Herd path adopters" help maintain all Wilderness Paths that the Forty-Sixers have rehabilitated.

The Forty-Sixers hope to memorialize Grace Hudowalski by renaming East Dix as "Grace Peak," and to recognize Russell Carson by renaming South Dix as "Carson Peak." The Adirondack Forty-Sixers organization emblem is ADK 46R, but Forty-Sixers is not part of the Adirondack Mountain Club (ADK); these two organizations, however, share many common goals and concerns.

Programs

Founded in 1972, the annual Outdoor Leadership Workshop is held the first weekend in May to instruct leaders in camping and backpacking. Designed for camp counselors, Y-leaders, scout leaders, 4-H groups, college outing clubs, and individuals, the workshop deals with all aspects of trip planning and execution. Since 1979, Forty-Sixer trailmasters and volunteers donate thousands of hours annually to trail maintenance, lean-to restoration, and construction of new bridges, lean-tos and privies. Volunteers earn the Conservation Service Award and patch by contributing 46, 146, 346 and more hours to projects in cooperation with the DEC. Nonmembers can also participate and earn these patches. A former mountaintop seeding project helped preserve rare alpine plants and flowers, and Summit Stewards on Mount Marcy, Algonquin Peak, and occasionally other peaks educate hikers about the fragility of this alpine vegetation. Hikers are urged to travel only on paths and bare rock on all summits. These projects and practices are an ideal

Forty-Sixer Historian and Correspondent, Grace Hudowalski, first woman to complete climbs of the 46 High Peaks, at 60th anniversary of her 46er finish. Photo by David White.

way to "give back" to the mountains. The Forty-Sixers support other organizations and activities that benefit the Adirondacks, as determined by its executive committee, which meets twice yearly. Dues are only $8.00 annually; members' additional donations support conservation and educational efforts. The Annual Meeting is held Memorial Day Weekend; Fall Weekend is in early autumn. The club's Adirondack Peeks magazine is issued twice yearly.

Safety in the Mountains

Safe climbing in any season requires knowledge and preparation. "Climbing the Adirondack 46," a brochure published by the Adirondack Forty-Sixers, recommends taking a wilderness first-aid course offered by hiking organizations such as the ADK and the Sierra Club, NOLS (nols.edu), Wilderness Medical Associates (wildmed.com), SOLO (soloschools.com), and the American Red Cross (redcross.org). The Forty-Sixers organization offers partial reimbursement upon completion of its Outdoor Leadership Workshop and for completion of other wilderness first-aid courses.

For emergency help, the Park-Wide Emergency Dispatch telephone number is (518) 891-0235, but cellular telephone reception is unreliable in the mountains. ADK's Winter Mountaineering School (winterschool.org) teaches the skills and equipment essential for a safe winter outing. Only hikers in excellent physical condition should attempt the High Peaks in winter, and it is recommended that one be familiar with the peaks and trails and always monitor weather (noaa.gov). Adirondack Peak Experiences is a book of true stories with some hard-earned advice, but it is not a guidebook; essential references are offered in the appendix.

REQUIRED 46 ADIRONDACK HIGH PEAKS

Name	Elev. in ft.	Trailed (TR); Minimally Maintained Wilderness Paths (MM)
Mt. Marcy	5,344	TR
Algonquin Peak	5,114	TR
Mt. Haystack	4,960	TR
Mt. Skylight	4,926	TR
Whiteface Mt.	4,867	TR
Dix Mt.	4,857	TR
Gray Peak	4,840	MM
Iroquois Peak	4,840	MM
Basin Mt.	4,827	TR
Gothics	4,736	TR
Mt. Colden	4,714	TR
Giant Mt.	4,627	TR
Nippletop	4,620	TR
Santanoni Peak	4,607	MM
Mt. Redfield	4,606	MM
Wright Peak	4,580	TR
Saddleback Mt.	4,515	TR
Panther Peak	4,442	MM
Table Top Mt.	4,427	MM
Rocky Peak Ridge	4,420	TR
Macomb Mt.	4,405	MM
Armstrong Mt.	4,400	TR
Hough Peak	4,400	MM
Seward Mt.	4,361	MM
Mt. Marshall	4,360	MM
Allen Mt.	4,340	MM
Big Slide Mt.	4,240	TR
Esther Mt.	4,240	MM
Upper Wolf Jaw Mt.	4,185	TR
Lower Wolf Jaw Mt.	4,175	TR
Street Mt.	4,166	MM
Phelps Mt.	4,161	TR
Mt. Donaldson	4,140	MM
Seymour Mt.	4,120	MM

Sawteeth	4,100	TR
Cascade Mt.	4,098	TR
South Dix[1]	4,060	MM
Porter Mt.	4,059	TR
Mt. Colvin	4,057	TR
Mt. Emmons	4,040	MM
Dial Mt.	4,020	TR
East Dix[2]	4,012	MM
Blake Peak	3,960	TR
Cliff Mt.	3,960	MM
Nye Mt.	3,895	MM
Couchsachraga Peak	3,820	MM

MacNaughton Mountain is now measured at exactly 4,000 feet, but is not required. The Forty-Sixers questionnaire asks whether the hiker has climbed it.

[1]Proposed new name, Carson Peak
[2]Proposed new name, Grace Peak

Part I:

ADVENTURES IN THE HIGH PEAKS REGION

I survey a sight not often seen on this or any other mountain in the Adirondacks. Not a square millimeter of the natural mountain—the rocks and the grass—is exposed. The entire cone is wearing a thick mantle of ice—varied textures of water ice and shining snow ice. Torrential freezing rain has sheathed it in a great dome of polished glass. I move up on the sloping rink, the squeaking crampons biting securely, but I have to jam down the dull ferule of the ice axe or it simply slips away. That alpine feel is exhilarating.

— Landon Rockwell, "Dome of Heaven"

Gloria and Cliff Daly climbing Gothics Peak. Photo by Arthur Boni.

1

MOTHER NATURE VERSUS
RECORD-BREAKING MOUNTAINEER

THE GREAT RANGE IN A GALE

Ted E. Keizer, a.k.a. Cave Dog

Introduction: The Hike Fifty Challenge—Adirondack High Peaks, New York
This challenge was a tribute to Bob Marshall, a leader of the environmental and conservation movement that began at the turn of the twentieth century. Marshall founded the Wilderness Society, helped plan the National Park System and the Appalachian Trail while working with the United States Forest Service, and was first to explore much of the Brooks Range in Alaska. He named six hundred places on our maps. As he traveled the country exploring national forests, he set a lifelong goal to do thirty-plus-mile day hikes in every state. He reached the low forties when he died at the untimely age of thirty-eight in 1939.

The Dog Team¹ partnered with Duofold to bring the team to all fifty states. The team invited hikers, runners, and walkers to celebrate Bob Marshall's ideals by joining them on the trail. Cave Dog targeted a three-mile-an-hour pace and encouraged anyone to hike with him for one to thirty-plus miles; others served as support teams.

The Dog Team began in Portland, Oregon, on September 15, 2005, and finished on November 29 in Lake Placid, New York. On this quest Cave Dog hiked the crown jewels of our national trails—climbing snow-clad mountaintops in New York, hiking a tropical paradise along the Na Pali Coast of Kauai in Hawaii, traversing the sand dunes of Colorado, scampering over the old lava flows of New Mexico, and admiring glaciers on the Iditarod Trail of Alaska. The Outdoor Life Network (OLN) made a documentary of his Hike Fifty Challenge, called Live Your Passion, for national television in winter 2006.

Bob Marshall designed the Adirondack route in July 1932, and it is possibly Bob's most famous route, including thirteen of the Adirondack 46er High Peaks— Big Slide, the Great Range over Marcy to Skylight, the MacIntyre Range — and Mt. Jo, altogether 13,600 feet of elevation gain. It was a great tie-in with the tribute to Bob Marshall, and Bob would no doubt have been enthused about this Adirondack adventure at the end of Cave Dog's Hike Fifty Challenge.

Cave Dog's Account of His Treacherous Day in the High Peaks

We knew this was going to be a monster hike in the best of conditions at this time of year. Local mountaineers had stated that it was humanly impossible to do it on November 28 because of snow, ice, and little daylight. Success would require optimal weather, but new snow had fallen. I wanted to give it a try anyway. If hazards made the route impossible, I would descend to lower elevations to finish the distance. We had no idea that I was about to embark into the center of a violent windstorm that knocked out power for the entire region. It would have made sense to start the hike at midnight so that the most difficult stretches were finished during daylight, but Bob Marshall had a restriction that each hike must be a day hike—finished within twenty-four hours. So I delayed the start to 9 AM, guaranteeing greater difficulty after nightfall, but making it more possible for everyone to join in a celebratory finish up Mount Jo the next morning.

The day started with an ascent up Big Slide with Sea Dog, Under Dog, Crag Dog, and Two Dog with the temperature far warmer than expected and the snow not too deep. Near the summit, though, the team saw that the route was going to be at least as difficult as anticipated. Blowdown from recent high winds and considerable ice slowed the pace. I shot down the trail to Johns Brook Lodge (JBL) with Sea Dog, having fun scrambling across ice-covered creeks and negotiating countless fallen trees. We joined Sugar, Rad, Mo, and Night Dogs at boarded-up JBL. The Dog Team has wonderful memories from there after our 2002 Marshall Mountain Madness Ultramarathon, and it was great to be back.

I headed alone to Lower Wolf Jaw to start the Great Range traverse; Night Dog headed directly to Haystack, where we would meet later. Rock-hopping across Johns Brook, I marveled at how beautiful the ice looked atop the rushing waters. The hike up to the crest of the Great Range was quiet and peaceful. The creeks trickled and snow melted under rising temperatures. As I climbed higher, the fallen trees increased and ice became a significant factor again. The last half mile to the Lower Wolf Jaw summit felt more like three miles. Ice was everywhere! The wind had picked up. Until then, I'd been reluctant to put on crampons because the ice had been intermittent, but I had no choice on the ascent of Upper Wolf Jaw—huge walls of vertical ice lay directly in my path. At times I had to kick the front two points of each foot into the vertical ice, and in lieu of having ice axes, pull myself up the cliff bands, grasping tree limbs. On the summit I received a radio transmission from Night Dog asking how I was doing; he had reached Little Haystack. I explained that conditions were more difficult, but I was still on pace.

Conditions got steadily worse. The wind was reaching gale force, especially on the summits. It was raining periodically, and the short day's light was dwindling. Atop Armstrong I radioed Night Dog that I was still pushing onward, and he said that he would start moving toward me. That would be the last time I would talk to him that night. The route presented a constant series of problems. When I found a solution and executed it, I'd encounter the next problem. There was no letup to ease the mind. I had trouble crossing the summit of Gothics in the gusting wind. I began to realize that I might have to call off the Great Range traverse. I was still on pace, but it was getting too dangerous. But now I was unable to reach Night Dog, and I could not leave him out alone in this treacherous windstorm.

The descent off Gothics is incredibly exposed. Fortunately, cables have been laid down, but even with cables I was being thrown about by the wind. In the Gothics-Saddleback col I post-holed through knee-deep snow; here was the first bailout point from the Great Range. However, without word from Night Dog and no way to contact him, I continued up to Saddleback's summit. I was still unable to contact him. The wind had reached a fevered pitch as I started my southern descent off the cliffs of Saddleback. With my headlamp on my forehead, I was unable to see my feet in the dense fog! The light lit up the moisture in the air too much. I took my headlamp off and held it at knee level, but this reduced my ability to brace myself against the wind. The rock was covered by a layer of ice too thick for me to see the directional blazes. In a hopeless effort to try to uncover the blazes, I chipped away at the ice with my poles and was proceeding on all fours to keep from being swept off the mountain by the wind. Not able to find the blazes, I crawled out in the most likely direction and came

Cave Dog climbing Cascade Mountain. Photo by Nancie Battaglia.

to the edge of a precipice. I shined my light into the abyss, but saw nothing below, so I crawled out in a different direction only to look over another edge with no known bottom. I was soaked from head to toe and no longer able to keep up a pace that would keep me warm. Here I decided it was too dangerous to proceed.

I ascended back up to a relatively protected area and tried to radio Night Dog, to no avail. I got out the satellite phone and tried his cell phone without success. There is phone service on Haystack, but only near the exposed summit. I called Sugar Dog, telling her that I didn't like this situation at all—somebody must get word to Night Dog. Sugar Dog said she'd continue calls to his cell phone. I decided to make another attempt off the south side of Saddleback; I couldn't leave Night Dog out there! Besides, I had no idea how far Night Dog had intended to proceed north. I was kicking myself for not setting up a bailout time with Night Dog. My second descent off Saddleback didn't end up any safer, and I was now getting sore from hammering ice in a useless effort to find blazes. Back at the summit for the third time, I called Sugar Dog, who had still not made contact with Night Dog. She had reached the rest of the Dog Team, and they were ready for action, but I was the closest to him. I was not that far from Haystack, but had no way to get there directly. I would have to descend north to JBL and then climb back up to the Great Range to reach Haystack. The only problem would be if Night Dog had moved northward on the Great Range.

My water-soaked body became cold extremely fast in the pernicious wind. I finished the call and got moving. Despite my numb body, the temperatures were unseasonably warm at the lower elevation. The snow that I'd hiked through in the morning was now gone. Moving at a good clip, I warmed up again. However, without the mental stimulation of the high-altitude labors, I was hit by powerful sleepiness. The intensity of my last month of the challenge, with twenty-six rugged hikes over fifty kilometers each, had not afforded me as much sleep as I needed, and now it was catching up with me. I was having trouble staying on my feet. I called Sugar Dog, but she still had heard nothing about Night Dog. I slapped myself, sang to myself, screamed at myself, but nothing kept me awake. I called Sugar Dog again; still no word. During a heated discussion about how much I disliked this situation, about how Night Dog couldn't be left out alone, I snapped out of the depths of sleep deprivation. Revived, I ran the rest of the way down to JBL and was amazed that the river I'd rock-hopped hours before was now knee-deep rushing water.

I called Sugar Dog again; Night Dog had called Sea Dog! Enormous relief swept over me. Sea Dog told Night Dog to get off the mountain immediately, hike to the Adirondak Loj, and Lucky Dog would pick him up. I wanted to join him, but Night Dog was too far ahead. I spent the rest of the night hiking at lower elevations to achieve the necessary mileage for the challenge, finishing at 4:00 AM, and caught a two-hour nap.

By 7:00 AM everyone had gathered for the hike up Mt. Jo, which I'd never climbed and was looking forward to. There were Solstice Dog and Crag Dog, Sea Dog and Mo Dog, Under Dog and Honey Dog, Rad Dog and Lucky Dog, Sugar Dog and many others. There were dogs running around all over the place, but there was one dog I was the most pleased to see—Night Dog. He was full of stories of shivering uncontrollably, blowdowns, hiking up and down the side of Haystack to stay warm, coming out at The Garden instead of the Loj, and wind, oh so much wind. He had a bit of a burnt look to him.

Many reporters and cameramen documented the final stretch. Everyone had a delightful hike up Mt. Jo, and I was pleased to see Adog and Snow Dog pop out from the summit trees. The summit was blustery and gave everyone a hint at what Night Dog and I had experienced hours before. On the descent, Solstice Dog was nearly crushed by a falling tree blown over by the winds! Luckily, surrounding trees kept the falling tree from making it to the ground. Solstice Dog was unscathed, but it gave everyone pause.

More people and reporters had assembled at the finish line, but two stood out—George Marshall's son, Roger, and his wife had come to congratulate the Dog Team. I was honored and excited to have these distinguished guests, who joined us for a pancake celebration at Adog's and Base Dog's house, the 2002 Marshall Mountain Madness Ultramarathon base camp. The foul weather caused a power outage in Lake Placid. The Duofold RV with its propane tank and stovetop came in handy again; ever-resourceful Lucky Dog pulled out a camp stove, and the Dog Team never lost a beat in its celebration.

The Marshalls took the team to see the great camp where James, Bob, George, and Putey Marshall spent their summers learning wilderness ethics from their father, values that have benefited us all. The team returned to base camp for more festivities, and I took a break from one of three Jacuzzi baths I'd taken in eighteen hours! Dacks Dog, at eight-and-a-half-months pregnant, and Gold Dog, fresh off an 8,500-mile rail trip, joined us. The team told stories of the last seventy-five days: the camcorder that filled irreparably with dust in a Kentucky cave; two professional video cameras smashed in New York and Hawaii, and a camera lost in Texas; District of Columbia police who thought Cave Dog was a fugitive murderer—for who else would be hiking around the monuments at night in the rain?—and who also pulled over the RV to make sure it was not going to bomb the Capitol; scores of armadillos in Louisiana; the Wyoming blizzard and fiery red sunset in South Carolina; a Nebraskan who said, "One of the great things about us Nebraskans is that we are bland"; saving a run-over dog in Ohio; the fear of flash floods in Utah; a huge brown bear catching fish in an Alaskan stream; the epic sand dunes of Colorado; an irate ranger in Tennessee; the fantastic waterfall in Missouri; mountain goats clamoring on tiny ledges in Montana; the fungus message in Vermont; kayaking around Alcatraz in California; the huge showing of hikers in Michigan; a difficult bushwhack in Alabama that almost took out an eye; the unexpected terrain of Oklahoma; the crashing waves in Maine; the moose sighting in Idaho; a rare moonbow in Hawaii; and this intense mountain experience on Bob Marshall's famous Adirondack hike. 🏃🏃

[1]Sea Dog—Ross Workhoven; Under Dog—Dan Schwachter; Crag Dog—Brett Rindt; Two Dog—Nancie Battaglia; Sugar Dog—Ann Sulzer; Rad Dog—P.J. Keizer; Mo Dog—Kelly Morris; Night Dog—Ralph Ryndak; Lucky Dog—Paul Lavoie; Solstice Dog—Beverly Hackett; Honey Dog—Heather Haggerty; Adog—Richard Kelly; Snow Dog—Marsha Finnan; Dacks Dog—Erica Loher; Gold Dog—Bill Stowe; Base Dog—Joan Kelly. For a complete list of the Dog Team, visit: http://www.TheDogTeam.com

*T*ed E. Keizer, a.k.a. Cave Dog, grew up in Oregon, graduated from Brown University in 1994 with degrees in geology, biology, and political science, was student body president, expected a political career, and then decided he needed to experience life before he could enact law. He set out to do his own study of society, people, and nature, and traveled the United States, living and working in fourteen states including sojourns in Indian country, the inner city, and the woods. He tried many means of employment—hot air balloon pilot, hotel accountant, steel construction, shoveling snow off roofs, enumerator, moving man, high-school teacher, legislative policy advisor, and ambulance driver. His only restriction was that he never did the same job twice. He visited 145 National Park sites, did a thirty-one-day solo in Glacier National Park under winter conditions, and paddled the 325-mile Maine Island Trail with Groove Dog.

Cave Dog set eight climbing records[1]: 46 Adirondack High Peaks in 3 days, 18 hours, 14 minutes; 48 New Hampshire White Mountain 4,000ers in 3 days, 17 hours, 21minutes[2]; 55 Colorado 14,000ers in 10 days, 20 hours, 26 minutes; Vermont's Long Trail in 4 days, 13 hours, and 15 minutes; 35 Catskill peaks over 3,500 feet in 2 days, 15 hours, 24 minutes; Barkley Marathons in Tennessee, a course record of 2 days, 8 hours, 57 minutes; 40 North Carolina and Tennessee 6,000-footers in 4 days, 23 hours, and 28 minutes; and the Duofold Hike Fifty Challenge, a 50-kilometer (31.1-mile) hike in each of all 50 states in less than 75 days. He married Ann Sulzer (Sugar Dog) in 2007, honeymooned in Indonesia, bought a house in Oregon, and ran for the Oregon State Legislature in 2008. He and Ann are expecting their first child in May 2009.

[1]For more information, visit www.TheDogTeam.com.

[2]Tim Seaver has hiked the 48 New Hampshire peaks in three days, fifteen hours and fifty-one minutes.

2

A WINDY, COLD NIGHT AT 4,500 FEET—
THE CAVE DOG ADVENTURE

EXTREME CHALLENGES IN EXTREME CONDITIONS

Ralph Ryndak, a.k.a. Night Dog

Ted Keizer, popularly known as Cave Dog, had spent the last seventy-five days pursuing one of Bob Marshall's dreams— hiking fifty kilometers in all fifty states within that time period. Bob Marshall was one of the first 46ers and an active environmentalist, but his life was cut short by a heart ailment at the age of thirty-eight. It would be fitting to finish this quest in New York's Adirondacks on one of Marshall's most famous routes.[1]

I kept track of Cave Dog's progress as he and his team journeyed from state to state. As a veteran support team member from the Catskill Challenge in 2002[2] and the Vermont Long Trail Challenges in 2003 and 2004, I agreed to accompany Cave Dog on a substantial segment of Marshall's Adirondack route, carrying support supplies and extra clothing to Little Haystack to wait for Cave Dog as he climbed over the Great Range. I would carry a water filter, five quarts of power drink, sandwiches, Power Bars, lots of snacks, and extra clothing. Many calories are consumed on a long hike with 13,600 feet of elevation gain! Although my route to Haystack was direct, I had a formidable hike from then on: Haystack, Marcy, Skylight, Iroquois, Algonquin, Wright, and Mt. Jo. Sea Dog (Ross Workhoven) reported that the team—Dan Schwachter, the OLN (Outdoor Life Network) cameraman, Brett Rindt, John Grimler, and Zack Rudland—would be ready at The Garden on November 28, 2005, for Cave Dog's hike of the Bob Marshall route, and I'd be ready to go at seven o'clock.

I had little sleep the night before because I was so excited to meet again with Cave Dog and the team. The last time I saw them was in 2004 at the end of the Long Trail Challenge. The Duofold RV arrived with the rest of the team, including the OLN photographer. I put on my heavily loaded pack and headed up the Johns Brook Trail, where I would wait at JBL (Johns Brook Lodge) for Cave Dog. It was a beautiful morning and the weather was mild. I had plenty of time, so I enjoyed the solitude of the forest. Hikers had said that snowshoes weren't needed, but crampons would be necessary. The Johns Brook Trail was so relaxing; I was serenaded with sounds of the babbling brook and birds enjoying the mild weather. After two hours Cave Dog and other team members arrived from Big Slide, describing the tremendous blowdown caused by an October storm. The mood was joyous; it was a great privilege to be on the same route that Bob Marshall had taken years ago.

After a last review, Cave Dog was off to the Great Range and our later rendezvous at Little Haystack at 4,400 feet. I headed up the Phelps Trail to wait for Cave Dog. It didn't take long to find out about the blowdown; I was going in between, over, and under it for long stretches! I was lucky to have tracks to follow, because trail markers were hard to come by in the debris. The air was very moist from the mild air mixing with melting snowpack, and fog was forming. The mesh bridge at Bushnell Falls had a tree over it and was twisted and slippery. The stream at Slant Rock was high, and I slipped and went in up to my knees. Fortunately, I was prepared with Gore-Tex boots and extra clothing. The higher I went, the more the upper section of Johns Brook was flowing thanks to the mild weather. The upper section of the Phelps Trail is close to Johns Brook, and I fell through the hard-pack into the stream. Between going through miles of wet blowdown and falling through up to my waist in cold water, even the best clothing was put to the test!

Nighttime was imminent as I neared the Range Trail. My progress had been slowed, but I still had plenty of time. I radioed Cave Dog, who was now on Upper Wolf Jaw. The same obstacles had slowed him down—blowdown, high water, ice and snow—but now the winds had picked up dramatically! On Armstrong, Cave Dog was slowed by the high wind, and I was being battered, too. Visibility was near

4,960-foot Mount Haystack (left), Little Haystack (center), Mount Marcy in background.
Photo by Steve Boheim.

zero in pitch dark and fog. Because he was still far off, I took the Range Trail to the col between Little Haystack and Basin to escape the high winds and ward off hypothermia. It was tough to stay stationary at 4,500 feet in high winds, especially when soaked through! Even though I had worn the best clothing, the dampness that filled the air and the gale force winds pushed the dampness through the Gore-Tex. I was wet to the core.

At the col I waited for Cave Dog, and when I radioed him, all I heard was silence with the sound of high winds on the peaks ripping through the dark night. I had to keep moving, so I headed back up to Haystack and was knocked to my knees with a gust of wind that sucked the breath out of my lungs. I had a hard time getting to my feet, so I radioed Cave Dog on my knees while resting against a stunted conifer. Once again, silence. It was very late, and he should have made it to Basin by now! I had to drop down to the col again to fight hypothermia. The game plan was for us to move swiftly over the exposed rock of the high peaks, not to spend a lot of time queued up waiting. I waited in the col and then moved back up Haystack to try to reach Cave Dog and to use my cell phone to call base camp. Silence.

I was now very worried about Cave Dog. My first thoughts focused on the icy conditions on the steep, exposed rock of Saddleback. Had something tragic happened? I prayed not. I had to make a call to base camp, now! The winds were throwing me around like a rag doll, and I was becoming exhausted. I had the base camp number wrapped in plastic and tucked away in my pack. But the winds were so strong that if I opened my pack, I had to make sure its contents were not blown away. It was hard to make out the phone number; foggy, dense mist blown by the gale buffeted my glasses and made my headlamp nearly useless. I had to memorize the number quickly because the numerals were being smeared by the rain and wind. I tried calling from the tree line. No bars. Nothing. I radioed Cave Dog. Nothing. What should I do? Leave the mountain and have him come up here and find no one there? Was it an equipment malfunction from rain-driven wind? If I weren't here, he'd be in dire straits in need of food and water.

I had to go farther up Haystack; higher up, there's sporadic reception. The rocks were icy and the winds so strong that it was more of a crawl than a climb. I got the phone out and struggled to see the numbers on the display. I had bars. Someone was finally going to answer. This would be the first time in hours that I had been able to talk to someone. It was Sea Dog! He said to get off the mountain, now! Cave Dog had abandoned his quest to finish the Bob Marshall route because of the conditions, and would fulfill the mileage requirement at a lower elevation. I was elated to hear that he was okay; I'd imagined the worst. Sea Dog told me to go to the Loj, but I had to return to The Garden, where I had left my vehicle and a change of clothing. It was now 11:30. I was soaked and had been blown about by winds that I later learned had knocked out power in Lake Placid. Trees were down in many areas. What the velocity of the wind was at over 4,500' on Haystack, God only knows! I'd reached my limit; I was tired from keeping myself in an upright position.

I made my way down eight miles over the blowdown and across high waters, with nothing more than a headlamp to guide me through fog that was so thick I couldn't see my wet, numb feet. I would need to follow my tracks to find my way in the fog through the blowdown. But the snow had melted, and the trail was obliterated! I did not even want to think about being lost in this quagmire of blowdown. I couldn't falter, because my body temperature was dropping with the falling temperature. I had to keep moving quickly; the hours of being stationary on the mountain had caused slight hypothermia. I wasn't afraid, however, because I did have dry clothes packed for such an emergency. After crossing swollen streams at Slant Rock and beyond, I found myself at the quiet empty Johns Brooks Lodge at 2:30 AM. I was okay now and looking forward to congratulating Cave Dog and the team for the completion of the Hike Fifty Challenge in honor of Bob Marshall. A mile from The Garden parking lot, I saw eyes ahead of me—a deer that refused to wander away. I walked five feet past it, and it did not move. A strange night indeed!

I headed over to the Loj, where the Dog Team met me. Lucky Dog, Paul Lovoie, gave me warm drinks and food, and Beverly, Solstice Dog, gave me a jacket and a hat. The area was filled with reporters, including the Associated Press and TV crews. Cave Dog and I were very glad to see each other! I also met George Marshall's son, Roger. What a day, and night—another adventure with Cave Dog and the Dog Team! ᛈᛈ

¹ To read more about their adventure, go to www.TheDogTeam.com.

² Described in *Catskill Peak Experiences*, Black Dome Press, 2008.

*R*alph Ryndak: When I first hiked Wittenberg Mountain with my brother Joe, the wonderful view captivated me and I couldn't wait to hike again. Nelson Shultis owned several thousand acres and let us backpack in many beautiful locations. He taught us about animals, trees, area history, and backwoods knowledge such as "Leave no trace." Maddy and I are regular and winter Catskill 3500 Club members; I'm a 46er, #4833, and recently completed hikes of all Catskill 3,500-foot peaks in each month of the year.

3

A MOONLIGHT CLIMB OF MOUNT MARCY

A MILE-HIGH ADVENTURE

Isaac Siskind

It was 1:20 AM on New Year's Eve as I crawled out of my sleeping bag, carefully trying not to brush any tent frost on my companion. I was fully bundled in protective layers of clothing, and movement was awkward. Twenty minutes earlier, in a half sleep, I'd been trying to grapple with decisions such as whether to answer the call of nature or to stay put and hold on until morning, or maybe to reach for a candy bar to stave off the cold and make the remaining hours a little more pleasant. My thoughts were interrupted by a loud whisper from outside. It was Ethan, our young cook group leader, excitedly wanting to know if anybody was interested in a night ascent of Marcy. After an overcast and windy day, Ethan reported that the night was calm and clear. As part of the B2 Section of the joint ADK-AMC Winter Mountaineering School, we were camped this night between Indian Falls and the Plateau area.

Realizing that we were extremely fortunate to be located so high on the mountain under these weather conditions, and knowing how difficult it would be to plan the time and circumstances for another venture of this nature, I said, "Okay, give me a few minutes to get myself organized." A muffled "hooray!" greeted my affirmative response. Ethan, already anticipating a favorable reply, had gotten his bivy sack and Ensolite pad. I began the laborious process of getting dressed, after which I tossed a stove and cooking utensils into my pack. The candy bar that I'd been thinking of eating (chocolate-covered halvah) went into my pocket for the calories I would surely need. My tent companion, Jeff, who was nursing a tender knee, wished us well and elected to stay behind. I wondered if my fifty-one years of experience and judgment were clouded by the exuberance of a nineteen-year-old.

The night was truly bright as we made our way up the trail toward the Plateau area to find the rest of our section. We awakened John, the section leader, and announced that we wished to climb Marcy and were looking for companions. After first saying, "All right, just fill out the sign-out sheet in the morning," John realized that we really meant to climb now. We checked the other tents, awakening twelve people and finally finding three willing to try the climb. While waiting, the cold was starting to penetrate. What seemed like a grand idea earlier was beginning to pale somewhat. The others appeared, and now that we had a strong party of five with all the requisite emergency equipment, things started to fall into place.

It was close to 3:00 AM when we passed the Phelps Trail junction and started the actual summit ascent. By now the wind had started to pick up, but the sky was still cloudless. There was ample light, making flashlights unnecessary. We agreed to travel as if roped, so that we would be close together in case of a problem. Above tree line the wind became fierce, and with icy patches the footing became precarious. Ethan wisely called a halt so that we could drop down slightly to the lee side of a large boulder, where we donned crampons and face masks. When asked if we were all comfortable using crampons, there were interesting comments. Bob mumbled something about having trouble keeping them on. I then remembered a field fix that he had made two days earlier, and now hoped that the fix was permanent. This was neither the place nor the time to improvise repairs. Someone commented that he was comfortable on crampons, but not always sure which was left or right; however, he had brought instructions in his pack. Again, the nagging doubt. I was congratulating myself on my foresight in checking my equipment, which was borrowed. My own crampons were too small to fit the Sorel winter boots. One crampon was on when the ankle strap on the second gave way; a mild oath and the announcement that I broke a strap must have aroused similar doubts in my companions. After minor fussing, I fished out a spare nylon strap that seemed custom-made for the job. Pleased with my good luck, I resumed the climb with confidence.

The moon was waning and longer shadows were being cast, but the lighting was still superb. We made the summit about 4:00 AM and spent ten minutes absorbing a fantastic sight. To the north and west we could clearly see the illuminated towns of Saranac, Lake Placid, and Tupper Lake, while to the south there were only

Hale-Bopp Comet. Photo by Ira Orenstein.

solitary twinkles of scattered lights. The heavens were crystal clear with more stars than I had ever seen before. The fact that this was the last day of 1979 seemed to weave a spell about us. The quick flash of a meteor heightened the drama of the scene. Before descending, we congratulated our leader for his imagination in recognizing an opportunity and his persistence in seeing it through. All agreed that this experience was the highlight of the year.

The descent went quickly, and our three companions from the Plateau group arrived at their campsite in time for the usual 5:00 AM reveille. They stayed up to join another group that was climbing Haystack. Ethan and I continued to our tents to catch a couple of hours of sleep to lull ourselves into thinking we had had the benefit of a full night's rest.

We broke camp in brilliant sunshine, a luxury after a week of cooking and camping in the dark. We moved our gear to Indian Falls in time to rendezvous with the rest of our section (nineteen people) for a New Year's Eve celebration. The festivities consisted of hot chocolate, a small piece of plum cake and animated discussion reviewing the past week's experiences. At 14°, there was much foot-shuffling and hand-slapping to stay warm. One by one, people began turning in, and at 8:50 the year came to a close.

Upon reflecting on the outing, and especially the previous night's climb, I found it refreshing to have observed the competence of the young folk in coping with problems unique to living outdoors in the winter. I heartily recommend participation in this Winter Mountaineering School. It was a wonderful opportunity to do winter climbing, meet new people and, in my case, to temporarily bridge the generation gap.

Originally published in the December 1980 Adirondac, *the magazine of the Adirondack Mountain Club, Inc. (ADK). This abridged version is reprinted with permission of ADK. www.adk.org.*

Isaac Siskind: My interest in outdoor activities started with two Harriman backpacks in college and a first climb of Mt. Marcy in 1953. My wife and I completed the 46 in 1981, #1702 and #1703, and the Catskill 3500 peaks. As a trail supervisor for the New York-New Jersey Trail Conference, I'm responsible for maintaining over 50 miles of trail in Harriman Park, field checking new maps, and proofreading guidebooks. I take great pleasure in my sons' outdoor accomplishments, particularly as they raise the third generation as "Greenies" enjoying the outdoors. 🚶🚶

4

A MARCY ADVENTURE

INTELLIGENCE: NOT MAKING THE SAME MISTAKE TWICE

Philip B. Corell

Winter climbing began for me as a high-school student in the early 1960s when my father placed me on a train and sent me off to hike with my former camp counselor, Jim Bailey (46er #233). During my summers at Camp Pok-O-Moonshine, Jim had led me up most of my 46 peaks. My most memorable winter trip took place during a January college break and taught me many lessons about self-sufficiency and, most importantly, about the hazards of making commitments to others when entering the woods.

My first "accomplice" was Steve Smith, a fraternity brother at Franklin and Marshall College. Steve was adventurous, gung ho, and intrigued by the challenges of the Adirondack Mountains in winter. With his family's borrowed car we headed to New Haven, Connecticut, to pick up Mark Gibson (46er #225) and an unsuspecting classmate of his. Mark and I had finished the 46 together as campers and were constantly looking for new adventures in the mountains. Having grown up in Iowa City, any location with mountains and trees had instant appeal to Mark. We planned to pack over Marcy and down the Opalescent River to Lake Colden, where we would meet Jim Bailey hiking in from Adirondak Loj. Having always planned trips with our glass "two-thirds full," Mark and I explained that we could easily make it to Plateau lean-to, then nine-tenths of a mile below Marcy's summit, the first night, and then on to Lake Colden—a mere five and a half additional miles—by the end of the second day. We were fairly new to winter camping and probably not in the physical shape necessary for the conditions we were about to face.

We arrived during a major winter storm, and we had no idea how unprepared we were to enter the mountains under these conditions. Over a foot of fresh snow greeted us at the Loj parking lot, with more coming down. We enthusiastically began our journey with the snow still falling. We were quickly jolted to reality when we found the trail above Marcy Dam unbroken. Mark and I weren't experts, but the others were just learning the "art" of snowshoeing with the added challenge of a sixty-plus-pound pack and borrowed equipment. The pace slowed and our goal of reaching Plateau lean-to became completely unrealistic; our party's unnamed fourth held us back critically. The unwanted tonnage of our primitive pre-"hi-tech" gear slowed us as well. We wouldn't even make it to the junction with the Hopkins Trail.

At 6:00 PM darkness was imminent, and we stamped out two tent platforms in the middle of the Van Hoevenberg Trail and set up camp. Mark owned a "finicky" and smelly Primus kerosene stove. The fuel odor permeated the air and, fortunately for me, he was sleeping in the other tent! A gourmet meal of Dinty Moore beef stew was heated in the can over the sputtering stove and washed down with soup and mandarin oranges. Our only source of water was melting snow that was basically unpalatable without added cocoa or Jell-o. Between the kerosene fumes and the debris of pine needles and dirt floating in the pot, the resulting liquid was extremely foul. Fortunately, all of the research on the importance of hydration hadn't been published yet, so we had no idea how much trouble we were soon to experience!

That night the snow abated and the temperatures plunged. By morning there was a thick layer of frost lining the tents, which showered us with every movement. Trying to get damp bags and tents back into stuff sacks became our first challenge. Our primitive canvas tents, laden with moisture, added substantially to our packs in bulk and weight. Wet cotton clothing was frozen solid, and most of our other belongings were damp from the spindrift blowing in the air. There wasn't enough time to melt drinking water, and the thought of the finished product did little to motivate us. With renewed vigor we hit the trail cluelessly, under-hydrated, but awed by the fresh winter beauty around us. Our heavy packs didn't help our pace, but ensured a quick warm-up on the unbroken trail. We finally made the summit of Marcy, a bit dispirited by the slow pace imposed by our weakest link and the retreat of the sun. The gray cold and advancing hours induced a vague anxiety about the travel remaining; Lake Colden seemed a distant and uncertain objective. We could see no markers or cairns because of the depth of the snow and the overcast conditions. Fortunately, we knew that if we headed for Schofield Cobble, we could pick up the trail at the tree line.

Below tree line we would periodically walk off the trail and find ourselves at the mercy of the "Adirondack Spruce Trap." To the uneducated, "the Spruce Trap" develops in areas where the spruce trees are four to ten feet tall. During major storms, light powdery snow covers the trees. At the bottom of the trees and between the branches, pockets of air are trapped. If the unsuspecting climber steps over one of these pockets, they will plummet into a welter of spruce boughs well below the surrounding surface. Feet and snowshoes are now entangled in the branches below. Removal is difficult, much like a porcupine quill once injected. Churning is to no avail. Escape usually requires taking off the snowshoe, removing your foot from the trap, and then reaching down to retrieve the

Summit, 5,344-foot Mount Marcy. Photo by David White.

snowshoe—all at considerable, energy-burning effort. This exercise inevitably moistens the climber, either from snow entering at collar and cuffs, or because of the additional perspiration generated by the struggle. This process taxes one's good humor if it occurs repeatedly. In unconsolidated areas, climbers have found themselves six feet or more below the surrounding surface. A climber must use whatever means available to build a ramp to reach more solid footing, or hope that there is someone to assist them—but the second climber often becomes an additional victim.

Wet and a bit discouraged, we finally attained the Lake Tear lean-to site. So much snow had fallen that winter that only a mound of snow marked the probable location of the lean-to roof! We had hoped that our progress would improve once we were down Marcy. But we could not find the comfort of trail markers most of the way to Feldspar lean-to, and floundered in deep, cold, new powder. Occasionally, by sheer chance, we'd stumble on a marker a foot or two off the ground, another hint of the snow depths with which we were dealing. In the early dimness of advancing winter night, dehydration, fatigue, equipment, and uncertainty were impacting our progress.

Early snowshoes—and the ones we had borrowed—had leather bindings. As the day progressed, the heat from our boots caused the snow to melt and soak into the leather. Under the strain of use, the wet leather now stretched and the bindings loosened, causing the snowshoe to fall off. Needed adjustment was deferred because of resulting wet, cold hands and the time involved in struggling with the stiff, unwieldy buckle and strap adjustment to prevent the inevitable step out of the shoe. Eventually, as you stepped out of your snowshoe, your leg would plunge down into the unconsolidated snow. This would result in a face plant with a sixty-pound pack firmly weighing you down! We soon became adept at turning our bodies as we fell to avoid a mouthful of snow, but grew tired from struggling up and wrestling to replace the shoe.

The toll of what must have been substantial dehydration and the reaction of sore, tired, water-starved muscles to a sudden and unexpected plunge now came into play. First was the plunge and scream of pain as the muscle cramped. One of your sympathetic companions would try to assist you. The pack had to come off, the leg straightened out, and with great difficulty the individual was assisted back to his feet. The resulting cramp could then be massaged. One couldn't bend down to put one's snowshoe back on, because the cramp would return. Soon, however, no one else in the group could bend down to help without their leg cramping. The need to place a new hole in the stretched leather so that the binding could be tightened added to the frolic. After repeating this process several times the wet, stressed leather would usually break, necessitating a repair with rope.

This scenario was repeated many times until 5:00 PM, when we finally arrived at Uphill Brook lean-to. We had committed to meeting Jim at Lake Colden, 1.8 miles farther, and we had the tents. Normal, sane folks might say, "This hasn't gone at all as planned. Let's spend the night here!" But how long could that relatively short descent possibly take? And, oddly, stumbling on seemed less daunting than setting up camp. As light made its final retreat, we continued to break trail in the two feet of fresh snow, searching for markers and traveling in the "general direction" of Lake Colden by using the Opalescent as a guide. What flashlights we had were soon ineffective, at best. The purchase of headlamps hadn't occurred to us, and the intelligence to bring extra batteries had eluded us. There were more falls, more cramps, and general resignation that we had to travel on, despite the fact that we had everything we required to make camp sitting on our backs.

Shortly after 10:00 PM we finally crossed the river near the Lake Colden camping area, picked up fresh tracks and followed them to Jim's lean-to. Jim correctly figured that no other fools would have ventured out in a full-blown storm to pack into Lake Colden via the summit of Mt. Marcy! It quickly became obvious that our concerns for Jim's welfare—one of our motivations for continuing—were completely misplaced. Jim had set up a windscreen with a poncho and was sound asleep in his two Army surplus down bags. He was obviously very comfortable and not particularly worried that we hadn't arrived.

We attempted to tend to our personal needs—tents had to be raised, snow-shoes taken off, and wet clothes changed. We quickly realized we were totally help-less. Mark was the only one who could bend down and take off his own shoes without cramping. Steve had spent two days with rubber pack boots that were a half size too small for his feet. Our unnamed fourth was helpless. We, who had come to "rescue" Jim, were entirely reliant on his assistance. He pulled our wet pants and boots off and got us into our bags. Each time someone tried to bend their leg, there would be a sudden cramp and yell of pain; the lessons on the effects of insufficient water intake and lack of conditioning had been learned in a painful and memorable fashion. Underestimating Jim's self-sufficiency and honoring our hastily thought-out verbal commitment had caused us to push our bodies unnec-essarily to the edge of exhaustion, but pushing on did afford us much-needed assistance in restoring ourselves for the night. Being Jim, he had brought in treats to eat, including a half gallon of ice cream! Despite his condition, Steve couldn't resist the temptation. To this day he remembers the taste of coffee that night and the instant effect the sugar had on entering his stomach. The next day we took plenty of time to relax, drink, eat, and pack before our trek back to the Loj and an eight-hour drive home.

My father was always philosophical about mistakes that he termed "learning experiences." He would often repeat, "As long as you don't make the same mistake twice, you're doing okay!" Looking back, it is clear that we courted grave danger. It would be some time before we really understood the critical importance of proper equipment, and the necessity of staying dry and drinking adequate fluids. Though we were not optimally conditioned, the resilience of youth and our intimate knowl-edge of the terrain had enabled us to avert possible disaster. Our "learning experi-ences" left many lasting impressions on us all. We continued to winter camp, and I can guarantee we never made the same mistake twice. I firmly believe that the challenge of "getting it right" motivated us to continue camping and climbing in winter. Mark, Steve and I did have further misadventures, but routes were planned more sensibly and options discussed. We didn't obligate ourselves to meet others, and we camped lower, where we had ready access to water in liquid form with the aid of an axe. Lean-tos were used as a base where we could have fires at night and take day trips, instead of moving long distances with heavy packs. We tried to be in proper shape for the goals we set. I fondly look back on those first trips and the practical knowledge we gained about equipment, planning and, most importantly, anticipating what might go wrong.

Mark, Steve, and Jim added their own recollections to this story. Steve remem-bers setting a blistering pace back to the car, promising himself that he would never enter the Adirondacks again. Fortunately, that wore off quickly and he was party to several more trips. Mark lives in the mountains near Salt Lake City, but gets back to the Adirondacks several times each year. Ten years ago, while climbing Marcy in January, I ran into Mark and his wife skiing from the summit. Jim has spent his life in the Adirondacks actively involved with the Algonquin Chapter of the Adirondack Mountain Club and serving as the Plattsburgh city historian. He has always been known to be "up for an adventure" in the mountains. ⚇

*P*hilip B. Corell: *My introduction to the Adirondacks began in 1956 as a ten-year old attending Camp Pok-O-Moonshine. I completed my first round of the 46 in 1962, and my first winter round in 1985, #224W. Some of my most memorable camping and climbing experiences were shared with my wife, Mary, and two sons, Jay and Mark, while they completed their 46. I spent four terms as 46er president, thirty-six years with the Outdoor Leadership Workshop, and currently serve as the club's treasurer.*

5

TREK TO THE TOP OF NEW YORK STATE

FROM BEARS TO THE BARE SUMMIT: A MARCY ADVENTURE

Lynne Christensen

"**I** think I'd like to climb Mt. Marcy,"
Minna said to me one day. She had heard Sandra Weber on the radio discussing
her book *Mount Marcy: The High Peak of New York*, extolling the virtues of the
southern route. There are several routes to Mt. Marcy, and the southern route from
the Upper Works trailhead is less heavily used. "Weber described it as being very
beautiful and it made me want to try it," Minna said. Weber is an enthusiastic pro-
moter of Mt. Marcy. She writes: "Mount Marcy is a jumble of jagged rock thrust
upward at the heavens. It is a cold, wet, windy wasteland—rarely noticed before
1836 and not fully explored until the 1870s. Yet it captures my attention and affec-
tion like no other mountain in New York State, or perhaps on earth." Not only the
wild beauty of Mt. Marcy inspires Weber, but also the age of the mountain—the
erosion-resistant bedrock, called anorthosite, is 1.1 billion years old!

We settled on the last week in August. We arrived at the trailhead at 2:00 PM,
and by 2:30 the rain had stopped, although the forecast wasn't encouraging. Shoul-
dering thirty-pound packs, with hiking sticks in hand, we set out. On a swaying
suspension bridge the trail crosses Calamity Brook, a beautiful clear mountain
stream cascading over enormous rocks. The trail follows this brook, which out-
lets in the Hudson River, crisscrossing it several more times to its origin at Flowed
Lands. We expected to encounter many fellow hikers, but the middle of the week
before Labor Day weekend turned out to be the right time to avoid crowds. Hikers
on their way out had vacated lean-tos; we would have our pick. One nice young
couple warned us to watch out for bears—the lean-to they stayed at had a bear
cable. We arrived at Flowed Lands, once a man-made lake created by a dam (since
breached) to increase the water flow along Calamity Brook for iron smelting and
log driving. It is now a sheet of water at the foot of Mt. Colden and Mt. Marshall,
its beauty rivaling that of one of the prettiest Western wilderness lakes, Jenny Lake
in the Grand Tetons.

We located the lean-to with the bear cable, a wire strung high up between two
trees from which to hang your food away from hungry, scavenging bears. But the
lean-to had a dirt floor and no lake view, so we found a lean-to set high on a bluff
overlooking the lake. Someone had strung up a rope between two trees for hang-

ing food. As we arrived, we heard rain on the roof. After crawling into our sleeping bags, we heard the distinctive activity of a bold bear near our food. Confident that the food was hung out of its reach, but uncomfortable about the proximity of a hungry black bear, I had a fitful night's sleep. In the morning it was clear the bear had played piñata, from the two ragged rips in the bag, but she failed to get the goodies. Before setting off, we hung it more carefully.

At 8:00 AM with the sun shining, we set off on our six-mile trek to Marcy. The first mile to Lake Colden over protruding tree roots, up large boulders and through much mud, was a little rougher than expected. From Lake Colden, the trail runs along the delightfully named Opalescent River, the most beautiful section on a gradual ascent beside the lovely river, which periodically serenades with the sound of rushing water tumbling over huge boulders. In some spots one can walk to the water's edge and commune directly with the river; at others, one can peer over a cliff to watch the water rushing through a narrow cleft one hundred feet below. We dawdled along this section. With two miles more—the most difficult, with an ascent of 2,000 feet—we began to worry about misjudging our time. Another mile brought us to Lake Tear of the Clouds, the spot where, on September 13, 1901, Theodore Roosevelt was having his lunch after climbing Mt. Marcy when a messenger delivered the news that President McKinley had taken a turn for the worse, and Vice President Roosevelt was being summoned to return.

The nearly cloudless sky had turned completely overcast with a few grayish clouds that appeared to hold rain. Would we get a view from the summit? We were too close to turn back. As you climb the last mile, the alpine terrain becomes evident. Mt. Marcy is one of only a handful of mountains in New York with alpine plants, specially suited to withstand cold and bitter winter winds. Trees and shrubs are short and scrubby, and tundra plants replace woodland plants. The summit of Mt. Marcy is bare rock face, and the final quarter mile is a climb up sheer rock carpeted with lichen. "How close are we to the summit?" I pathetically asked a descending hiker. "Just put one foot in front of the other and you'll get there," was his cheery reply. "Was it steep?" we were later asked. "Yes, quite steep." Breathing hard and walking ever slower, I took the hiker's advice. One foot in front of the other, looking down, I kept going. But wait, the trail had leveled off. "Where's the summit of this thing?" I asked Minna. "Oh, we just passed it," she said.

I walked back to the identifying plaque. Mt. Marcy had first been climbed (by white men) in 1837. The party of twelve included scientists, professors, an entrepreneur, an artist, and five guides—three of whom are listed as "unknown woodsmen." Three additional men who were not on the initial climb got their names engraved for posterity. I also learned that the Native American name for the mountain is *Tahawus*, meaning "Cloud-splitter." After "Tahawus" was used by a nineteenth-century poet to describe Mt. Marcy in an 1837 newspaper article, readers believed that this was the original name of the mountain and the rumor was impossible to stop.

The sky had cleared and the view was spectacular! Emerging onto the large, open summit of Mt. Marcy after trudging through thick woods is like being born. The mountainous terrain of the High Peaks spread out before us on all sides. We

Summit, Mount Marcy; Mount Haystack in near background. Photo by Steve Boheim.

regretted not having started out earlier, because we longed to linger on the summit. At 2:45 PM we headed down and were back by seven o'clock, just in time to make a nice hearty dinner in the little remaining light. Exhausted, we hung the food bag and went to bed. In the middle of the night, Minna jostled me awake. "I hear the bear," she said. It was nosing around the food bag. I peered around the side of the lean-to, hoping. Our luck had run out; the bag was gone.

Another beautiful day dawned the next morning and we'd hoped to do more exploring, but the bear had changed our plans. There was now only one thing to do—hike out. We stopped by the suspension bridge over Calamity Brook for a rest, where we encountered someone spraying water onto a large rock. This man was friendly and insisted that I look at something. I was tired and hungry and not in the mood to talk to strangers, but not wanting to be rude, I did. He explained that the rock was embedded with the mineral labradorite. He wet down a portion and had me look at it from two different angles. From one angle, it appeared gray, but with the sun shining from a different angle, the embedded crystals were brilliant blues and greens. Ah, now I knew how the Opalescent River got its name—its rocks are also full of labradorite.

We toasted the bear and the trip at a restaurant. Sore, hungry, and tired, I thought that I wouldn't do such an ambitious trip again. "The thing about a trip like this," said Minna, "is that afterward you swear you'll never do it again. But later you start planning the next one." Sure enough, just days later we were talking about going back to Mt. Marcy, wiser about the conditions and the bears.

The presence of black bears in the High Peaks shouldn't stop anyone from backpacking there. Unless provoked, they don't attack humans. Bears have learned that there is likely to be food in certain locations, but there are effective ways to keep it out of their reach. Visit http://www.dec.ny.gov. The Department of Environmental Conservation recommends keeping food in a two-pound bear canister, which can be rented or bought. They can be placed on the ground. Use official bear cables installed by the DEC, strung at the proper height. If hanging food, use a counterbalance system rather than tying the rope off to a tree. A brochure that describes this system is available from the DEC. 🐾

*L*ynne Christensen: *My adventures in the outdoors began as a child in Califor-nia, hiking and camping with my family in the Sierras. My father, an avid fly fisherman, instilled in me a great love of the outdoors. In New York City, I joined the Sierra Club and hiked many areas in southern New York. Then I met Minna, who introduced me to the Adirondacks and some of the most beautiful places on earth.*

GOOD GRIEF!
NINETEEN YEARS OF HALLOWEEN HIKING

AN EPIC EPICUREAN EXPERIENCE

Donald P. Berens Jr.

In late October 1976 I drove to the Roaring Brook trailhead below Giant Mountain. Conditions were right for an early start to the ice-climbing season, and I planned a solo climb up the eastern cirque of Giant followed by a solitary, contemplative night in the lean-to north of Giant. I ascended to the col between Giant and Rocky Peak Ridge and bushwhacked northward to the east face of Giant, which glistened icily in the glorious sun. Mindful at every step that I was utterly alone and that a slip would be followed by a very long slide, I carefully picked my way upward, occasionally chopping steps with my ice axe. After an hour I reached the top of the slide and bushwhacked through snow to the summit of Giant for a lunch break. I had completed the difficult part of my project and anticipated a quiet night of reflection in a remote lean-to.

I met another hiker who was lunching, and we asked each other where we had come from and where we were going. He, too, was headed for the lean-to north of Giant and invited me to join him and his thirteen (!) companions for dinner—there went all hope of a quiet weekend. But I had little choice since I had counted on that lean-to for shelter, and the offer was intriguing. A diverse crew bearing remarkable cargo began to arrive from the north trail. These strangers were as hospitable as their companion whom I had just met. They, too, invited me to share their supper, the ingredients for which they began pulling from their packs. First, they produced champagne—twenty-four bottles! Next, champagne glasses—two dozen, each painted fluorescent orange on the base for easy identification in the wilderness twilight. *Pâté de foie gras* and French mustard were spread on crackers. After the appetizers came the bouillabaisse, chili, lamb stew, and apple crisp with freshly whipped cream. In the face of these gourmet delights, I left my planned supper of granola and dried fruit buried deep in my pack.

What I had encountered was the Blueberry Marching and Chowder Society (BMCS) It had been meeting once annually for several years on the weekend closest to Halloween to eat fine food in the forest and to pay its sincere respects to the Great Pumpkin. I was about to witness secret rites known only to a privileged few.

A rubber mask now transformed my mountaintop acquaintance into a ghoulish high priest of the occult. A forty-five-pound pumpkin (yes, it had been carried in with the champagne) was eviscerated and filled with a concoction of rum, champagne, and candy corn. The pumpkin was passed around and toasts were drunk. The celebrants then each contributed a knife stroke to carve a face in the great gourd. Exhausted by the day's events, or overwhelmed by the spirit of the evening, I soon collapsed into unconsciousness. On Sunday morning the carved pumpkin was carried to the summit of Giant and a candle was lit within it. I had experienced something out of the ordinary realm of Adirondack culture; I gave them my address and phone number, hoping that somehow I might once again experience a similar epiphany.

A chance encounter like mine had played a formative role in the history of the BMCS. In spring 1968 a weary hiker, Jack McIntosh, stopped in the Blueberry lean-to on the trail from Duck Hole. Three other travelers, Chip Bookman, Larry Brooks, and Jay Sulzberger—undergraduates at Columbia—joined Jack. They discussed Adirondack trips they would like to take and agreed to meet again. That fall the Blueberry Marching and Chowder Society was born: "Blueberry" because of the site of conception; "Marching" because that is obviously necessary for backpacking; "Chowder" because, largely thanks to chef Larry, the group eats well; and "Society" because its members are social (translation: they like to party).

Their first Halloween trip was to Mt. Marcy via Indian Falls, but the hike was sparsely attended. Their tent pitched on top of Marcy was blown over by the Great Pumpkin. But that trip was instantly realized as a tradition in the making. The pumpkin ceremony was instituted and endures; the greatest Great Pumpkin, eighty-four pounds, was carried to Mt. Marcy in 1972. Their second trip marked the beginning of another tradition—the Sunday evening debriefing at Chez Pierre, a marvelous French restaurant in Wilton, New York. It was hardly necessary after the sumptuous dining in the woods to add another lavish meal, but then, if measured only by the standard of necessity, the whole Halloween hiking enterprise is inexplicable. Dinner at Chez Pierre became firmly ensconced in the tradition.

Mt. Marcy was the traditional destination for seven of the first eight trips, until the Lake Tear lean-to was destroyed and BMCS members got tired of carrying their feast so far into the woods. The pumpkin has now been placed on Giant four times, Colden and Gothics twice each, and Haystack, Armstrong, and Seward once each. The tradition that does not vary is fine dining in rustic surroundings. Champagne and pâté are staples. Soups have included oxtail, leek, carrot, and potato, all made with ingredients fresh from Manhattan's markets. Entrees have included lamb curry with chutney, Peking duck with moo shoo pancakes, beef Bordeaux, and chicken Florentine. Only the finest of candy corn is used for the after-dinner sweets.

The cast of characters comprises a modern, eccentric version of the nineteenth-century Philosophers' Camp. There is the patriarch, Jack McIntosh, chairman (then) of the Wesleyan University physics department. He is responsible for recasting paleontologists' views of the shape of the brontosaurus's head. Rollie Rollefson was another Wesleyan physicist. IBM has contributed physicists Tom Worthington, Bob Scranton, and Celia Scranton. Tom was the solo hiker I met on Giant. Jay Sulzberger is a mathematician, but to call him a mathematician is to miss the measure of the man—Jay is a man of reckless enthusiasms, a raconteur extraordinaire. No one could forget his detailed plans for franchising Captain Gull fast-food restaurants with the distinctive ship's funnel décor and the powerful, hidden intake fans to supply customers with all the gullburgers they could want. It is he who carried the eighty-four-pound pumpkin to Lake Tear. My profession, law, has provided its share of pumpkin worshippers. Most notable is Larry Brooks, who labors in the outdoor kitchen with superb results. His wife Marcia, also a lawyer, is a regular. Rochester has contributed history professors Tina Isaacs and her husband, Mack Knox, the biographer of Mussolini, and Kodak chemists Allan Sowinski, Jerry Klein, and Jack Freeman.

Years before Jack Freeman was elevated to the secretariat of ADK, he practiced as scribe to the BMCS, recording its oral history. His task was made difficult by the fact that the oral history changes from year to year, indeed, moment to moment. Participants have been multigenerational. Larry Brooks's parents, Jim and Fran, have attended more than once. Barb and Karen Thompson have been coming for five years, since they were four and six years old.

With many scientists on these trips, and thanks to unusual field conditions, incredible natural discoveries have been made; for example, wintergreen Lifesavers, when broken on one's teeth, emit a green luminescence visible in the dark. Of most significance possibly since the unified field theory is the Principle of Conservation of Jacks. All the fieldwork for this theorem has been done on BMCS Halloween trips in attempts to explain a fundamental fact: Jack McIntosh and Jack Freeman are each frequent participants in the Halloween trips, but no one has ever observed them together. Tantalizing predictions have been made that both would attend a single trip, but first one would have unexpected surgery, or then the other would have an engagement to sing Renaissance motets. In 1985 Jack McIntosh, in Connecticut, recovered from the flu and decided to come at the very hour that Jack Freeman, in Massachusetts, succumbed to the flu and decided to stay home. Clearly, those who expected both Jacks to appear together have misapprehended the nature of the universe. Great strides have been made toward understanding this phenomenon; the data suggest that they are two manifestations of a single Jack. At any given moment Jackness may manifest itself in one mode or the other, but never in both. Indeed, there may be Jack and anti-Jack, apparently similar but actually bearing opposite charges, and if McIntosh should ever shake hands with Freeman, the universe would be obliterated.

The BMCS is aging more or less gracefully. Gone forever is the era of the summit circus tent. Minimum-impact camping in valleys is now the norm. Our children now accompany us. Most of us can't walk as far or carry as much as we used to. But the irreverent whimsy of BMCS continues to attract professionals and scientists, young and old, from all over the United States into the woods for one annual weekend of supernatural good fellowship. 🏃

Originally published in Oct./Nov. 1986 Adirondac, *the magazine of the Adirondack Mountain Club, Inc. (ADK). This abridged version is reprinted with permission of ADK, www.adk.org.*

*D*onald P. Berens Jr.: *A list maker since my Boy Scouting days, I have completed the Adirondack 46 (#1741 and #27W) over ten times in all seasons and most months, the Northeast winter 113, #22, and the high points of the fifty states, #8. I lead hiking and snowshoeing trips for the RWMS and the Albany Chapter of the Adirondack Mountain Club. I bicycled across the United States in 2008 and would like to pedal in every state. My wife Maureen and I live in Latham, New York, with one of our two children.*

7

THE TRAP DIKE

DON'T LEAVE THE DIKE TOO SOON

Gloria Daly

The most frequently asked questions when I tell anyone from home about my mountain adventures are, "Why do you climb mountains?" and "How did it all start?" It all began when my niece asked if my daughter and I would accompany her on her quest for the 46, and in our ignorance we readily agreed. The day I climbed my 46th peak, the question of "What's next?" was answered with, "Let's climb them all again in the winter!" We've had many other climbs and adventures, including the Trap Dike. The seed was planted for that climb when my husband, who had climbed it years before, said, "I would never climb the Dike again!" I leafed through Barbara McMartin's *Discover the Adirondack High Peaks* and came across this warning in bold letters: "DO NOT LEAVE THE DIKE from the third level where an apparent opening appears." The Dike can be a veritable waterfall, so climbing it in a season of low rainfall would provide a drier, safer passage.

The summer of 2000 was a dry season, so July 5 was the date we chose for the climb. Our friend and guide was Francois, who had been on this trip with my husband. The rest of the eager participants were my daughter Shannon, my niece Andrea, and her husband Robert. As we descended toward Avalanche Lake we saw the slopes of Mt. Colden, but it wasn't until we reached the second bridge on the "Hitch-up" Matildas"that there was an impressive view of the Colden slide with the Trap Dike. As we climbed the jumble of loose rocks at the base of the Dike, there was no sound of water trickling under them—a good sign. We relaxed and enjoyed scrambling up the rock steps and steeper pitches, feeling protected by the rocks on either side. When we arrived at the critical pitch, we stood in awe of this magnificent channel above us—still no significant water. To avoid the steep rock face ahead, three of us crossed over the main channel onto damp, slippery rock. Shannon chose to continue up the rock face to meet up with Francois, who was directly above her checking out the grade of the slide. She climbed about halfway up a steep rock and ran out of handholds. The rock was nearly vertical, so she couldn't see below to reverse her ascent.

It was the only time in all of my climbing trips that I felt at a loss to find a solution. I was having a mother moment: should I have brought my daughter on a hike this dangerous? I knew that, at twenty-two, this athletic young woman was strong of body and mind, but I also knew that she couldn't hold on forever. The solution was a "blind faith" move, with Francois giving precise instructions from the top of the wall as to where Shannon could get a handhold and a foothold to get around the rock. This would put her into a crevasse, where she would be in a better position to continue upward. Andrea, Robert, and I all held our breath as she swung one hand around and made contact. The foothold was a little more difficult to find, and she made three attempts before finding a safe perch. She still had to swing her body around and get a four-point contact on the other side before climbing to where Francois was. I looked down to what now appeared to be a very steep, unforgiving rocky pitch below. No mistakes could be made here! She made it, but there was no applause, only a deep sigh of relief.

From that point on, there was no turning back. This is what lay ahead: the Dike narrows, so that the water was coursing down the left channel with broken slippery rock to the right of the waterfall. The pitch is about forty feet high, and the section we climbed was nearly as steep as the waterfall. We often had four-point contact using hands and feet to crawl up, and any mistake at that point would have been fatal. To the right of the waterfall there is a three-foot-long narrow chimney cut in the rock. Francois showed us how to navigate this section—three or four steps up to the chimney, then, facing inward, wedge the body into it and start look-

The Lower Trap Dike. Photo by Neil Luckhurst.

ing for hand- and footholds. They are not obvious, and you have to be creative. We took our time, pausing after every move to study the moist rock above. At the top of the chimney is a boulder that would require rock-climbing skills, which we did not have. So the best exit was to go left, stepping into the back of the chimney and, trusting it would hold, step onto a small rock ledge about two feet wide, swing the left foot up and over the chimney—and you're out. There was more climbing from there, but it looked easier. Looking back, we realized that there was a serious fall-off beneath us. The climb through the chimney is not all intuitive, and we were thankful for all our past climbing experience. A second sigh of relief.

Past the third waterfall, it's a scramble up steep steps where the ground levels out a bit and the sun starts to filter through, even though the walls still hem you in on either side. Above this pitch there is a break in the dike, and Francois went over to check out the slide. Barbara McMartin's warning came to mind: "Don't get out of the Dike too soon!" We soon had a report from Francois: "Don't come out here; the slide is near vertical. Keep to the left and head up to the cairn." We could see the cairn, but missed the way out to get over the steep walls, so we ended up on a narrow, steep slide that runs parallel to the Colden slide. Our path went up to the left across the top of the slide and then disappeared into very nasty krummholz.[1] After twenty minutes of being stabbed, jabbed, and whacked by unforgiving, thick mountain woods, we emerged near the top of the main slide.

Although the view is breathtakingly beautiful, the pitch of the slide is not for those who have any fear of heights. We were all laid out flat on the slide, belly crawling up on the sticky slide surface to the summit rock. Andrea and Robert had no problem with the steep grade, but were uncomfortable with the wide expanse of the slide itself and kept to the low scrub at the edge of the slide. The slide dropped us onto the trail near the summit, where we took a moment to look down, each of us having the same thought: "I can't believe we climbed that!" 🥾

Note: *On March 16, 2007, an avalanche in the Trap Dike sent trees and rocks cascading down into Avalanche Lake and up onto the shore on the other side.*

[1]Stunted forest characteristic of timberline.

*G*loria Daly: *I live in Ottawa, Canada, with my husband Cliff. I started mountain hiking at age 43 and am still climbing at 60. We lead mountain treks and do trail maintenance, and I'm a member of GORP (Gals on Rugged Peaks), five friends who have been climbing mountains together for years. On completing my 46 in 2000, #4959, the question arose, "What next?" The answer was, "The winter 46." Recently asked, "What's next?" I replied, "To keep climbing until I'm old!"*

8

CLOSE ENCOUNTERS OF THE BEAR KIND

BRUIN BUDDIES TOO CLOSE FOR COMFORT

Anita Stewart

Of the many great experiences I have had in the Adirondacks, I still get shivers when I think about this one. I agreed to accompany Gloria in her ongoing 46er quest, hoping to bag Saddleback and Basin even if it was the muggy, buggy time of year. We've shared many hikes, skis, backpacks, and cups of tea, and I wouldn't pass on an opportunity to spend more time in the woods with a good friend. We hiked in to Johns Brook Lodge campsite, where we met Scouts who had lost all their food at Flowed Lands, a common occurrence in the High Peaks. We were sure that this wouldn't happen to us—we had the new bear canister. At the same campsite, a ranger had once chastised us for hanging our bear bag above the trail. "Bears use the same trail, you know," he said.

After we set up camp, we enjoyed supper and our usual "cuppa tea." Then we carefully stashed our food in the bear canister and threw it into the bush, thankful that we didn't have to spend an hour trying to find a viable tree and getting the ropes and bags rigged up. We retired to our tent and, not thirty minutes later, heard a loud rustling at the canister, about thirty yards away. A bruin had found it and was desperately trying to break into it. He worked that thing for forty-five minutes as he clawed and tossed the canister. We wondered where he would look next when he realized there was no free lunch, but he never came into our campsite or thankfully, close to the tent. The next morning we found the canister, fifty yards from where we'd left it. The bear had put up a great fight, but the canister had won, even though it had deep claw marks all over, with many on the top. When we returned after successfully climbing Saddleback and Basin in the rain, we showed the canister to the ranger and fellow campers, who were all duly impressed. We were the talk of the camp.

Fast forward to the following week. We were with our children—Eric, nine, and Kirk, six. They were already seasoned hikers and campers with several High Peaks to their credit, including Big Slide and Whiteface. The plan was to camp past Marcy Dam overnight and attempt Colden the next day, then Phelps on the day after that before hiking out. I called DEC to learn when campsites fill up on a Friday night, since we had to travel from Ottawa and, with kids, we wouldn't have as much flexibility to move. "By the way," the woman at DEC said, "do you know there are bears in the area?"

"Oh yes, we had an encounter with the canister last weekend."

"I recommend that you eat dinner early," she warned, "because they are now coming out before dark and charging people while they are eating."

Just what we need, I thought, *when we want our kids to have a positive camping experience!*

We marched in full of vim and vigor, set up our two tents and a tarp, and had a sumptuous dinner of stir-fry, all cleaned up before dark. It was a bit eerie, however, because nobody else was in the area. We put the trusty canister *far away* this time and looked forward to a good night's sleep and adventures the next day. It was close to dark; Kirk was in bed, and Mom, Dad, and Eric were enjoying quiet time outside.

Lo and behold, I saw a dark, large, bear-like shape meandering close to where the canister was stored. I immediately pulled Kirk out of the tent in just his underwear and shirt and shepherded both boys over to the lean-to. Bill said that I should take a hiking pole. I replied that if the bear got that close, I didn't think a pole would do much good. Bill stayed behind to watch and inform us when it was safe to return. It was one of the longest thirty minutes of our lives, although it was an opportunity to discuss bear behavior with the kids. I told them that bears are normally shy of humans. The ones around here were only looking for easy food, since the area is so heavily used and they are probably often successful in getting food bags. The children were worried about Dad; while quaking in my boots, I had to be calm and reassuring. We had our ears and eyes on high alert, wondering what was happening and where Bill was.

Thirty minutes later—by then it was fully dark—Bill came to the lean-to and reported that the bear had come into the tent area, sniffed around the kitchen area, and then rambled off. If we'd been without the kids, I would have packed up and marched out; with the kids, we decided to stay. We figured we were safe for the night, since the bear had found no food. We put the kids back to bed, and Bill and I stayed up to see if anything lurked in the shadows. To be extra safe, Bill took *all* kitchen-related gear and placed it with the canister, while I constantly scanned the area.

Suddenly, I saw two beady yellow eyes behind the tents—a bear! Whether it was the same bear or not, I had no idea, but I also didn't care—it was big and too close for my comfort. Bill was on his way back from stowing the cooking gear, and I urged him to move faster without telling him why, since I didn't want the kids to hear.

This bold and brave bruin walked less than ten feet past us. He was not at all scared that there were glowering two-legged humans shining a light on him.

He looked at us and continued on his merry way. What a feeling, knowing that the two most precious things in the world were inside a flimsy tent, oblivious to this, and we did not have a lot of control over the situation! We stood sentry duty another fifteen minutes and then decided that, since the bears didn't seem to be bothered by humans, we'd rather be in the tent and not *see* them than stand outside shivering.

Eric and Kirk at Marcy Dam junction on trek to Phelps Mountain. Photo by Anita Stewart.

If I slept forty-five minutes that night, I'd be exaggerating. Initially I couldn't stop shaking. Adrenaline must have been raging through me at full strength. Finally, that stopped, but every time someone moved, or maybe a little critter outside scratched something, I was certain that there was a huge black bear outside the tent, ready to sniff us out. We made it through the night, but not easily!

The next morning we decided *not* to tell the kids of the second encounter. We told them that, since the chance of an encounter with another bear was fairly high—and Mom and Dad couldn't handle another sleepless night—we'd pack up, climb Phelps and move to a civilized campground, without bears, for the second night. They understood, but were disappointed. They were scared silly waiting in the lean-to the night before, but now they moaned, "But it's so much fun, can we please stay?" It was music to a parent's ears, but our sanity had to prevail.

The kids got another 46er to their credit—Phelps—and Mom and Dad had a better night's sleep. I'm not sure the children will remember as much about the bears as we did. When you are fully responsible for your children's safety and wish to ensure a positive experience, an incident like this remains imprinted in memory. Although we love backpacking, we will only backpack into less-bear-populated areas now. We don't want the stress and the risk of encountering the "rogue" bear that is hungry and frustrated because he can't get enough "easy eats." It truly amazed us that these animals showed absolutely no fear of humans. 👫

*A*nita Stewart: *I started hiking after marrying and vacationing in Alberta, where my husband Bill was raised. Bill climbed the 46 and Kirk and Eric are aspirants. Kirk climbed his first, Big Slide, at a tender age of four. The other hiking family is GORP (Gals on Rugged Peaks), five friends who for years have enjoyed girls' weekends ranging from long, grueling hikes to couch hikes with wine and lots of laughs. I enjoy ticking off mountains, but prefer a nice hike over bagging another peak.*

OF MOUNTAINS AND CHILDREN

WILDERNESS THROUGH THE EYES OF CHILDREN

Daniel Kriesberg

Like all fathers, I have dreams for my sons. These are not dreams that Zack and Scott will become sports stars, doctors, lawyers, or multimillionaire businessmen. My hopes and dreams are that they become lifelong backpackers. So far things are looking good. The boys and I have done our share of backpacking. We usually hike in a mile or two, set up camp, day hike, and hang out. These are great trips, and the boys love the chance to be out and free in the wild.

Last summer's trip was different. At ages ten and seven, Zack and Scott were attempting to climb Mt. Marcy. The allure of climbing New York's highest peak caught their imagination, and they were more excited than on any of our other trips. We reviewed the plan—walk four miles each of the first three days, and eight on the last. Scott asked, "Why don't we stay an extra day? That way we wouldn't be as rushed." "That is a great idea," I replied. So we made plans to add a day. My kids wanted to backpack longer! There were no sweeter words this father could hear.

We started at 2:00 PM and had a 4.5-mile walk to Calamity Lake. With the packs at their heaviest and only five hours or so of light, I told them we wouldn't be able to do much hanging out on the way. Zack and Scott always find a lot to look at when they hike, which is a great way to hike unless you are carrying a sixty-pound pack and trying to get somewhere by dark.

I thought about our other big trip this summer. My parents took our family to Juneau and Glacier Bay. The boys had ten days of hikes, boat trips, and fun with their cousins. We had seen whales, bears, mountain goats, and much more. Would they be disappointed here with the lack of wildlife or bored without their cousins? At the sighting of the first toad, however, I remembered that small wildlife is great, too! The boys caught every toad and frog on the trail. Seeing a grizzly bear was great, but holding a squirming toad and laughing at your brother when it pees in his hand was great, too. While there is something grand about being in relatively untouched Alaskan wilderness, there is something wonderfully hopeful about being in a second-growth forest where moose have returned and even wolves may come back.

The distant thunder became less distant. At least I had them dressed right. The rain did not bother them, but Scott was getting tired and needed a break from his pack. Zack volunteered to carry it and strapped it over his belly, and we kept going. In the car there had been several bickering fights. I talked, well, maybe I yelled, about how we would need to help each other and the only way for us to be successful was to work together. I guess they actually listened. I didn't realize how much help this had been for Scott until Zack got a little tired and I took Scott's pack. My pack was so heavy, the only way to get it up was to sit down, put the straps over my shoulders and use a tree to pull myself up. The rain stopped and started and stopped. We took a break under a huge rock overhang. I was feeling the pain of the first day's hike and began looking for a possible campsite, but the boys wanted to get to Calamity Lake, so we pushed on.

We set up the tent and ate hot dogs. I hid the bear canisters, and we climbed into the tent, proud of overcoming our first challenges. Zack and Scott fell asleep after just a couple pages of the book I was reading to them. Later, when shuffling sounds outside the tent woke me up, I laughed to myself. "Ha, ha, bear, this is not like last year when I did not have a bear canister. I got you this time." My lack of respect came back to haunt me. I awoke to see food wrappers scattered everywhere. The bear had somehow pried the top off one of our bear canisters. I wanted to cry. I couldn't hike the boys back. I cleaned up the mess and told the boys the bad news. Zack was comforting, "It's not your fault, Dad." It was, but I tried to turn it into a lesson on being careful—mostly for myself.

I sorted through the food to see if there was a way to save the trip. Luckily the bear had left the canister containing our breakfasts and dinners. If we could ration the Pop Tarts as lunches, we might be okay. I would skip a few meals. For breakfast I ate some of the tortillas that the bear had not finished. It was the only thing left behind besides one cookie. People camping nearby heard what happened and gave us a bag of trail mix. I have to admit, I was hoping we could score a handout or two. A little while later, a couple walked by. When they mentioned they were hiking out that morning, I decided to tell them our story. We got a Cliff bar, a bag of M & M's and two cheese sticks. We were set. Scott's comment made my day. "Dad, people are so nice here." There was trail magic. The bear had taught us two lessons already.

We were handling our challenges and began backpacking to Feldspar lean-to, three and a half miles closer to the summit. We walked in our "positions"—Zack led, Scott walked in the middle where he was "more comfortable," and I brought up the rear. Hiking with Zack and Scott was so different from hiking with my other partners. The boys never stopped talking. It was nonstop about Star Wars or Legos. Scott talked about the light saber he wants to invent. Zack talked about baseball. I chimed in on occasion with a thought or two. They asked me to tell stories, but quickly interrupted and took over with their own ideas. Mainly, I listened to the music of their voices. The only thing that interrupted the talking was a toad or frog. They caught them, petted them, named them, sometimes kissed them and let them go. We got to our campsite in time for a relaxed dinner.

In the morning, powered by oatmeal and leftover pasta, we set out to climb Mt. Marcy. It was raining, but the boys had no qualms, so off we went. The rain stopped by the time we got to Lake Tear of the Clouds, the sun shone through, and I was happy. I had made a bargain with the weather gods: "I'll take whatever rain you have this summer, just give me a sunny day on Marcy." After a rest,

Scott, Dan, and Zack on summit of Mount Marcy. Photo by a fellow hiker.

Zack and Scott pushed on without any complaining. I was in awe of them. The trees were getting smaller, and suddenly we were out on exposed rock. This was their first hike above tree line. Zack was a little nervous. I was surprised. He is the rock climber of the family, and I usually have trouble keeping him off boulders. He wanted to turn back. Scott was telling me he was tired. He wanted to go back. I told them there was no way we could turn around. The summit was in sight. They settled down. We picked small goals and hiked from one cairn to another. Suddenly we were on top! Out of the wind, Zack whittled, Scott drew Star Wars spaceships and I watched them as much as I watched the mountains. They humored me and let another hiker take our picture. I hope they will someday look at it the way I remember my father, my brother, and me when we took the LuLu City Trail in Rocky Mountain National Park. I pointed out that no one else up here was even close to their ages; proudly we made our way down to a great night's sleep.

In the morning I made pancakes. They didn't turn out quite like the ones Mom makes. They were more of a mush of half-cooked dough drenched in syrup. Scott called them scrambled pancakes and thought we should make them at home. I ate their leftovers; at least it was filling. The bear-imposed backpacker diet was a good one—the better the scenery, the less food one needed to eat.

Our plan was to hike back to Calamity Lake, with long stops at swimming holes on the Opalescent River. At the pools I stripped down but, to avoid traumatizing Zack from embarrassment, I kept my shorts on. Scott dunked a few times too. Few things are as exhilarating as a dunk in cold, clear water. Clouds began to build and I thought of pushing on, but the boys discovered the joy of throwing sticks into the waterfalls, then racing and chasing them downstream. The sticks would get caught underwater, pop up, spin around, get stuck, and then get moving again. They watched with such joy and laughter, I decided to just be in their moment and not worry about rain or the rest of the trail. I joined in collecting and throwing sticks and thought, "Does it get any better than this?"

The clouds passed, and when it was eventually time to go, Zack said, "But we just got here." "Zack, we have been here two and a half hours," I said. He laughed and thought that was great. So did I.

In Jack Turner's book, *The Abstract Wild*, he writes about loss of the wilderness experience. He bemoans the fact there are few places to see for the first time. I agree in many ways, but one antidote is to see wilderness through the eyes of children. They are not tainted by worries of global warming or acid rain. Mt. Marcy was simply a great mountain to climb. They were out there the same way they eat ice cream and candy—enjoying the pure taste and pleasure without any worries of calories, cavities, or cost. I envied them, and it saddens me that it will change. I hope that our time backpacking gives them the strength that when the change does come, they will have enough wonder, hope, and just enough anger to protect and restore, to last a lifetime. Backpacking has given me this and many other gifts. I want to share them with my children.

When we finally left, it only took an hour or two to get to our last campsite. We set up camp and went down to the lake to look for frogs. Scott was soon up to his knees in muck. I have to admit, I was getting grouchy and losing patience with the mess. Then I reminded myself that it was *my* idea for him to put on sneakers and look for frogs! We finally cleaned up and I made dinner. After dinner we sat by the pond and watched a frog and lots of leeches. The leeches were amazing, and it was good to just watch a frog instead of catching it. Mount Colden loomed over us, and Zack asked lots of questions about mountains we could climb. We made future plans, from Mt. Kilimanjaro to the high peaks of the Catskills.

We hiked out in morning rain, making one stop at a bridge for a swim. The clouds cleared and the boys played. Scott and I took showers under a small waterfall. They wanted to stay longer, but it was a long drive home and Mom was expecting us.

I dream of the boys being backpackers, but I have no idea how I am defining that dream. Are there a certain number of trails to hike, mountains to climb, nights sleeping out? Is the dream that in twenty years they will ask me to go on a trip together with them? Does it mean that the two of them will go together at forty-plus years? The answer is that backpacking is only part of my dream for them. My dream is that whatever job they have, wherever they live, that they will live life in relationship with the rest of the natural world, not against it.

A few days after the trip, I told them about Bob Marshall and showed them his list of the top ten mountaintop views. I thought that might be a good goal, to climb all the mountains on the list. Zack read the list aloud, and when he announced that two of the mountains are named Nippletop and Dix, they both collapsed in giggles. Me, too. 🏃

Daniel Kriesberg: Growing up in Syracuse, New York, the Adirondacks were woven through my life—family weekends, first backpacking adventures in high school, summers as a Long Lake waterfront director. It is the place to which I compare all else. Now I live on Long Island, and the Adirondacks are still the place I take my own children for backpacking and other adventures.

10

DOME OF HEAVEN

ALGONQUIN PEAK ENCASED IN ICE

Landon G. Rockwell

The rain lasted for two days, heavy and steady and cold. Today, with a brilliant sky again, the deep fluff of powder snow that had covered the North Country is a thick and saturated sponge. When I see Algonquin Peak from the road by Cascade Lakes, it is obvious that something different happened up there. The cone looms like alabaster, and every curve and every plane of the alabaster is polished. Obviously, up high there has been a deluge of freezing rain these last two days and I'll surely need crampons.

Out an hour, the snow is deep and hard. There is no need for the snowshoes I have as a hedge against breakable crust or possibly softer snow at higher elevations. After a short steep pitch paved with green-water ice, around which I zig and zag, I reach the waterfall. About halfway in distance, but not in time, it is a captivating spot on a level section of the trail to pause, cool off, and drink. The waterfall is in winter storage, mulched by enormous bulges of ribbed green ice. No water is either visible or audible. I think of those who have been by here in the summer but never in the winter, and what sense of wonder they would have at this salient, shining, static sight. But as I watch, while fueling on chocolate and hot tea, it is anything but static. Even in deep freeze, it flows with arrested movement and glows with a brittle light that gives me the illusion of being pelted with rays of extreme chill.

I recall when I was a kid and came by here with another boy. We thought it would be a good adventure to climb the rocks of the waterfall, follow the brook up to where it petered out, and then bushwhack up to the top of Wright Peak, from which the brook flows. It seemed very daring to climb that steep wet rock and it probably was, given our total lack of both experience and judgment. It seemed like the day before yesterday, although it was close to fifty years ago. By now the extreme chill is no illusion, and I continue steadily to the Wright Peak junction. There is a good view of the cone of Algonquin along the way, better than in summer because you are standing on several feet of snow. This close view confirms what I'd seen earlier: a dome of heaven. I see the entire Seward Range and there, too, rock slabs are sheathed in ice and I can almost hear them glitter in the cold brilliant light.

At the junction the crunchy crust is modulating to boilerplate, and it is crampons from here on. The neoprene crampon straps are beautifully flexible in the zero cold, but my hands are not when I finish the job. Beyond here is more or less straight steep pitch, all rock in summer, leading to a short level shelf and, above that, the cone. The crampons take the boilerplate on the steep pitch much better than boots on rock. Up on the shelf I am curious about the snow conditions, since I've had problems here—the last time was only a year ago. A lot of hiking had created an excellent foot pack on Big Slide, and that should have prevailed on Algonquin, so on a fine winter day I had blithely set out for Algonquin without snowshoes. Excellent snow pack, even on the steep pitch above the Wright junction. *Just like a sidewalk*, I was thinking as I reached the shelf below the cone. Then I disappeared in some six feet of snow. I had fallen into an air hole bred by a buried spruce. As snow builds up around the tree, the branches act like an umbrella shielding the spaces between their whorls from accumulation of snow. When the tree gets completely buried, the space above is a sure booby trap for anyone walking without snowshoes or skis. It took me five minutes to swim and wallow back onto the hard snowpack. The snowpack had been covered for the last quarter-mile by new-blown snow, so there was no obvious track. Well, it would just be a problem of sniffing out where that packed snow was in these relatively open woods. I took a couple of steps. Plunk. This time only up to my chest! I spent over half an hour floundering around in the snow on that damned shelf. I doubt if I made forty feet beyond where I first went in. That lovely snowpack had vanished, covered by several feet of newly drifted unconsolidated snow. I finally settled for climbing Wright, where I met a couple of guys to whom the same thing had happened. They had seen my tracks on Algonquin, wondered what had happened, and soon found out.

Today there is no new drifted snow! The seamless boilerplate flows right up to a sheet of light gray ice, sealing the cone directly above me. I take off the sack, unlash the snowshoes and leave them, saving a small amount of weight and making everything much more accessible. Before climbing onto the windy cone, I have to perform a distasteful operation frequently required by the normal perversity of my body's thermostats, particularly in winter. I've worked up a big sweat even though I've been traveling in the minimum of clothing. I strip to the waist, shed a soaked duofold and put on a dry one. By the time I'm ready to stuff the wet one into my sack, it has already started to stiffen.

I survey a sight not often seen on this or any other mountain in the Adirondacks. Not a square millimeter of the natural mountain—the rocks and the grass— is exposed. The entire cone is wearing a thick mantle of ice—varied textures of water ice and shining snow ice. Torrential freezing rain has sheathed it in a great dome of polished glass. I move up on the sloping rink, the squeaking crampons biting securely, but I have to jam down the dull ferule of the ice axe or it simply slips away. That alpine feel is exhilarating. About halfway up the cone, there is a vertical escarpment of rock about four or five feet high, interrupted midway by a little horizontal ledge two or three inches wide. In the summer two long steps will get you up. Now it is encased in several inches of totally smooth black ice. Nothing could have been easier. I simply slam the pick of my axe into the ice on the ledge above, kick in the front points of my crampons, and walk straight up it.

The summit cairn is a squat icicle, and I am alone on the top of Algonquin in conditions that may not soon prevail again. On the way up I had glanced back at my track out of curiosity—there was none. As far as visual impact went, I might as well have flown up. I was so astonished that I bent down for a close look to be

Rocky, enjoying the mountains he loved. Photo contributed by Heidi Rockwell.

sure I still had my senses. The tracks were invisible from a standing position. The ice hadn't fractured—just a faint pattern of pairs of ten very unobtrusive dents, but those slight indentations had been enough to give me complete security. Then I suddenly realize that it could be a tricky matter coming off the cone with no track to follow. I'd been up this route scores of times; nevertheless, anyone familiar with varieties of weather above the tree line knows how disoriented one can become even on well-known terrain. But today the sky is cloudless, the wind is mild, and the cold is not severe. If Algonquin had been thickly socked in, I wouldn't have been up here alone in January, regardless of surface conditions.

On the summit I rough up a section of ice with the adze of my axe so that when I sit down I will stay there! Hot tea laced with rum, a very cold sandwich, and Algonquin's comely view produce a satisfying lunch. As I tour the gently convex summit, I am pleasantly aware of my total isolation in this small realm to which I have come and with which I am briefly one. Life's flailing motions not far away lie still, and all around fortissimos of silence rise. The village of Lake Placid, sharply visible a dozen miles away, spreads like an irrelevance in this world of ancient, tumbled, frosted rock. Physically I am not far from home; otherwise, I am simply a note or maybe merely a rest mark in the endless cosmic score. *Magnificor.* The only lack is someone with whom to share the elegance and the mood. But there had been no one to go with, and this was not a day I would be content to spend in the lowlands. Companionship and mountains are almost redundant, but going alone is not without its rewards; sometimes the experience can be more intense, more inward, and more relaxing when solo.

Never travel in the mountains alone. Whenever I note that prudent counsel, I agree in principle and perversely continue to follow my lifelong mountain travel patterns, which have probably included well over two hundred solo trips. I know all the arguments, and they are impeccably rational. But mountaineers are an indi-vidualistic breed and do not suffer all conventional wisdom easily. I have no moun-taineering friends who have not traveled solo many times. Even the experienced are vulnerable; they can get hurt like anyone else. But that is a risk one takes, mostly without dwelling on it. One of the subconscious attractions of mountaineering is the potential element of risk. Almost everyone is a risk-taker. Most people fall in love sometime. Consider the risk of that. Most people drive cars. Consider the risk of that. But if the axe does fall and someone gets lost or hurt and needs rescuing, what about the burden of responsibility that is thrust on others for search and res-cue? If someone gets lost—really lost—they are either inexperienced or have poor judgment. The two usually go together. *They* should *never* travel alone. What about the experienced person who has a bad throw of the dice and gets disabled? That's a tough one, unless you can banish all solo traveling, which you cannot.

Now it is time to go. The January days are short. I want plenty of margin for the trip down and, besides, I am getting cold. For an instant I imagine what it would be like to be stuck here without crampons, fancifully ignoring how you could possibly get here without them. There would be no way of getting down intact, yet I was to have the easiest and most direct descent of the cone I'd ever had. I thought of John Fowler on Mt. Washington in early April of 1936. He and a companion climbed the mountain via Tuckerman's Ravine in search of good skiing on the summit cone. The skiing proved impossible because of heavy wet snow, so they continued to the summit carrying their skis and spent time in the then refuge hut. The temperature dropped substantially, freezing the snow hard and smooth. On the descent, 200 yards from the summit, Fowler slipped and slid 900 feet on frozen corn snow down the entire cone of Mt. Washington to the rocks of the Alpine Garden and death. Two of my close friends found the body. It had given me early in life an enormous respect for winter slopes above tree line in the Northeast mountains.

At the foot of the cone, I stop and turn for one long upward look at a sight few will ever see again. 🏃

Originally published in the June 1978 Adirondac, *the magazine of the Adirondack Mountain Club, Inc. (ADK). This abridged version is reprinted with permission of ADK, www.adk.org.*

*L*andon G. Rockwell, "Rocky," was a member of the American Alpine Club and the Alpine Club of Canada, and climbed extensively in the Alps and the Canadian Rockies, but his heart was always in the Adirondacks, where he built a cabin in Keene Valley in 1950. Rocky had been a fan of U.S. Supreme Court Justice Douglas, both for Douglas's powerful defense of the First Amendment and for his mountain writings; one of Rocky's treasured moments was hosting Justice Douglas on the deck of his cabin. Rocky died in 2003, leaving his wife, Heidi, two children by a previous marriage, and three grandchildren.

11

WE SHAN'T BE LONG

A HIGH PEAKS THANKSGIVING

Landon G. Rockwell

It was the day before Thanksgiving and all through the house every creature was stirring—pie fillings and cranberry sauce and turkey dressing and cups of coffee. Outside it was a stunning day with fresh snow, the sky unblemished blue, and a windless twenty-five degrees. After lunch nobody is stirring anything, including themselves, and suddenly I have a severe attack of my chronic restlessness. "Let's go somewhere—anywhere."

"Win, how about going up Cascade?" Win is subject to the same malady I have.

"Sure—we can easily make it back by dark."

"We shan't be gone long," we agreed.

There was a new trail up Cascade that I hadn't yet hiked, and that is one of the reasons I proposed Cascade. I have an irrational compulsion to know all the trails in my area (roughly a ten-mile radius from the summit of Marcy) well enough to have a guidebook picture of them in my mind at hundred-yard intervals. It was time to hike the new trail, virtually a moral duty! Alone once on the old route, I almost collided with a bear. Well, not quite—he was ambling toward me and I toward him, each of us absorbed in our own concerns. I saw him a split second before he saw me; I froze, then he saw me and froze. Thirty feet away he cased me in a dumb bear-like fashion. He couldn't figure me out. Windless, he could not smell me; he had not heard me on wet leaves from morning showers. But the fuzzy form he saw was obviously not supposed to be there. For a full three minutes, he stood there puzzled. Then, wanting to be underway, I moved. He galumphed off to his right, which happened to be parallel to the trail, and I followed, running, to get another look at him. A hundred feet beyond, he stopped and looked back, curious. I was definitely not his cup of tea, so he took off full throttle. It was the longest sight I had ever had of a bear. He was a big one, three hundred pounds or more.

We are now on a moderately steep pitch leading into a broad col at about 3,000 feet. We are the sole travelers in a small world of glittering woods spiced by the wonder of discovery—we had never been on this ridge before. A half hour of moderate grade brings us to an Adirondack wonderland, a little step-down ledge and then a series of open glades sprinkled with contrasting clumps of birch and balsam, which are loaded with fresh piles of powder snow. Above that, the roof of uninterrupted blue. I scan a small segment of infinity with my eyes, but I cannot scan it with my mind. I recall St. Paul's words: "Faith is the substance of things hoped for, the evidence of things not seen." Perhaps I grasp infinity a little better now, here, the day before Thanksgiving. The color contrasts alone are as dazzling as I remember in anything but alpine surroundings—dark green, white, cobalt blue, so intense that the colors themselves seem three-dimensional. Fantasy. But what would experience, never sparked by fantasy, be like?

We reach the open rock at the top of the crest, then up to the rocky cone and the summit of Cascade. Except for the forest fire of 1903, the cone would be an undistinguished hump of woods. We snack and sip tea, two specks overwhelmed by the vast brilliance of white and blue, indulging in the best of two worlds—an entirely winter scene, but without the chill or wind of winter. Pure joy. We resist leaving; Win proposes what I had dismissed as too late to do. "Let's go over to Porter." Well, why not? There's a full moon for travel light, and it really isn't right to turn our backs on a scene like this until we've fully drained it in. "Sure, let's go over to Porter."

From Porter all the topography is defined in sharp contrasts of light and shadow, the faces of Giant and Gothics lit like beacons with alpenglow. Perched on a rock blown clean of snow, we watch the mountains fade from forms to silhouettes. Our night vision takes over, losing all color discrimination, so we see only in degrees of gray despite the considerable light beginning to be shed by the enormous Hunters' Moon. We rise to leave, and I start down where we'd come up. But Win again has another idea. "Let's go down the other trail." The "other trail," longer than the one we'd come by, descends to The Garden parking area and comes out right at our house. The same thought had occurred to me, and we take off through untracked snow. "The girls will worry about us." "Why should they worry? They know we know what we're doing." "They'll still worry—we'll be way overdue." "Maybe, but a little worry won't hurt them!"

There are substantial drifts to wade through on the ridge before the junction where we descend the face of Porter. This is our first encounter with snow this season; it is good. I remember a verse from the book of Job: "Hast thou entered into treasures of the snow?" Like almost anyone else who has experienced snow extensively, I had not always regarded it as "treasure." I had wallowed in it exhausted, I had been scared to death of it on exposed steep Alpine slopes and knife-edge ridges, I had been totally disgusted with it in late April when it tilted with daffodils as to which would prevail. But now it was treasure sealing our little world with its seamless hush of white.

We make our way diagonally down the south face of Porter in moonlight, more or less following the trail and shortcutting occasionally. Most of the forest cover here is birch with smooth branchless trunks. The birch shadows on the snow are so startlingly sharp, our reflexes almost rein us up short several times lest we trip over them. Finally we see the rocks of Little Porter loom dimly ahead of us, scramble up and are stopped in our tracks by the haunting view. Keene Valley is an island of lights below us to our left, directly below us is the dim trough of Slide Brook valley, and above, staccato patches of pale white on the open rocks of the Brothers, all crafted by the sovereign splendor of the moon. We sit there for half an hour or more.

"We better get going, the girls will really be worried—we're already more than two hours overdue." Reluctant to forsake the spell, we continue following the trail along the crest of Little Porter. We're back a little after 7:00 and discover a big sign outside that tells us the girls *are* worried—an absent car. I phone Dave Ames, our local ranger, and leave a message with his wife. Fifteen minutes later the girls return, angry but relieved. "How could we know—you said you wouldn't be gone *long*."

It was a memorable experience to have shared with my son. 🏃

Originally published in the October 1977 Adirondac, *the magazine of the Adirondack Mountain Club, Inc. (ADK). This abridged version is reprinted with permission of ADK, www.adk.org.*

For biography of Landon G. Rockwell, see "Dome of Heaven."

12

Night on Bare Mountain

Below Zero in Your Birthday Suit

Mary M. Holmes

Well, no, the mountain was not actually named "Bare," and we weren't on top of it exactly, but let me explain by telling the whole story. My brother-in-law's younger brother Rick and I had gone on several outings in the Adirondacks, backpacking and canoeing, but he wanted to share the exquisite joys of winter backpacking with me and suggested a January ski trip to Mt Marcy. In the mid-eighties, the idea of spending overnights in the mountains in winter was fairly new, so we were on the proverbial cutting edge. It was exciting. We made the date, and I put together my gear. I had a zero-degree synthetic sleeping bag, an insulated parka, and long johns. Rick had lots of good gear, since he had done this and almost everything else in the "Dacks." I felt that I was in the company of an experienced guide.

The weekend of our outing arrived. I picked up Rick and we drove to the trailhead at Heart Lake. There was lots of snow—a good three feet of snow pack, great for skiing. When we pulled away from the register box, it was ten degrees under a clear sky. We skied to a Marcy Dam lean-to and had the whole place to ourselves as the sun went down. I had worked up a lot of sweat in over two miles of skiing, and being inexperienced in winter camping, I simply wrapped up tighter and got into the sleeping bag as soon as I could. The temperature was plummeting. In the gathering darkness we put on our headlights and saw our breath forming great clouds of fog around our heads. We ate a hot meal that Rick fixed on the Coleman stove, and then it was time to sleep.

I had experienced very low temperatures. I had taught at the New York State University at Potsdam for a year and was familiar with winter's extremes. What I had not experienced was sleeping out in such weather! I was amazed at how everything froze, and very quickly. We had not washed our cooking pots, thinking that we would do that in the morning. That was a mistake. We had stacked them together, and they froze that way. It also made them more enticing to raccoons, and several times during the night the creatures banged them on nearby rocks to get them apart. They failed, but their antics were simply a footnote to the night's main attraction—my surviving those degrees below zero. Rick was fond of saying that the degrees above zero were very different from those that dip below, and I agree.

We got into our sleeping bags and tried to drift off. Rick succeeded, but I was shivering. I tossed and turned, and Rick woke up. He realized my situation and was concerned that I was becoming hypothermic. Then he did the most chivalrous act that one could expect a hiking partner to do—he offered to exchange bags with me. I was very surprised, but accepted. He had a –30° bag, whereas my bag was rated at 0°. I noticed a distinct improvement after the exchange and once again tried to find the way to Nod. I still felt very clammy, however, and it dawned on me that I'd have to completely change my clothes if I were to get some sleep. It must have been near midnight when I roused myself from the relative comfort of the puffy bag. Reluctantly I got out of it, took off the parka and began to strip down to the skin. I changed into a fresh pair of long underwear. I really don't remember being cold while doing this, but I remember the darkness and my flashlight trying to penetrate the clouds of vapor produced by my breathing as I worked very quickly to cover my bare skin.

Those are the "bare" facts and the "bare" part of the story. The next morning Rick and I retrieved our pots, boiled water and separated the pots, packed and skied out to home and comfort. At Rick's house we learned that the temperature the night before had dipped down to –40°! Not unusual for the mountains, but it did explain why no one else was foolish enough to occupy the other lean-tos. We felt a real sense of accomplishment to have coped with such an extreme. I felt the accomplishment all the more, since I had undressed completely, in true polar bear fashion, leaving nothing between my tender flesh and the not-so-tender care of Mother Nature. I've learned much more about winter hiking since then. I have gone out many times into the Adirondacks to experience the beauty revealed when everything is covered in snow, but that maiden voyage of winter camping will always remain special because of the learning, the sharing, and the extreme temperatures. 🏃

Mary M. Holmes: I've always enjoyed exploring the outdoors and never feel more in touch with myself than when my feet are wandering a forest path. I consider the Adirondacks the cradle of my backpacking interest. After retirement from the FBI, I completed the Appalachian Trail, the Colorado Trail, and the John Muir Trail. But my home and my heart are in the Adirondacks, so I bought land and designed and built a log cabin. I've maintained trails with ADK and still maintain a portion of the Northville-Placid Trail.

13

BEAR ENCOUNTERS ON JOHNS BROOK

CLOSE ENCOUNTERS OF THE FURRED KIND

Taryn Bukowski

When I suggested a multiday hiking trip to my husband, it reminded him too much of his army training and he couldn't understand how it could be fun. My sister-in-law, however, was game. She is an avid cyclist who has ridden across the country, and I felt sure that she could handle the trip—in spite of living her entire life in suburban Chicago. My father and I outlined for her the important details of hiking the Adirondacks—water filtration, etiquette in cooking and cleaning up, where to make camp if no lean-to is available, and most importantly, the art of hanging a bear bag. She was skeptical of the last, sure that we were just trying to get a rise out of the "city girl" with our warnings of marauding, thieving bears.

After gearing her up appropriately and carefully plotting our route, we set off via the Johns Brook Trail past the lodge to claim one of the lean-tos upstream. The first one was vacant, and our first task was to refill our water supply, so we found the filter, gathered water bottles, and rock-hopped into the creek. There wasn't much chitchat; we were tired and thinking about setting up camp.

Squatting with my back to shore, it was relaxing to enjoy the outdoor sounds, the babbling creek, and singing birds. I noticed Karen had gone a brilliant shade of white and thought maybe she'd gotten her first feel of mountain-cold water on a misplaced foot, but she was looking directly over my right shoulder. I turned around and there it was—a black bear that had the same idea we had, that "a cool drink sounds good right about now." I don't think the bear realized we were there until I had moved to look at what had scared the color out of Karen. She grabbed onto my leg with a vice grip, and I returned the favor on her arm. Once he saw us, the bear was none too happy. Fortunately, he just splashed once in the water and took off toward the lean-to.

I joined Karen in the "Whiter Shade of Pale" category. Granted, bear encounters were nothing new to me in my many hiking trips. This, however, was the closest I'd come to a bear in the wild, and I don't mind saying that it didn't sit very well with me! Most of my experiences had been in waking up and finding my bear bag dismantled and my hiking trip over. Karen and I looked at each other to verify that this had, in fact, happened in real life and wasn't just a delusion brought about by

Forest Pre-serve bear.
Photo by Paul Misko.

fatigue. It took only moments for the realization to set in before Karen was on her feet pointing toward the lean-to and exclaiming, "Our food! Our packs with all our food! They're up there!" I shifted my vice-like grip to her leg and calmly and eloquently pointed out, "What the hell do you think you are going to do about that? I sure as sh*t am not going up there any time soon!"

Luck was definitely with us, as the bear had not bothered to inspect our gear and had moved along to a quieter watering hole. That night, as we were settling in, reality again intruded and we couldn't pretend he wasn't out there, somewhere, waiting. It is amazing how, under the right circumstances, a field mouse inspecting a hiking boot can sound exactly like a black bear preparing to eat you alive! We didn't see him again, but he was there. He checked out our bear bag that night, but was unable to get more than a few scraps of trail mix out of a tiny seam he tore open.

The next night we warned fellow hikers nearby to take every precaution. It's too bad they didn't heed our advice. The next morning they found they had lost their whole stash and bemoaned to us how the bear had not only gotten their mangoes, but also the chocolate-covered espresso beans. It was hard not to laugh, but all Karen and I could envision was this poor bear, running around the woods all jacked up on caffeine, hyper as can be and crapping like crazy all day long! I am proud to say that Karen and I have since had multiple successful forays into the Adirondacks, and while we have had other bear encounters, we have never since had quite the experience that our first trip together gave us. 🚶

Taryn Bukowski: My father's deep appreciation of all nature has to offer was shared at home in DeRuyter, New York, on family camping trips, and during my hiking trips with Dad to the Adirondack Mountains. I shared his knowledge of the wilderness and how to have minimal impact with my own children and extended family. If we all do this, more people will appreciate the environment and the importance of preserving the natural gifts we have been given.

14

A DOG'S DAY IN THE HIGH PEAKS

A PUPPY'S PEAK EXPERIENCES

Michelle Hamilton Scott

On an ADK Iroquois Chapter outing to the High Peaks, I decided to take along my teenage son Emlen, his friend Kevin, and Onyx, the Guiding Eyes dog my daughter is raising. Onyx was ten months old, seventy-five pounds of clumsy, lovable, adolescent Labrador. A brief word on the Guiding Eyes program: we obtained Onyx from the Oneida County 4-H Office of the Cooperative Extension Service. Puppies, six to twelve weeks old, are given to families for one year to be raised with love, attention, and basic obedience training, but then must be returned for three months of intensive training for their future lives as "eyes" for the blind. Most of the dogs are Labradors or golden retrievers and are bred especially for their intelligence, eagerness to please, and gentle disposition.

When we arrived at The Garden parking lot at nightfall, Onyx's pleasure matched ours as we all inhaled the damp, woodsy smells. The hike into Winter Camp was uneventful, except for a short stretch when I loaned someone my flashlight and used my Guiding Eyes puppy as my "eyes"—not successfully. In her enthusiasm she led me off the trail into mud and to the discovery that bushwhacking in the dark leashed to a dog causes great tangles.

At Winter Camp in late September, it is appropriate to sleep on the porch, where the sounds of Johns Brook can be fully appreciated. Onyx, confined to the kitchen at home, was thrilled to find humans joining her on the porch who were even willing to share sleeping bags.

Saturday morning, as friends set off in various directions, the four of us headed for Basin and Saddleback—my twenty-first and twenty-second peaks, and Emlen's third and fourth. For Kevin and Onyx, these were to be their first peaks. Excitement and energy levels were high, and all morning I delighted in watching dog and teenagers climb every boulder, leapfrog the lead position, and cross streams in the most unorthodox ways. Onyx, our water dog, would linger in every puddle or stream until we were nearly out of sight, then catch up to share sprinkles of mud and water with everyone.

After Slant Rock and a healthy-sized snack, we began the climb up Basin in earnest and soon got an inkling of problems to come. Every time we came to a boulder or ledge more than two feet high, we'd have to coax overcautious Onyx over or find a way around it. There were numerous places with steep ledges to clamber over and with no way around, so I'd have to set Onyx's front paws on the top of the rock, have Emlen hold them to prevent her from retreating, then lift her back end, sighing with relief as she scrambled up the trail. The problem seemed to be that she was afraid and did not trust her own agility. I theorized that, with patience, she would gain confidence and learn how to climb most of the obstacles. Near the summit of Basin, we came to a twelve-foot rock face with a log ladder. I suggested that we might give up on Onyx and turn back, since I couldn't imagine wrestling her seventy pounds up a ladder. But Emlen, eyeing the summit ahead, proclaimed this obstacle no worse than what we'd already overcome. I didn't share his confidence, but helped pull and push our panicky pooch up the ladder. She "climbed" it once she realized we were not going to let her turn back.

The hike went on like this—fifteen minutes of hiking, followed by ten minutes of coaxing, pushing, pulling, and lifting Onyx. She became more timid and shaky as the day wore on, and I was patient only because of the boys' helpfulness and my guilt at bringing a clumsy, heavy puppy on a trip that was far too strenuous. We had our humorous moments, too. As I was edging Onyx up a particularly steep, open rock face, four hikers passed us on their way down. They looked at my mud-covered legs and arms, and with large grins agreed that they had never encountered a hiker quite so dirty. Anyone who has a Labrador knows that its thick tail spins like a helicopter blade whenever it feels it is losing its balance. Having been at the hind end of the lifting most of the day, I was wearing more than my share of the mountain.

Reaching the summit of Basin, we felt sure that going down would be a breeze. We enjoyed the views and celebrated Kevin's first peak. To our chagrin, the descent presented the same problems; Onyx was afraid to jump down more than a foot or so. The only thing in our favor now was gravity.

As we began the ascent of Saddleback, we met a couple who said we'd never get the dog up the cliffs. Our faces must have reflected our emotions, for they quickly began softening their remarks. I assured the boys that nothing could be much worse than all the obstacles we had already overcome. When we came to those cliffs, however, I must admit that in my three years of hiking, with numerous adventures, I'd never felt more discouraged. Onyx lay down, exhausted, while we edged our way around looking for a more reasonable approach. Other disbelieving hikers must have done likewise, since there are two dead-end paths on either side of the cliffs. I sat down by Onyx, wondering how I might lift her up this six-foot perpendicular ledge. (I was even having doubts about getting my own 115 pounds up.) As I watched Emlen and Kevin cautiously edge their way up to scout for help, I realized that the cliffs were surmountable—as long as you have hands.

Onyx was shaking from cold and exhaustion. As I wrapped her in my spare jacket, I saw that her footpads were badly cut in several places and that three toenails had been ground down past the quick by the rough granite. I felt terrible and saw myself as extremely foolish for forgetting that Adirondack mountaineering often requires hands as well as feet. I felt so badly over Onyx's anxiety and pain that tears filled my eyes. Emlen and Kevin returned with two hikers coming our way; one was in the same shape as Onyx. With too much gear, he was barely able to climb down the cliffs himself. He stood apologetically below while his companion stated that he was exhausted as well and unable to help. He suggested that we go back the way we came. It was after 2:00 PM and we'd covered the first five miles at a much slower pace than expected. The thought of taking Onyx back over Basin seemed an absurd alternative. It took me many minutes to persuade this hiker that I needed only a little extra muscle to lift Onyx overhead. (It occurred to me later that he might have been intimidated by the dog's size and possibly have been worried that he might get bitten.) We hoisted Onyx up the next few cliffs using the pull-push technique we'd perfected. Eureka! We had made it. We explored the top of Saddleback and looked back over the trail to Basin, enjoying the expansive feeling one gets from a successful climb.

It was literally all downhill after that. Our energies were renewed with food and drink and we bounded down, discussing how many plates of spaghetti we'd eat upon reaching Winter Camp. We arrived at sundown, soaked our tired feet in the icy waters of Johns Brook, and cleaned up. Onyx had soaked herself entirely in the brook, so she had to be dried off to prevent chilling in her exhausted state. She fit nicely into my heavy polypropylene turtleneck, if I rolled up the sleeves, and she was sufficiently weary that she was not even embarrassed about her ridiculous appearance.

Kevin now has a consuming interest in climbing. Emlen and I are eager to return, and Onyx, who will spend most of her life in a harness as a Guiding Eyes, has some first-rate and some woeful memories of her adventure. If you plan to hike with a dog, know your trail beforehand. If you have a dog you can easily pick up, you shouldn't have major problems. If your dog is very large, be sure it can climb up and down steep places, cross teetering bridges, etc. Do not leave dog excrement on or near trails. Bury feces if possible—for the same reasons you bury your own. Keep your dog leashed around other hikers. Do not take dogs that bark a lot—this is not in keeping with wilderness and getting away from it all. The Department of Environmental Conservation requires that your dog be under control; they advise that any dog caught running after deer can be shot. This is particularly important in the spring, when the deer are heavy with fawn or have wobbly fawn in tow. Consideration of these guidelines will help prevent passage of rules banning dogs from trails, as has happened in many other wilderness areas. 🚶🚶

Originally published in September 1985 Adirondac, *the magazine of the Adirondack Mountain Club, Inc. (ADK). This abridged version is reprinted with permission of ADK, www.adk.org.*

Michelle Hamilton Scott: My love for the mountains was sealed when I took a SUNY field ecology class, which included studying and camping in the High Peaks. While working, raising children, and pursuing my degree in nutrition science, I became a 46er, #2324, climbing many mountains several times in all seasons. When I can share my love and enthusiasm for the outdoors, it brings enormous satisfaction. As people learn about and appreciate the natural world, they will protect it.

15

SLEEPING IN THE SNOW, MAY 1943

THESE GIRLS WERE SOMETHING ELSE

Helen Colyer Menz

For several years we took a week's vacation time from work around Memorial Day to make trips to the mountains. Our friend Ruthie Prince (later King) would also take time off. Bess Little was an older lady, maybe in her sixties. She and Ruthie trusted us to plan trips and to bring them back in one piece. We decided to climb Allen Mountain from Keene Valley. We didn't have gas to drive (because of World War II rationing), so we took a bus to Keene Valley. It was spring-like, and our trip almost ended at Black Brook because the water was so high that we had to take our boots off. As I tossed one boot to Mary, it went into the brook and started to sail to Johns Brook, but Mary plucked it out just in time!

At Johns Brook Lodge the famous rhubarb was up. Since no one was at the lodge, we pulled some to cook, then hiked as far as Hogback lean-to the first night. We had homemade sleeping bags, made of balloon silk dyed brown and wool batts. Most of the ADKers made them that way. We had a tie party to fasten the batts to the material; some people even put zippers in theirs. Our pots were "beer" buckets with wire bails. Most of the food was canned or awful dried mixtures. The "Klim" (milk) was the worst.

The next morning we went to Bushnell Falls, where we would have to wade because there was no bridge. The water was wild! Bess said that we could cross if we wanted to, but *she* would camp out at the upper lean-to for the week. We couldn't find a safe place to even think of crossing, and decided we would go over Marcy instead of over Haystack to get to Allen. Easy to change plans, with a week to do the job! We weren't far above Bushnell Falls when we began to run into snow; turning back wasn't an option. The snow got deeper. We had shorts on, but decided not to put long pants back on because they would get wet—at least we'd have dry pants at night.

When the snow got up to our knees, we gave up on Allen and decided to go to Indian Falls. What a trip down! The snow got almost to our waists. We'd go four or five steps and fall in, take the packs off and crawl out. It was interesting. Bess's sleeping bag was around her shoulders; it kept falling off, so we took turns carrying it. No one groaned or complained; we just kept going. About 4:00 PM Mary said that we should find a place to sleep before dark. Bess was horrified. Ruthie was too tired to care, and so was I. Mary was the only one with energy.

We picked a flat place, trampled down the snow, cut a few boughs and spread our oiled silk over them. Sleeping bags went on top. We started a hole in the snow for the fire, with a layer of thick sticks as the base. We were so tired that we just cooked our breakfast oatmeal and then crawled into our bags. We had an extra oiled silk that we put over all of us. Our packs full of tin cans were our pillows, but we actually slept. There were some clouds blowing by in the open sky. We thanked the mountain gods that it didn't rain!

In the morning the fire hole had melted down two feet. We had spaghetti (which had been meant for last night) for breakfast. We knew that the Marcy Trail wasn't too far off, so we worked our way up. We were glad to get to the intersection. The snow on the way down to Indian Falls was quite deep and had the added pleasure of six to eight inches of running water under it. The sun was hot on that side of the ridge. The upper Indian Falls lean-to was a welcome sight. We set up housekeeping at once and hung things out to dry.

Marcy Brook was flowing fast near the fireplace, so we looked for a place for shelter in case we needed to evacuate. There were two, quite large, brand-new, one-holer johns. Ruthie saw a mouse in one, so she didn't think that staying in them was a good idea. The lean-to on the brink of the falls was in the direct line of the wind and was cold and damp from the mist from the falls. We decided to stay where we were, even if the water came up. Maybe we could build a dam.

That night was the first time in our lives that we couldn't start a fire. The candles didn't work, we had very little paper, and the wood was soaked from the mist. We had a cold meal with *no* tea. Emergency gear was kept in the lean-to— blankets, toboggan, and first-aid kit. We had borrowed the blankets and used them carefully. We had our *Readers Digest* with us, and for two days we read to each other. In between we snuggled under the covers and took naps. We finally got the fire going and had good food. The stream came close to the fireplace, but did not get into it.

After a day or two, we got our boots on and explored. Indian Falls was fantastic. There was so much water going over the falls that there were rainbows all over! The water had receded somewhat, so we waded across the brook and hiked down to Heart Lake, where we stayed at Mt. Jo lean-to. The Loj people told a hiker that the snow was too deep to do Mt. Marcy without snowshoes. That hiker talked to us, and we told him how deep the snow was. I guess he thought a bunch of girls were exaggerating, but he didn't make it much farther.

I called Uncle Ray in Saranac Lake, and he took us to Keene Valley for the bus. I got my patch for five winter peaks, but this trek didn't count. A. T. Shorey, who planned trails in the High Peaks, told us that the following spring he was on the Bushnell Falls trail and saw burned sticks that just might have been from our fire. 🚶🚶

~~~~~~

Helen Colyer Menz: My sister, Mary Colyer Dittmar, and I grew up in Saranac Lake. Our dad included us on his fishing and hunting expeditions. I had a rifle and a hunting license, and we were very comfortable in the wilderness. In 1935, after Dad died, we moved to Albany and I got into Girl Scout work at our church. The Albany Chapter of the Adirondack Mountain Club invited scout leaders on a hiking trip and thus began our sixty-four-year relationship with the club. Mary and I met our husbands, Ditt [longtime treasurer of the Forty-Sixers] and Bill, in the ADK, where we also met Ed and Grace Hudowalski [historian and correspondent for the Adirondack Forty-Sixers for fifty years]. I worked with Grace for many years recording and numbering new 46ers, and then worked with her on the first 46er book. I've climbed nearly four rounds of the 46, #42, and our children are all 46ers.

16

ALGONQUIN SUNRISE—AUGUST 1944

ADVENTURE IN THE NIGHT

Helen Colyer Menz

My sister Mary and I got the bright idea that it would be great to see the sun rise from 5,114-foot Algonquin Peak. Our friends Ruthie and Mabel were always up for an adventure. Since it was during World War II, we didn't have enough gas to drive to Heart Lake, so we took a bus from Albany to Lake Placid after work and then a taxi to Heart Lake. Our friends were waiting for us with a fire and a feast at the Mt. Jo lean-to, our favorite. Our taxi driver even helped take our things to the lean-to. He worried about the "girls" being out in the woods at night, but the most exciting thing that happened was the breaking of a bag of potatoes. We had quite a search for them in the dark.

Summit, 5,114-foot Algonquin Peak. Mount Colden in background. Photo by David White.

Around midnight we packed our breakfast, snacks, and water and set off. With a half moon we could see the shadows of trees and, partway up, the extensive white birch groves looked sort of spooky. We refilled our canteens at the waterfall and made good time even though we didn't rush. It was too early for sunrise, so to keep warm we went up Wright Peak first. From the summit we heard voices from Mt. Colden and occasionally saw a light. It was strange to hear voices in the dark from another mountain. We would learn more about that later.

We were on top of Algonquin as the sun rose. Gray light gradually transformed into various colors—it was beautiful, and we just sat and looked, lucky that it was a clear day. We were surprised to see the shadow of the entire MacIntyre Range on Wallface and MacNaughton Mountain. We went over Boundary to Iroquois and back, and cooked breakfast at the first brook on the way down. We met rangers who said they'd heard voices in the night, saw lights on Wright and figured they'd have another rescue on their hands. Why would anyone be on Wright Peak at three o'clock in the morning? The rangers were on Mt. Colden because people had gone up the Trap Dike and got off too soon onto the open rock face; it was so steep that some hikers were terrified and couldn't move. Someone went for help, and rangers came with ropes to help them back into the dike, where they waited for morning. One time a party of ours went out on the Colden face too soon, but we didn't want to be rescued. It would have been a blot on our record and ruined our reputations! What we did was to take off our boots and socks, being sure that they didn't roll down to Lake Colden, and went barefoot back to the dike. Bare feet worked like flypaper on the steep rock face.

This trip was unforgettable—the mountains at night, sunrise on Algonquin, the shadow of the MacIntyre Range, and distant voices in the night. 👫

For biography of Helen Colyer Menz, see "Sleeping in the Snow, May 1943."

17

LEADERSHIP

"TOUGHING IT OUT"

Jeanne Goehle Sternbergh

One must go on a beginner's trip with the Rochester Winter Mountaineering Society (RWMS) to qualify for further backpacks, and my first peak with them was 4,240-foot Big Slide Mountain. After my first winter season, the society's members advocated that I complete the Winter 46 with them; I would be the first woman in the group to do so, five years later. On Fridays we would drive to the Adirondacks and stay in an inexpensive hotel, four to six people per room. After breakfast we'd backpack to a high base camp and climb one or more peaks, hike out Sunday and stop for a big dinner. The longer ranges required three-day trips. A leader planned the number of tents, the occupants of each, and the lead for each tent, which held three to four people. The tent lead purchased and prepared the food; good cooks were chosen repeatedly for tent leads!

We tried to establish camp and quickly change into dry clothing before it got dark. I never quite got accustomed to the cold while camping. On very cold days I dived into my sleeping bag and stayed there through dinner and breakfast, only leaving to collect snow or go to the bathroom. We had to melt snow for dinner and our next day's supply of water, which was a long process—a pan full of snow seemed to melt to nothing. Dinner always tasted good! We would have a hot after-dinner drink and tell stories until we fell asleep, exhausted. After a really hard day, we could sleep for twelve hours.

I remember two participants on a slower-paced family trek that I led to Mt. Colden—the wife of one of our strongest hikers, and the son of a fairly new hiker. The wife was a positive and enthusiastic person. Her husband carried her part of the communal gear, as well as most of her gear, and he still could have sprinted up the mountain. She found the climbing very difficult, especially holding the snowshoe horizontal when trying to kick into the previously formed "step." Finally her husband hand-placed each of her steps and gave her a push on the rear to help her make it up the mountain. Although she said she would never do it again, she loved the camping and was exhilarated when we got to the top of Mount Colden. She had gained a better understanding of her husband's addiction for climbing mountains in the wintertime.

The father/son situation was more difficult to handle. The son was not dressed appropriately. Although he had poly long underwear, he was wearing jeans, and that's an absolute no-no for winter hiking. Jeans get wet and freeze; they don't wick moisture and can contribute to hypothermia, which I mentioned to his father. Because I'd brought extra clothes, I decided to let him go with us anyway. A couple hours later the son was struggling to keep up. At first he had been running and jumping in the snow, but soon he ran out of energy. I knew we wouldn't make the summit if we slowed to his pace and, in addition, he had started to feel cold. I had to make a decision, so I called for a break so that I could talk with him. I offered to take his pack off so that he could have a better rest. I was shocked! His pack was as heavy as mine. He was around twelve and of slight build—no wonder he was so exhausted. I questioned his father and found out that the boy was carrying part of the communal gear; his father thought he should tough it out. I reminded the father of the purpose of the family trip—for family members to enjoy their experience. His son would have to "tough it out" on another trip.

I gave the father a choice: either I would walk them out, or all decisions relative to the boy would be made by me. First, I emptied his pack. The father couldn't pick up much of his gear, so I divvied it between the more seasoned backpackers. Second, I thought up challenges and games the son could play while he climbed. We joked and laughed a lot. When we camped, I insisted he strip off his jeans, and we gave him dry clothes to wear while he slept. Fortunately, he remembered the fun part of the trip and enjoyed the experience immensely. The family trip was a success! Spouses experienced firsthand the beauty that drew their husbands to the mountains most winter weekends. This was my first time as a trip leader, and I was proud of how I handled the trip. 🏃

Jeanne Goehle Sternbergh: At Kodak in Rochester, many coworkers backpacked and we got the hiking bug. My husband and I "passed" the Rochester Winter Mountaineering Society's required beginners' trip. While not the strongest hiker in RWMS, I was nowhere near the weakest. I stayed in shape in numerous ways because I wanted to be a strong and capable hiker, to carry my own weight both on my back and in my participation. I am 46er #1960W.

18

THE DETHRONING OF THE KINGS

THE PRIDE OF LYONS

Hannaleah Lyon

I grew up in suburban New York City, close to that expanse of green and mountain that grows into the Catskills and to the Adirondacks, with black bears, ice-cold streams tumbling over boulders, ponds edged by the work of nature's toothy engineers, high peaks stretching into the clouds, the quiet before dawn and pause on a sun-white mountaintop, the calm between dusk and dark—quiet the city does not know. I spent afternoons in the trees and poison ivy surrounding the stream that ran between the subdivisions, daring friends to jump with me into mud that squished up to our thighs. We followed raccoon tracks, ate wild onions, cut arms and legs on thorn bushes. But I dreamed of real woods, bursting with the promise of adventure.

My parents sent me to camp near the Adirondacks; like my older brother—the grasshopper-eater, fish-catcher, tripper of the year—I loved backpacking. We sang as we scrambled up the bare rock of the high peaks and scrunched into our sleeping bags as we told scary stories, listening to wild animals and ghosts creep around our lean-to. I learned how to start a fire with birch bark, pee in the woods without harming my boots or dignity, and hang a food bag high enough to thwart even bears that had spent years training at Marcy Dam.

I began to write, question, and wonder. Struggling with existential demons, I realized that the woods offered holy stillness that I was supposed to find in religion, but never did. I read Thoreau and Emerson. Sitting across a beaver-dammed pond at sunrise, I all of a sudden understood that it went much deeper than the sheer joy of pinecones and deep pools in snowmelt streams. The woods were shining all around me, and from within me.

The sun dips beneath the horizon and the Lyon pride pauses to reflect on the incoming chiaroscuro, thinking of *Walden* perhaps or of a horror movie in woods like these. The eldest and most distinguished, a Dartmouth assistant professor, takes a minute from contemplating his vanishing knee cartilage to muse, "The nice thing about twilight is that it gives you a pause between day and night to reflect on just how @#^&* physically disabled you're about to be." Heads nod at this revelation, but no Lyons laugh. Only hours ago the hubristic middle child had said he was too good for hikes without high peaks, and the Lyon clan had been unscarred, unscathed, and unsoiled.

It's been a trying day, one could say, but one could also say that Algonquin, the monolith from hell they were slowly crawling down, was a mere mountain. If the Lyons run into any ranger who cheerfully chirps out something to that effect, there is no doubt that the family will slaughter and possibly eat the well-meaning woodsman. Spirits are running dangerously low and the family has run out of trout jerky. They must resort to drastic measures—the father does his job, checking the trail conditions by falling lavishly and repeatedly on his face to get a closer look. The eldest son does what he can—whimpering whilst imitating the eldest living Lyon, Granny Bea, the grandmother with a pig's heart and plastic knees—while his dear sister fantasizes about knocking him unconscious and dragging his body down the trail so as not to have to listen to his pitiful whines. The middle child, the painting brother, eventually breaks down and piggybacks Dr. Stupid, the crippled music professor, over the obstacle course of a path.

As the last traces of dusk fade, the group hobbles down the trail—the little sister at front, giving a running commentary on trail obstacles as her young eyes are the only ones still working; the two brothers in the middle, relying on the painter's legs, one quietly moaning up top and the other huffing his exertion below; and the father in the rear, sporadically toppling into the dark when diabolical boulders and roots get in his way. As the girl clicks on a cell phone to help her squint out the status of the trail, a *deus ex machina* in the form of an intelligent man with a flashlight comes bobbing down the trail. Tony sees the Lyon family and realizes his mistake (as a kind person, he'll help them), but it's too late for him—he's been sucked into the Lyon family hike. He hands his flashlight to the girl and attempts to carry the eldest brother, grunting, "You weigh three hundred pounds or something?" before flinging him to the ground, panting. This brother was the smallest male Lyon, weighing 130, but the dark distorts eyes and back muscles—Tony the savior can be forgiven. The liberator and the painting brother act as crutches, carrying the cripple betwixt them. In no time, compared to what might have been hours without their rescue, the Lyons and the intelligent man with flashlight reach the parking lot. The girl, previously teased by the painter for being an idealist greenie, realizes this is the only time she's ever been glad to see asphalt. The family tries to take their savior to dinner, but he's had enough and exits as quickly as he can.

Several days later when the professor was able to talk through painkillers, he wondered at the resurgence of his knee injury. "I'd had no problem walking around my house," he notes, but the rest of the Lyon clan had learned their lesson. Never again would the painter brother be the deciding factor when choosing a mountain to hike. Never again would the professor be allowed on such a vigorous excursion without a new set of knees, and never again would they be caught in the woods without a flashlight. And a stretcher. 🚶

*H*annaleah Lyon: *The near disaster of an adventure on Algonquin, above, inspired my family to explore hiking trails closer to home. We came together in the same woods that Ernst, my father's father, a devout atheist Jew and refugee from Nazi Germany, used as his temple in America. Though not able to be under one roof, we remain together in shared memories of picking blueberries as fat as marbles, throwing rotten mushrooms at each other, starting fights with geese in the middle of Pine Meadow Lake, and charging after wild animals—camera in front, common sense left behind.*

I went to college in rural Vermont and struggled to understand the American landscape—its suburbs, prisons, and projects—instead of enjoying streams, birches, and lakes. I went to San Francisco to volunteer in the county jail and saw system-ized pain, hopelessness, and despair. I wanted to reach back into memories and grab all the fireflies I'd caught and the birch bark I'd peeled and use it, somehow, to make the sadness lighter. Instead, it burrowed into me. I spent my college years organiz-ing against the prison industrial complex. I opened my heart to the city's pain and pleasure and to its people. I work at Constellation Energy, America's largest energy provider, and join the struggle to provide renewable energy, fighting from within to bring power to the people.

19

CLIMBERS FOLLOW GHOST UP MOUNT MARCY

A LEGEND TRACKS A LEGEND

Ed Hale

Six climbers bushwhack up a slab-sided wilderness chasm. "If Old Mountain Phelps is watching," trip leader James A. Goodwin says, "he knows we're now on a 'random scoot.'"

As a Forest Preserve centennial event, the hiking party is following the original trail up Panther Gorge to the state's highest peak—5,344 feet above the Hudson River's mean tide level. Phelps cut it in 1861, marking it with ax blazes on trees and piled-stone cairns on the bare rock.

"It took him maybe three weeks," Mr. Goodwin says, "a week in the gorge alone." Women drove him to cut the route. In about 1859, he guided the first two women—Fannie Newton and Mary Cook—to reach the summit. His success gave Phelps his first local celebrity.

"Sure," Mr. Goodwin says, "that trip was the incentive for the trail."

It was abandoned in 1873 when Verplanck Colvin cut the present southeast trail for his surveyors.

"Colvin thought the Phelps trail was too rugged for his surveyors to get instruments up there," Mr. Goodwin explains. "And he wanted a practical route from the Ausable lakes to Lake Colden."

Phelps's blazes and cairn are gone now. A section of the gorge is choked with fallen trees crisscrossed from the 1950 hurricane and mounded with beaver dams. Mr. Goodwin, though, remembers it when he was a boy guide at Keene Valley's Interbrook Lodge in the 1920s.

"The gorge had big spruce trees then and a waterfall off Marcy," he says. "It was beautiful, a little Yosemite Valley."

It's fierce now. So the boy guide grown to a man of seventy-five avoids blowdown because Phelps would. He starts seven-tenths of a mile west to avoid this gorge's center where the big spruce once grew.

The four men and two women climb on the edge of history. On slabs tilting forty degrees they search for hand- and footholds, almost upright with both hands and feet on the wall. They avoid wet spots, rootless grass, spalling surfaces, lichens. Mr. Goodwin climbs deliberately. "The moss is slippery," he warns, pointing at a velvety cluster on the route. He looks where he's going, but glances behind often, adjusting his pace to make six into a team with a single mind.

"There's a good handhold there," he says. "Pass it along."

On a crossover step, he clears away loose rock and dirt to make a foot-long transition stable. The green ridges become dense with cripple bush—tough balsam with dwarfed arms tugging against sweating bodies and hiding holes two, five, even twenty feet deep. The 1.3-mile bushwhack caps Saturday's 16.8-mile-day centennial trip.

𝕏𝕏 𝕏𝕏 𝕏𝕏

The climbers' day begins early. After six-and-a-half hours' sleep, Mr. Goodwin arises at 4:45 AM in his Keene Valley home. He's been hiking for seventy years. Before he was seventeen he'd climbed Marcy fifty-five times, and now he's preparing for his 188th trip.

"It's embarrassing," he says. "It's the only mountain I've counted continually."

He's a quiet, almost shy man who wants the day to belong to the memory of Old Mountain Phelps through the efforts of the centennial hikers, representing the Adirondack Trail Improvement Society. He has headed that group for seven years as president.

Despite his diffidence, Mr. Goodwin spent a lifetime leading hundreds, perhaps thousands, of boys and men, girls and women—as English, history, and geology teacher, Adirondack guide and World War II climbing instructor for the Tenth Mountain Division with service in Italy.

Five others are preparing for the trip—each climbing for a different reason. On East Hill in Keene, Nina H. Webb, fifty-seven, is researching a Colvin biography.

"I'm interested in Adirondack history," Mrs. Webb says, "and it's a chance to climb with Jim Goodwin."

She picks up Robbie L. Ticknor, a sophomore at Franklin and Marshall College, in her station wagon. "It's an adventure and fun," he says. He's interested in Adirondack route-finding and history.

Ronald P. Miner, thirty-three, a Keene Valley guide and caretaker, waits in the ramshackle lean-to at the head of Panther Gorge for the others to reach him.

"Our history is important," he says, "and events like this should be relived."

Barbara M. Hale, fifty-nine, and her reporter-husband, sixty, crowd into Mr. Goodwin's 1983 red Chevette.

"I like being part of an unusual hike," Mrs. Hale says, "led by the Adirondacks' most knowledgeable mountain leader."

"And," her husband says, "it's a story."

At 6:12 AM the Webb station wagon and the Goodwin Chevy reach the Ausable boathouse. The five Forty-Sixers (Mr. Goodwin has climbed the 46 peaks over 4,000 feet fifteen times) launch a green Old Town war canoe into Lower Ausable Lake at 6:25.

"Old Mountain Phelps complained that others used his guide boat," Mrs. Goodwin says, "so he may have paddled up the lake in a canoe."

As an osprey circles overhead and a crest of mergansers scurry along the shore, the climbers launch the twenty-six-foot canoe, hop aboard and paddle the length of the lake. Ashore again, they walk a mile to the Warden's Camp at the Upper Lake's outlet near the trailhead of Old Mountain Phelps's original route. The existing trail follows Phelps's 1861 one for 2.8 miles.

Boots are tightened; packs are checked. The easy part is over. A six-hour climb—with more than half spent on the 1.3-mile bushwhack up Marcy's rock-scarred flank—lies ahead. In good spirits, the party begins the 1,800-foot ascent of

Standing, left to right: Bobby Hale, Ed Hale, and the late Nina H. Webb. Sitting, left to right: Ronald P. Miner, Jim Goodwin, and Robbie L. Ticknor. Photo courtesy of Watertown Daily Times.

Bartlett Ridge at 7:30 AM. The boulders of Shanty Brook show through the trees. At Crystal Brook at 8:20, the leaf-covered footpath rises more steeply.

"Did Old Mountain Phelps tread this trail?" Mrs. Webb asks.

"Sure," Mr. Goodwin answers, "I see his footprints just ahead."

As the trail rises steeply, talk dies like wind at day's end. Mr. Goodwin fields the inevitable questions: How far?—and how long?

"When you tell them it's a two-hour hike," he says, "they tend to slow down." Time and distance are relative, Mr. Goodwin adds, depending on the climbers and the problems they confront.

After passing the Mount Haystack trail junction, they begin a six-hundred-foot descent to Panther Gorge. Mr. Goodwin stops and points:

"There's Marcy," he says.

The whiteness of a new rock slide singles it out from the gray of the other five-hundred-to-seven-hundred-foot slabs.

"We'll start at the bottom of the white one," Mr. Goodwin says, "and work our way diagonally across to the other higher slides on the left."

They reach the ramshackle lean-to with its rock-secured plastic roof where Mr. Miner, the husky Keene Valley guide, joins the party. Mr. Ticknor changes from shorts to long pants for the bushwhack. The six head into the unmarked wilderness of this gorge at 10 AM. Marcy's peak hides 2,000 feet above, beyond some of the state's wildest terrain. The party scrambles up a brook draining the white slide that's reached at 10:41.

"Don't put too much weight on that rock," Mr. Goodwin says, maneuvering always upward. And he recalls the work of Charles D. Warner—nineteenth-century author, *Hartford Courant* editor, and climbing companion of Old Mountain Phelps—who wrote: "The pleasure of such an ascent consists not so much in positive enjoyment as in the delight the mind experiences in tyrannizing the body."

That's the kind of things they talk about as the steepening rock sucks breath from the climbers' lungs and pulses pound 180 beats a minute. They hardly glance at Haystack (4,960 feet) towering to the hikers' right and Skylight (4,926 feet) rising over their left shoulders; these third- and fourth-highest peaks—close enough to discern hikers on their ridgelines—are yardsticks to measure progress.

"Did Old Mountain Phelps carry a rope?" a climber asks as the slide angles to forty degrees with only nut-sized knobs and no cracks to grip.

"Sure," Mr. Goodwin replies, "But Mary Cook (Phelps's heavy but courageous client) refused to use it."

Near the top of the white slide, Mr. Goodwin leads the party into cripplebush to reach an older slab with sloughing rock that stretches still higher toward Marcy's summit.

"Old Mountain Phelps is up there laughing at us," Mrs. Webb says.

Progress slows in the dense balsams. Mr. Goodwin searches for solid terrain beneath the thicket in which a hiker could drop from sight. He finds lines of least frustration—avoiding concealed cliffs and hidden holes, finding occasional islands of rock to change the pace. The hikers climb with arms and legs, grabbing balsam boughs for balance and testing the stability of lower branches with kicks.

Mr. Goodwin whistles, because climbers behind him are hidden in the hedge-dense growth. He whistles for reassurance, too, so others can follow his lead.

"You're a great bunch," he says, "regular mountain goats."

He says things like that often. It helps those whose only thought is the next step—can it be taken again and again, one foot after another, to the top? Each step up brings more peaks into view. But in the last forty-five minutes, the climbers have seen only green branches and a patch of green beneath the summit that looks like grass.

At 1:30 they arrive for lunch at the grassy patch, 100 or so feet below the summit that is alive with hikers. Assistant forest ranger David Chapman sees the group and is worried that its presence amid the alpine plants will tempt others to lunch there. He climbs down to herd them to the rocky summit, but stays to chat when he learns of their centennial mission. He radios that he's lunching on Marcy—below the summit, in the grass.

The static and summit voices bring the world of marked trails into stark contrast with the wilderness experienced during the three-and-a-half-hour bushwhack.

"I don't recommend this tough, tough route to just anyone," the burly Mr. Miner says.

Mr. Goodwin, always a caretaker, passes out plums. They taste better than crackers, cheese, and salami.

Old Mountain Phelps described his emotion upon standing on Marcy's peak as "heaven up-hi'stedness." Each climber, though, has his or her own delight.

"Joy is proportional to the effort to get there," one centennial hiker feels.

The group holds a hand-lettered banner in a twenty-mile-an-hour wind. Mrs. Webb, vice president of the Ausable Club, made it from a sheet. It reads: FOREST PRE-SERVE CENTENNIAL 1885–1985, ATIS MT. MARCY EXPEDITION VIA ORIGINAL ROUTE LAID OUT BY OLD MOUNTAIN PHELPS IN 1861.

When a curious hiker from Ottawa learns the group has bushwhacked up Marcy from Panther Gorge, she says, "You must have used compasses."

"No," she's told, "we had Jim Goodwin."

At 2:55 the climbers descend on the marked trail, and at 7:05 they launch the war canoe for the 2.5-mile return trip to the boathouse. Mr. Goodwin drops off his last passenger in Keene Valley and steps into his kitchen, puts down his pack and smiles. His wife hands him a squat glass of Old Crow, ice, and water.

Home is the climber, safe from the hills.

This abridged version is reprinted by permission of the Watertown Daily Times, *Bob Gorman, managing editor.*

[Editor's note: Jim Goodwin made his last ascent up Marcy at age eighty-five with his sons Tony and Peter, their wives Bunny and Susan, and his five grandchildren, Morgan, Robbie, Liza, Hunt, and Jon.]

Ed Hale: I've traveled from the South Pacific in World War II to the Arctic. Finally, though, I settled in the Adirondacks during the 1970s with wife and family and bought the weekly pre-Olympic Lake Placid News. *After selling it, I became the Adirondack correspondent and columnist for the* Watertown Daily Times. *I've climbed the Adirondack's 46 high peaks twice, #714, been a mountaineering instructor for the National Ski Patrol, and helped to train and found the 1980 Olympic Nordic patrol. Since retiring in 1990, I've taught Telemark and Alpine skiing at Whiteface Mountain. And all the while, I worry about too many using too much stuff on our glorious planet.*

20

A RIDE TO REMEMBER

ACCIDENT ON MISERY HILL

Donna I. Ellis

You could call me a flatlander, one of those weekend warriors from New Jersey who drives north to enjoy a very special part of the world—the Adirondacks. As a seasoned hiker and cross-country skier, and a former emergency room nurse, I thought I was ready for anything.

On one backcountry ski trip, the weather was near zero, but the sun was out and there were patches of blue in the sky—a beautiful day with a dusting of fresh powder. Two of us left from the Adirondak Loj area and skied through Avalanche Pass to the Lake Colden Interior Outpost. Even though I felt I was careful in negotiating the downhill turns, accidents do happen and a freak fall is always possible.

We were on the way back when I had one of those unexpected mishaps along a section of trail sometimes known as "Misery Hill." I felt my shoulder *pop* as I landed on the snow. When I couldn't get up, I knew I was in trouble. It was two o'clock, soon to get even colder with early darkness, and we had miles to go. I would have to keep moving to stay warm—and alive! My friend skied out to get help as I hobbled along very slowly in ski boots, supporting my injured arm with my good arm, extra careful not to lose my balance or step into a deep snow pocket that I would be unable to pull out of—which without the use of either arm is much more difficult than it sounds.

Alone in the woods, it doesn't take long for one's mind to take over, imagining a worst-case scenario. It was the cold that frightened me, I think—below zero all week—and knowing how cold it would get as the sun set. I think I started to hyperventilate, and then I became thirsty, but I had water and survival gear in my backpack that was still on my back. Oops, I couldn't reach any of it because of my injury. Any upper body maneuvering sent a new spasm of incapacitating pain. *Keep moving,* I said to myself, *baby steps … just do not fall.* My balance was off, but I couldn't grab a tree or use a pole.

It felt like a miracle when a ranger eventually appeared. This backcountry ranger wrapped me in a space blanket and put me on a rescue sled, and then a snowmobile driver—who slowed down on the bumps—took me to Lake Placid volunteer ambulance drivers. My ride out of the woods, flat on my back, gave me a whole new view of the great outdoors—a ride to remember!

On a picture-perfect autumn day the following year, we were looking for a short hike to stretch our legs. Our hostess recommended a loop over Big Crow and Little Crow, a pair of small mountains in Keene. We came across a lone hiker with his dog. The hiker looked like a local to me, a friendly sort, not in a hurry. We struck up the usual hiker conversation—how good it was to be enjoying the woods, the weather, what great views, etc. I noticed a small ax hanging off his belt and asked if he were a trail maintainer. He modestly replied, "Sort of." I told him about my mishap and how lucky he was to live where such a professional rescue team operated. He asked me where my accident happened and when. His name was Peter Fish, and he was the park ranger who was first on the scene that February day near Avalanche Lake when I was hurt. He was the one who wrapped me in a space blanket, radioed for help, and stayed with me until the rescue sled came. You might say he saved my life. Talk about *timing*—if we had not stopped to chat, or if our conversation had not taken the direction it did, we would have passed each other and never have known the history we shared.

You never know who you will meet in the woods. 👫

Donna I. Ellis: My favorite childhood memories are of Girl Scout camp and family vacations spent in the Adirondacks. Although I've hiked for years, only recently did I become connected with the "hiking community." I responded to an ad in a paper about a group hike, and it changed my life. I made a whole new circle of friends. They, like me, enjoyed outdoor adventures and encouraged me to accomplish goals I never thought possible, such as completing my Catskill 3500 peaks.

21

INTO THE TEETH OF THE TEMPEST

THE DAY THE WEATHER GODS USED IT ALL

Brian Hoody

The evening's forecast did not deter me: "Chances for scattered showers." *Not too bad*, I thought, *Better than the constant stream of storms that were passing through the North Country.* I wanted to catch the sunset from Phelps Mountain to test a new digital camera. It was slightly after 5:30 PM and the heat remained. The air was saturated with moisture.

The weather prediction came true halfway to Marcy Dam. Rain came down steadily, and soon my gear and I were soaked, but I was making good progress and was right on time to catch the sunset, so I pressed on.

At the dam the sun was out again! Perhaps I had foiled the weather gods and would have time to mess around with the million or so settings that the digital camera offered. Humidity increased and another chance of showers felt very possible, but the rain held off, so I started up Phelps.

The trail was very slick in spots, but on cue I broke through tree line and onto the summit cliffs just as the sun was setting. Clouds obscured Marcy, but Tabletop was still visible. The sunset, however, caused my stomach to knot up—an angry reddish-orange streak behind which loomed massive thunderheads. A cold wind whipped the summit. I took a few pictures and quickly headed for lower ground. The wind was fiercely hammering the upper portions of the mountain as I dropped off the summit cliffs; the rumbling began.

I got down the two steep areas near the top before darkness fell. I dug out my headlamp and continued on quickly, trying not to slip on the damp trail. So much for dinner on the mountain! A swig of water was all that I had time for. The booms of thunder got louder and were joined by flashes of lightning that cast an eerie illumination over the woods. I seemed to be in slow motion. Total darkness had fallen, and my sodden boots offered little traction, making for slippery moments.

As I arrived at the intersection with the Van Hoevenberg Trail, all hell broke loose in a raging thunderstorm, and I still had three and a quarter miles to go. Rain poured down and was lashed about by a howling wind. Peels of thunder crashed one after the other, and lightning flashed like a strobe light. A ground fog had developed, so thick that I could not see my feet! My headlamp was incapable of penetrating the gloom. I didn't want to stop, but not being able to see where I was

Summit, 4,161-foot Phelps Mountain. Mount Colden in background. Photo by David White.

going meant the possibility of injury. I had an extra flashlight and, to my relief, I could penetrate the ground fog enough to make my way if I used the flashlight in tandem with my headlamp.

The rain slackened as I neared the dam. *Possibly the worst is over,* I thought, but again I was proven wrong. I hurried across the spillway, bright bursts of lightning illuminating the choppy water. No bears tonight! The constant booming of thunder followed me into the woods, and then the rain came down in sheets—the worst had been yet to come. The trail became flooded and, coupled with the fog, it was now impossible to tell where the trail lay. I was torn between whether to stay put and hide someplace, or to keep going as quickly as possible. My fight or flight instincts appeared to be shut down. I was totally drenched and the only person stupid enough to be out in this mess, so the flight option finally won out. The lightning helped me find my way—the flashes were so bright and so frequent that the surrounding forest was lit up.

With the swaying trees and that strange light, I felt like I was on some kind of bizarre dance floor. I laughed to myself at my earlier attempts to keep my boots dry. For half an hour the tempest raged around me. I was dead tired when I finally saw the parking area. The storm followed me all the way back to St. Regis Falls; the rain slackened, but the noise and light show kept up into the wee hours of the morning.

In a couple of days, my stuff dried out and I noticed how clean my pack was! Years of dirt and dust had washed off in a few hours. I vowed the next time to use the washing machine to get my pack clean, as a never-ending High Peaks thunderstorm did not appear to have a gentle cycle. 🏃

*B*rian Hoody: *I spent my formative years in the northern Adirondacks searching for brook trout with my brother and friends. I am 46er #4410, a 46er correspondent and director, and a regular volunteer on the 46er trail crew since 1999. I enjoy exploring not just the higher peaks, but many parts of the Adirondacks. I authored* Notes from above Treeline *and was instrumental in the republication of the 1958* Adirondack Forty-Sixers. *Karen and I have two daughters, Maeve and Ryne.*

22

CURSE OF THE FOUR CORNERS

THE LEGEND IS TRUE

Brian Hoody

The legend is true. I had dutifully toted a rock up from the famed Four Corners to Skylight's summit cairn, and my first two climbs of Skylight featured fine weather.

For those unfamiliar with the legend: when the weary climber reaches Four Corners to climb to Skylight's summit, they must carry a rock to the summit or it will surely rain. Four Corners links some of the highest, most rugged peaks in all of the Adirondacks—the trail off the south flank of Marcy connects with the trail east out of wild, remote Panther Gorge or west past Lake Tear of the Clouds, source of the Hudson River, and south up Skylight, our curse.

On my brother's first climb of Skylight, I distinctly remember running off at the mouth about how we must pay due diligence to the legend and each carry a rock to the summit. We enjoyed extensive, beautiful views and brisk winds on the summit of Skylight, but we had one crucial problem—we had not a single rock between us. Even after my banter about the legend, we had forgotten to pick up a rock! It was a gorgeous day, though, with hardly a cloud in the sky—we had some-how circumambulated the legend. Reluctantly we left the summit, heading toward Lake Tear of the Clouds and our final objective, Gray.

The curse began to unfold as we ascended Gray on a steeper and longer path than I remembered. On the summit the sky still looked perfect and the views were superb. But the curse had a curve ball it was waiting to throw at us. When we descended, the curse took hold—not an immediate deluge of rain from a cloud-less sky, but a more methodical punishment. At the outlet of Lake Tear, I thought we would head towards Feldspar, but the consensus was that we head back over Marcy and out the easier Van Hoevenberg Trail. So we hiked back to Four Corners and began the long haul up 1,100 feet to the summit of Marcy. On the long slog up to tree line, I knew we were not going to make it out before dark.

The last light petered out after we crossed the bridge over Phelps Brook. Stum-bling through the dark, we eventually came out to Marcy Dam and the blessed truck trail, which would lead us back to the trailhead. Home free, or so I thought.

The first mile went fast, and we possessed a renewed sense of energy. Then I felt it—a drop on my arm. Condensation or something, I thought. I saw a sky

Summit, 4,924-foot Mount Skylight. Photo by Brian Hoody.

full of stars. Another drop, then another. And then it rained so hard that it was almost impossible to see. We broke out our jackets. All talking and joking ceased. Still, the stars were out. We must have been under the one cloud in all of the Adirondacks! The rain completely soaked through everything, and we sloshed through big puddles. After twenty minutes of this downpour, as suddenly as it started, it stopped; we were ten minutes from the trailhead. The stars were still shining brightly.

The moral of this little story: carry a rock a mere six hundred vertical feet from Four Corners, unless you're the gambling sort. If you don't wish to add to the huge cairn on the summit of Skylight, perhaps you should carry a rock up and then carry it back down—for safe measure, naturally. 🥾

For biography of Brian Hoody, see "Into the Teeth of the Tempest."

23

THE NORTH FACE OF GOTHICS

LIKE CLOCKWORK

Laura Waterman

The *North Face of Gothics*. Guy, our mountaineering friend Art Fitch, and I packed into the Orebed Brook lean-to to ensure an early start the next morning. The North Face had been living in our dreams all winter, and we were fit and prepared with our twelve-point crampons, ice axes with the elegant drooped picks, and the shorter wooden-handled alpine hammers. First generation Chouinard tools, all very cutting edge in 1972.

The morning of February 6, we snowshoed up the Orebed Trail to where we left the trail and began bushwhacking until we hit the Face a little way up its left-hand edge. A wide sweep of ice-and-snow-plastered rock led straight to the summit, not visible yet. We strapped on our crampons and, with ice tools brandished, Guy started out onto the Face in a rising traverse. We had a rope, but decided not to employ it until need became apparent. I followed. Then Art emerged a short

The North Face of Gothics. Photo by Neil Luckhurst.

distance, and stopped. "I'd say we should rope up here." He drew our attention to the fact that the Face, as we moved out onto it, swept away beneath us a hundred feet or so—and if one became detached ...

Guy, who had the rope, had almost reached a clump of stunted firs out on the Face where the real climbing started. I was right behind him, feeling that I'd rather keep going. It was a fine day, not windy, and I was rather enjoying the exposure. There was confused calling back and forth. None of us was argumentative by nature, but we were getting into a heated discussion about this rope with Art, who remained standing at the edge of the Face. Suddenly, the winter air was split by a ringing that lasted the length of a telephone ring. Guy slapped his chest, shutting off his alarm clock that he carried in his shirt. "It's for you, Laura," Art said, and this made us laugh. Then Art stepped onto the Face and skipped across the exposed traverse to join us in the comfort of the clump of firs; we roped up and got on with the day's amusement of climbing the North Face of Gothics. ⚔

Laura Waterman: In 1971 Guy and I decided to homestead—living on the land, for the land—in a cabin in the Vermont Mountains. We called our 38.8-acre homestead Barra, after an island in Scotland's Hebrides, Guy's ancestral home. Our objectives were to live simply, inexpensively, unhurriedly, concerned with basics like food, shelter, and fuel, and to maintain our mutual interest in climbing and hiking, literature, music, and writing. For nearly three decades we ate food we grew ourselves, using no running water or electricity. We built our own shelters and used wood from our land for fuel. We authored many books, including Forest and Crag, Wilderness Ethics, *and* Backwoods Ethics, *and were instructors in the ADK-AMC Winter Mountaineering School. After Guy's death in 2000, I wrote a memoir,* Losing the Garden: The Story of a Marriage.

24

THE GREAT RANGE

WINTER MOUNTAINEERING SCHOOL INSTRUCTORS CHALLENGE THE RANGE

Laura Waterman

The Great Range. We arrived after dark on February 7, 1974, and spent the night on the side of Route 73. Our friend Mike Fye slept in his car; Guy and I stuffed ourselves into his tiny canvas bivouac tent used for such purposes. That way, we could leave our mountain tent packed. It was a reasonable 15° above zero when we went to sleep, and an unreasonable 15° below when the alarm went off. It was dark, but it was morning. I fell into a bad mood thinking about Barra, our homestead in Vermont. We had put anything that would freeze—winter squashes, begonia, and ivy—in the root cellar. We'd planned to be away six nights, a long stretch for our unheated cabin.

On the walk into the ranger station, we passed a party coming out whom we knew—that was how it was if you hiked in the Adirondacks in winter back then. They'd stayed at Johns Brook Lodge and climbed the Brothers. The trail up to the Wolf Jaws was not broken, they grinned, eyeing the size of our packs. We broke the trail up to the Wolf Jaws and on to Armstrong—what a steep trail! When we reached the summit I was tired and we set up camp, our tent nestled into the deep snow and the scrub. The temperatures hadn't budged from the single figures all day. The night was screeching-bright with stars.

A magnificent sunrise brought us to life in the morning; it was –6°. We bounded down Armstrong and fought buffeting 30 MPH blasts on the Gothics ridge. The descent over steep ice-covered rocks bordered on the technical. After gathering our breath in the Gothics col, we broke trail up Saddleback, crested and hit an even steeper descent on the other side. Basin took the heart out of us—it's a big mountain and has two peaks with a col between. So when you think you've made the top, you have to lose ascent and then fight your way up another three hundred feet to the true summit. We kept switching leads to keep up the momentum, and from the summit plunged downward to Snowbird lean-to.

I was delighted to be at high-altitude, legendary Snowbird lean-to, and we set up the tent inside for a cozy night. We got the jump on a long, nine-and-a-half-mile pack out to The Garden by starting for Haystack in the dark. We made good time to the col, where we dumped our packs and shot off for the summit, wanting

Gothics and Pyramid. Photo by Neil Luckhurst.

to salute the sunrise. We were on top of the world as the sun illuminated the Dixes, with Marcy and Skylight aglow across Panther Gorge.

At noon we enjoyed a luxurious lunch on the porch of Johns Brook Lodge; Guy hung out the thermometer and we watched it rise to 15° above. We were in shirtsleeves on this sunny, windless day, sitting on the railing dangling our legs.

I fell into a grumpy mood on the drive home, worrying that our root cellar had gone below freezing. It had bottomed out at 31°. We had seedlings down there, too—tomatoes and peppers that we were foolish to have started so early. They were goners, as was the begonia. I cared about the begonia, but I loved the ivy, and it was alive and forgave me for running off to the mountains. 🀫

For biography of Laura Waterman, see "The North Face of Gothics."

25

SUBZERO BACKPACK

OVERNIGHT IN A COLD LEAN-TO

Dick Levine

Ed McGittigan called me after New Year's. "Dick, we're planning a hike in the Adirondacks on Washington's birthday weekend; would you care to join us?" I'd been hiking and backpacking for four years, ever since I increased my weekly running mileage to fifteen; two weeks before my forty-ninth birthday I completed my first marathon. Running put me in condition to hike and backpack—something I hadn't done since the 1940s, but which I'd enjoyed. I had been planning a winter hike, and a hike with Ed and others in the Adirondacks was appealing. "That sounds good. Yes, I'd like to go; I can arrange my schedule."

The Northeast had a cold spell after February 4. The daily mean temperature in central New Jersey where I live and work dropped to 10° or below—more like Arctic conditions. This continued to the Washington birthday weekend, when record cold was predicted. The coldest temperatures in the country were recorded in the Adirondacks at −40° to −50°. The February 16, 1979, *New York Times* had this front-page article:

> This small, cold Adirondack Mountain town at −42° was the coldest spot in the country. ... Saranac Lake lies in the heart of Adirondack Park, six million acres of the largest and wildest wilderness areas in the contiguous forty-eight states. Nearly every year hikers and campers die and sometimes disappear among the forests and high peaks ... a pair of searchers had to be rescued themselves the other week, one so far into hypothermia, the dreaded cold-weather killer, that he was hallucinating.

The coldest winter weather I had experienced on an overnight was 10°, and I was concerned about strong subzero temperatures. None of the hike organizers called about a change of plans, however, but only to discuss equipment to share. Seven people were planning to go.

We left at 6:00 AM with the temperature 5°. Three people had second thoughts about going. That left three hikers, not an ideal number for a winter hike under these conditions. I went with Tom Dincecco, fifty-two, insurance underwriter and experienced hiker for many years, and Paul Rohrbacher, forty, electrical engineer, hiker, skier, and hunter, also experienced. We arrived at 2:00 PM at Adirondak Loj. Our plan was to hike 6.5 miles through Avalanche Pass—a steep climb—then across frozen Avalanche Lake and Lake Colden, set up a base camp, spend the next day climbing Gray Peak and back to base camp to leave the following day. A ranger stopped us as we started.

"Just realize it's cold and will get colder, and I hope you're well-equipped. I see you have wool clothing." Tom walked a few feet and then turned around.

"Maybe we should discuss this. Should we go on?" I replied that I had two sleeping bags and down booties, and wasn't concerned about being warm at night. "It's all right with me," I said. I was concerned about cold feet during the hike itself; I had silk under socks, a lightweight pair of wool socks, and heavyweight wool socks in my hiking boots.

The trail was hardpacked at the beginning. After two miles we put on snowshoes, which we had to keep on for the rest of the hike. I reached Tom and Paul, who had been setting the pace, and we began the steep climb through Avalanche Pass. "Look at that frozen waterfall," Tom pointed out. "On one side the water flows into the Hudson River, on the other the St. Lawrence."

"Have you ever seen the view of Avalanche Lake from the pass?" Paul asked. "You have a treat coming."

Appearing gradually through the trees was a snow-covered lake and almost vertical cliffs. The sun was setting and the sky was orange in the distance as the day darkened. I had a little difficulty keeping up, but I kept them in sight. My glasses would frost over and I had to take them off, even though I'm near-sighted and things appeared slightly fuzzy. My woolen balaclava became wet from perspiration; it iced over, and my beard was encrusted with ice.

The afternoon went on and on. All I was aware of were the fifty-plus pounds on my back and heavy plodding steps through the snow. Tom and Paul were a few hundred yards in front of me across the frozen lake, surrounded by dark, striking peaks. Finally, Tom suggested we stop and look for a lean-to instead of setting up our tent. The lean-to was roomier, and water wouldn't freeze and condense on the walls. We found one that was not too filled with snow, unloaded our packs, and set up camp. Tom boiled water to mix with our dried foods. As night came it got colder and we climbed into our sleeping bags. I was not cold as long as I didn't roll off my foam pad that insulated me from the ground. I slept from one to two hours at a stretch in all my clothes and my down jacket, but a few times, when the cold would bite through, I wished I were in my own bed. About 5:00 AM Tom said, "I was cold all night and didn't sleep at all. I feel all right now, but the thought of hiking and climbing nine or ten hours today and coming back to another sleepless night doesn't sound too good. What do you think about ending our trip one day early?"

A Colden igloo beats a cold lean-to. Photo by David White.

Paul and I agreed without much hesitation. We decided to lounge around the lean-to in the morning, go for a two- to three-hour hike, come back to a hot lunch and then hike out. The temperature was −18°. We snowshoed across Flowed Lands; the sky was cloudless and the sun brilliant. On our left was Mt. Colden. On our right were Algonquin, the second-highest peak in the Adirondacks, and Boundary and Iroquois peaks. There was a mild breeze blowing across the lake. My nose felt strange.

"Paul, would you look at my nose?"

"Dick, there's a white circle about the size of a half dollar around the tip and nostrils."

Paul immediately took his gloves off and covered the tip of my nose with his hands. I did the same, and the color returned. I then pulled a scarf over my nose, and later put on a facemask. I was getting the early stages of frostbite.

By 11:30 AM we were back at the lean-to. After a leisurely hot lunch— improved with brandy, warm water, Tang, and freeze-dried peaches blended together—we packed up and headed out. It was a four-and-a-half-hour hike and, despite the cold, I had constant visions of a cool glass of beer and a milkshake. We had a good steak dinner in the Elm Tree Inn in Keene and returned to New Jersey as a twenty-inch snowstorm was beginning. I spent the next day shoveling out three-foot drifts from my long driveway. 🎿

Dick Levine: I grew up in the Bronx, hiked and camped as a Boy Scout. Raising four sons, I didn't begin hiking again until my mid-forties. I became a 46er, #2758, and Catskill 3500er, hiking many peaks in winter for over twenty years. I'm attracted to winter hiking because one is focused on the immediate, and while many problems in "the outside world" still exist, we can view them with a fresh perspective.

26

WALLFACE

ONE OF THE HUNDRED HIGHEST YOU PAY FOR

Denise M. Mongillo

Randy Caldwell and I were to meet Mike McLean at Upper Works trailhead at 8:00 AM. We waited until 8:30 before we started out for Indian Pass. I wore my Tubbs snowshoes, which are lighter weight; soft snow would stick to them less than it does on MSRs. Soft shell pants and uninsulated leather hiking boots seemed like a good choice in these warmer temperatures. The snow was melting, creating wet and muddy conditions. My snowshoes kicked up water from behind, causing my pants to get wet from the seat down.

Soon after the Cold Brook Pass junction we hit a brook crossing with the remains of a bridge—just two logs suspended high above the water that seemed dubious to cross. We bushwhacked upstream, found a downed tree and scooted across on our butts, legs dangling—a tricky task with backpack weighted with snowshoes, gripping a hiking pole. Past a lean-to in a beautiful spot next to the stream, we narrowly avoided sloshing into tributaries of Indian Pass Brook and the drainage from Wallface Ponds. I tried to think positively and enjoy the sunny, blue-sky day.

Soon, the dramatic Wallface Cliffs appeared ahead. There were postholes everywhere. Since the ground was still frozen, it was difficult to gain traction because the crampon on my cheapo Tubbs snowshoes couldn't dig in where the postholes were. This, combined with wearing my leather boots for the first time in months and snowshoes I hadn't worn all winter, was proving frustrating.

The views of the Wallface Cliffs were getting better. We met two young men observing a falcon nest. They didn't want to join us, because they'd heard that it can be "pretty thick" up there and they didn't have snowshoes. An ice-encased ladder over sheer rocks made me extremely nervous, because I did not have confidence in my equipment. We left the trail to bushwhack to the summit, a steady, steep ascent. My pants were getting wetter, and the water had begun to seep into my boots. My feet were getting very wet. I ignored the discomfort and pressed on. It all seemed trivial as we reached the shoulder of Wallface and had a spectacular view of Algonquin and Iroquois! We were five hundred feet from the summit. Off trail was like walking across land mines; Randy fell in a spruce trap up to his waist. The temperature was getting warmer. We reached the summit sign at 2:00 PM.

We planned to continue over the summit and bushwhack southeast until we regained the trail above the lean-to at the drainage from Wallface Ponds. Randy expected some steep contours, but if we followed his projected course of GPS points, we could give it a fair shot in fairly open woods. We came upon a cliff where I freaked out. Our only way down offered no hand- or footholds. I had to jump. I was terrified, as the ice was thick and I had no confidence in my snowshoes. Randy descended and positioned himself to break my fall. I had a meltdown, admitted that I was terrified, and tears welled up. But I was set to give it a go, when I slipped and went crashing down six feet. I knocked Randy over and we both fell to the ground. Luckily no one was hurt. I said, "I'm sorry, I didn't mean to do that. I slipped." I asked myself, *why do I do this?* After all, the fear of injury isn't fun. The adrenalin was flowing and I was sweating.

We had a long way to go, and it seemed we'd never get down. The trail seemed far away. We were lucky if we were going a third of a mile an hour. My arms were growing tired. It was all I could do to push myself through the thick branches. Then Randy yelled up, "I think we've reached a dead end!" He reported that it was too steep to go any farther and there was no relief in sight. "I hate to say it," he said, "but we have to go back up and out the way we came." *Ugh!* I tried to wrap my mind around this—retracing up that steep descent that was about to become our ascent! Okay, let's do it. But how would we get back up the six-foot drop that we'd just cleared?

Randy took another compass reading and headed up in a different direction. I was relieved. My snowshoes were not gripping; one step forward, and then back. As soon as I gained momentum, I'd get hung up on a tree branch that pulled me back. If that wasn't enough aggravation, one of my snowshoes fell off. I wanted to scream! I was worried about time, and constantly adjusting my snowshoes was frustrating. I took them off in hope of an easier time, but snowshoes strapped to my backpack provided more ways to catch every damn tree branch. My boots weren't providing traction either, so I put the snowshoes back on. I could barely pull myself up the thick, steep slope. Clinging to the side of this mountain, I broke out in tears—I wanted this nightmare to be over. I dreamed of a rescue … a helicopter would fly overhead and I'd signal for a basket to be lowered. No dice. Buck up and press on. Daniel Powter's song, "Bad Day," played over and over in my head … "because you had a bad day."

We reached the summit for the second time at 5:00 PM. We would be coming out in the dark, with five miles to go. I was sloshing around in my boots like I was wearing fishbowls. I changed my socks and put on Gore-Tex rain pants. Within minutes the fishbowls were back.

The descent was steeper than I recalled—down, down, down. Slide, slide, and slide. Rolling ankles. Tired and shaking muscles. Fishbowl feet. We finally hit the

Wallface. Photo by Denise M. Mongillo.

trail and found more obstacles to hurdle. The trail ascended a narrow, steep slope that I could barely climb. My snowshoes provided no traction. I was rushing to keep pace, and normally I can. The snowshoe fell off again. I was having another meltdown—*can't this be over!* I lifted my leg over a tree across the trail and ripped my Gore-Tex pants. More cussing. *Can one more thing go wrong?* We reached the ladder, and the adrenalin flowed again. *Can I do this?* My knees felt weak. I had to sit on my buttocks, do a slide-jump and hope for the best. *Whew, made it without injury!*

We put headlamps on at the lean-to. We still had that difficult brook crossing to face, scooting over that log—if we could find it. It was dark when we reached the remains of the old bridge. Randy thought we could probably maneuver over it, and he went first. The two remaining timbers of the bridge were sloping upward from the bank to a concrete footing on the opposite side, one higher than the other. Randy leaned against the top one and used the lower one to rest his feet and shimmy himself over. That didn't look too bad; I can do it. I heard the raging brook below in the dark. *Here I go.* Simple; I was across and we were home free.

The last two miles were as frustrating as the rest of the day. More mud, water, rock hopping—in the dark. My feet kept sinking and sticking in the mud. Pulling my feet out felt like I was lifting cement blocks. We were on the final death march. Squish, squish, squish … finally the trailhead, at 9:10 PM. I was never so happy to be finished and to put on dry clothes. Another Adirondack Hundred Highest conquered, but we paid for it. 🏃

~~~~~~

*D*enise M. Mongillo: *I was bitten by the "hiking bug" at age sixteen on Crane Mountain. It was during my 46er quest that climbing mountains became an obsession. In five months of 2004, I climbed my remaining 42 peaks. I became a Winter 46er, #5532W, and a Catskill 3500er by 2007. In 2008 I completed the Adirondack Hundred Highest and the 48 White Mountain 4000ers on a Presidential Traverse—twenty-three miles and eight 4,000ers in fourteen hours.*

27

The High Peaks Bear: A Love Story

Three's a Crowd

Will Nixon

Sunset glowed salmon pink on Mount Colden's gray rock, across Flowed Lands. The mountain resembles a volcano with its cone profile and long, smooth, stone slopes. We needed to find a lean-to—we had started late and hiked slowly. Hoping for less competition, I chose the south side with the dead-end trail. This trail was tough. Muddy and knotted with roots, it roller-coastered up and down the hillside embankments. Elizabeth fell behind, but getting a lean-to was more important than being polite. A camper brushing his teeth at the first lean-to directed me down the shoreline. To my great relief the next lean-to, in a secluded clearing, was empty.

While I pitched our tent, Elizabeth made dinner—garlic mashed potatoes and sautéed chicken thighs. A marvelous cook, she wasn't conceding to common backpacking fare like Ramen noodles or dehydrated cardboard Stroganoff. Three young Canadians arrived carrying a year-old baby. I didn't think we could refuse them the lean-to, but Elizabeth felt intruded upon—she'd wanted us to spend this evening alone, and after two nights of fitful sleep preparing for this trip, she feared she'd lie awake listening to crying. She walked to the shoreline to eat by herself. She was exhausted, and I let her go; I didn't share her hostility toward the newcomers.

The dinner tasted delicious, much better than my bachelor cooking. But the chicken juice greasing my hands, chin, and pants left an aroma sure to attract bears. I washed the dishes with stream pebbles, rinsed off my face and hands, and flung leftovers into the water. Had I made a dumb mistake? My headlamp revealed potato globs and pale chicken thighs on the shallow brown rocks, like unidentified body parts. The cold water would preserve them for passing hikers to ponder and scorn. I should've lobbed them into the bushes. The Canadian appeared with his dishes and warned us, "My wife just saw a bear."

My method for hanging food bags was simple, elegant, and easy—throw a line over a high branch, tie the end to the first food bag, pull it right up to the branch, tie the second food bag onto my end of the line, then push it upward until both bags dangle side by side in midair. This time nothing worked—the line over the branch had so much friction that I nearly strangled my hands pulling up the first bag, and then it snagged in lower branches. The second bag stopped at seven feet, an easy reach for a bear. I pushed and pulled at the bags to shift them to an equal height with a branch, but they merely swung back and forth, mocking me. Now, my turn for a meltdown! I felt an urge to smash the bags open like piñatas, spilling our food and ending this cursed trip. I slammed the branch on the ground, again and again, and called the Adirondacks names not listed in any guides. Elizabeth waited, her headlamp casting a yellow circle on crumpled leaves. When I finally stopped punishing the ground, she suggested tying another line to the second bag so I could pull it down beside the first bag. Her idea worked.

We went to bed. I heard the baby only once, a gargling hiccup rather than a howling cry. Elizabeth snored fitfully in and out of sleep.

In the morning Elizabeth persuaded me not to abandon the trip. Washing our pot, I saw that something had eaten our potatoes if not the chicken thighs. The sight helped restore some enthusiasm. We treated ourselves to an easy day, hiked to the end of the dead-end trail and found what we wanted—a lean-to far enough away for privacy. It was a romantic spot on a secluded point. Someone had arranged weathered logs like a rustic coral around the tent site, adding panache. An earlier downpour had given way to a sweeping blue sky. Our wet tent began drying in an evaporating mist. A towering birch tree with a high branch stood beside the lean-to, and we hung food bags better than ever—suspended fifteen feet above the ground, they slid up and down as easily as if on a pulley.

We explored Flowed Lands' sandy beaches; a small island was offshore. We could walk wherever we wanted through soft, knee-high grasses. Sulfur butterflies flitted by like lemony guitar picks. We savored the scents and wallowed in sunshine. We puzzled over the stunning purple flowers of the closed gentians that had five tall petals that apparently never opened. We looked for raspberries, hopped across streams, left footprints in the virgin sand, and absorbed the spectacular scenery from driftwood benches.

That evening we found five young men camped near the lean-to in two tents and a bivouac sack. Dozens of young people were at Lake Colden, as if MTV had gone camping. Now in my forties, I felt nostalgic. I'd backpacked in the High Peaks at that age, during the Medieval Period of external frame packs, heavy leather boots, stiff wool socks, and Svea stoves that sometimes flared up and singed my eyebrows. Observing this new generation I felt rejuvenated, but also wiser. I was no longer male bonding, as Elizabeth often teased me. We shared zip-together sleeping bags.

We kept a polite distance from the guys, cooking a tasty supper of gnocchi and pesto at the beach. Our neighbors skipped stones, boasted loudly, and galloped across the stream, splashing and whooping, stripped to their boxer shorts. They looked thin, fit and foolhardy, unburdened by bad knees, soft bellies, or other middle-aged worries. They were excited about finding leeches, and I was entertained by their rambunctious energy. Flowed Lands became a magical basin under darkening purple sky and the first pinpricks of stars. Yellow lights wiggled—campers on the opposite shore. We heard distant voices and the twanging banjo call of green frogs. We kissed and climbed up the path to bed.

I soon heard grunting, snorting, and the sound of a rotten log being ripped apart—a bear hunting for grubs. It was powerful, gutting the wood with its claws and snapping off branches as if cracking baseball bats. We weren't in danger—black bears have an omnivorous appetite, but they won't touch humans. It didn't keep me up long; in the woods I wake up and fall asleep a dozen times.

I woke to the faint sound of rattling and pictured the bear shaking the cooking pots I'd hung on a nail below the roof. *The bastard*, I thought. *He'll crush the pots for nothing more than the smell of a scrub pad inside.* Elizabeth pulled on her camp slippers, grabbed the flashlight and crawled out in her underwear. How good of her, I thought, to save our pots from the bear. Or perhaps she didn't know about the bear; she returned from the outhouse full of excitement. She'd heard the bear loping ahead of her flashlight beam into the blackness. "Ka-thoonk, ka-thoonk, ka-thoonk," she said, describing its uneven gait. "It got their food," she added, amused rather than frightened. Our neighbors had made a tenderfoot's mistake of hanging bags too low. She'd seen wrappers for marshmallows, Pringles, and other teenage dietary staples. "It's a total mess!"

"Did it get our pots?" I asked. "No, it got *their* pots." "Good," I said and fell asleep.

In the morning I saw their plastic bags strewn in the brown duff twenty feet from our tent. The conifers were too small for throwing a line over a branch; the branches were too weak. The campers had probably hooked the plastic bag handles on the highest trunk spikes they could reach, and the bear plucked them like fruit. Still, I never would've guessed that ripping open food bags could sound so violent that I would mistake the noise for the gutting of a rotten log.

"Can't you even hang a frigging bear bag?" said a youngster sitting safely inside his tent. I smiled. Doesn't every crowd have a critic carping from the sidelines? A strapping young man in plaid boxers studied the packaging detritus. "There goes staying out until Tuesday," he said.

"I think I heard it fart," said a third. "Yeah, that was loud!" "I want to pet it," the youngster said. The guys recovered enough food for one more day and left on a hike up Mt. Marcy. We prepared breakfast on the beach. It was another sunny day, with dragonflies darting over the grasses and a song sparrow singing. We chose Mt. Colden; the trail from the lake climbs 1,950 feet in 1.6 miles to the summit, an aerobic workout, but Elizabeth didn't mind. She hiked up faster than she

*A safer place for food—a bear
worked hard to open this, and
failed. Photo by Anita Stewart.*

descended. Halfway, we climbed a log ladder built up a cliff and ascended a series of stone slabs. I treasured a hard workout like this, and we had the trail to ourselves! Cool winds blew through my wet shirt as we reached the summit shoulder and viewed the spectacular panorama. The massive MacIntyre Range arched for six miles across the valley that plunged out of sight below; Flowed Lands revealed more open water, and the blue gems of Marcy Dam and Heart Lake lay in the forest carpet. These were the Adirondacks I wanted Elizabeth to see. "You take me to all the best places," she said, her favorite line on our recent Alaska vacation. I was glad to hear her say it again.

A friendly woman in a ranger shirt greeted us, a summit steward who instructed hikers not to trample the delicate ecology of dwarf trees and miniature plants. "Do you know the flowers?" I asked. I'd just seen a blossom that looked like mountain laurel, except that it was pink and grew as low as my boot. "Sheep laurel," she answered. "Plants are my specialty." She identified the tiny, white mountain sandworts, the blueberry-like shrubs of bog bilberries, and the mossy pincushions of diapensia in this alpine rock garden. We had seen similar pincushion plants in the Arctic and recognized names like Lapland rosebay. After thanking her, we descended the other side of Mt. Colden, rested by a secluded pond, and crossed bog meadows on log planks. Twice we stopped for lunch, first for homemade butterscotch bars loaded with nuts and seeds, and then for beef jerky and rye crisp crackers. For a steep mile we hiked along the Opalescent River that plunged down in waterfalls and pools through deep clefts in the rock like a Western slot canyon. By evening we arrived back at Flowed Lands, which seemed like home.

"To our first 46er!" I raised hot chocolate in a toast to Mt. Colden. "To a beautiful day," Elizabeth said, raising her tea. She made an Asian soup with fresh carrots, bell pepper, Ramen noodles, tofu, and Asian oils and spices. Pink light deepened in small cumulous clouds above the basin. In three days I hadn't yet added a warm layer over my short-sleeved shirt, because the temperature remained so balmy, even at night. This was camping at its cushiest. Elizabeth poured two bowls of delicious soup.

"*Get away!*" shouted a camper in the woods.

"GET AWAY! … Get Away … get away ..." echoed the hills. *Uh oh*, I thought, *the bear is back*. We ate faster. If the bear walked down the beach, Elizabeth wondered, should we abandon the food? Absolutely not, I insisted. Once, I had watched a black mass sniffing through tall grass in Yosemite Valley and waited for it to catch my scent and run away. But it kept ambling in my direction, and I retreated briskly, not wanting to panic and run. The bear galloped to catch up with me—it wanted my lunch—so I handed over the prize. A horse train of tourists rode by. "Did you see the bear eating some idiot's pack?" asked a man. Later, the ranger showed no sympathy—I'd reinforced bad behavior. I should've thrown rocks at it. *This* time I wouldn't run. I reassured Elizabeth that we didn't need to panic—just finish our delicious dinner, wash and hang our food bags, and everything would be safe.

Two campers marched toward us, carrying flashlights. "We don't mean to alarm you, sir," one said, "but there's a bear in these bushes." His yellow beam shined into the dark shrubbery. "It's really *big!*" the other added.

"*Hey bear!*" I shouted. "It doesn't respond to human voices," the first camper said. Hidden in the bushes, *Ka-thoonk, ka-thoonk, ka-thoonk*. We forgot about seconds, tossed the leftovers, and recruited the campers to carry food bags and gear to the other end of the beach. After washing, I ran the bags up the birch tree and felt relieved as they hung high overhead. As we undressed, I said, "These kids are going nuts over the bear. Think what would happen if they saw naked breasts."

"Wouldn't you like to know," she said.

I awoke, startled by rattling pots. *Could it be? No—relax. A spooky dream. Things are fine.* But I'd heard the bear ransacking our neighbors' bags again. In the morning the campers surveyed the damage. "Look how frigging close! Right here! Look at the claw marks on the tree." Apparently, one youngster had tried guarding his food by sleeping beside it. "Hey, it left a pooh!" "That's real bear shit." I loved their excitability and foolishness.

Elizabeth had been to the outhouse. "Will," she said, "it got our bags." How could anyone hang food bags better than I had? A blue stuff sack lay empty beside foil wrappers, pots, and food packages. The second bag wasn't in sight. Fresh claw marks scarred the tree where I'd lashed the loose ends. The bastard had beaten my system! I found carrots, Ramen wrappers, instant oatmeal packets, toothbrush and toothpaste, a shredded root beer can, ziplock bags buried in conifer needles— we were in a graveyard of spoiled camping trips. To atone for the garbage I would leave, I picked up several piles, using the trash bag that had been my waterproof pack liner. At least the bear left us coffee; a morning cup would make us much nicer people.

"Do you have my stove?" It was in the lost bag. A future explorer would find it and wonder what slob was so rich and lazy that he hadn't bothered to pack up his own stove. I'd been robbed of more than pride—that was $99.00 down the drain! For breakfast we were reduced to powdered humus mix, carrots, and half a bell pepper. We ate in silence.

The blue sky had hazed over with humidity. Plodding down to Upper Works, Elizabeth tripped and hit her head; I feared disaster, but the blow didn't draw blood. She rested, drank water, and lamented her lost Power Bars. Not until we'd found an ice cream parlor in Newcomb did our moods improve. A newspaper reported bears raiding campsites, cottages, dumpsters, and beaches, blaming the driest Adirondack summer on record. "I still haven't made you the brownie mix," Elizabeth said. That treat had been meant for our final night. I knew we'd be back.

This abridged version of "A Bear in the Pantry" originally appeared in the September/October 2002 issue of Adirondack Explorer, *a bimonthly magazine covering the Adirondack Park. Reprinted with permission.*

W*ill Nixon: In 1996 I moved from mid-town Manhattan to a Catskills log cabin—trading Chinese takeout, $4 cappuccinos and car alarms for a wood stove, a footbridge to the road, and night skies so clear that I saw more stars than I could hope to identify. Now I live in Kingston. I contributed to* The Adirondack Explorer, *have published two poetry chapbooks,* When I Had It Made *(Pudding House) and* The Fish Are Laughing *(Pavement Saw). A new poetry book,* My Late Mother as a Ruffed Grouse, *appears from FootHills Publishing.*

28

MY TAYLSPIN OF A WEDDING ON WHITEFACE MOUNTAIN

WHY GET MARRIED ANYWHERE ELSE?
(EXCEPT FOR THE GUESTS)

Belinda Spinner Taylor

In 1995 I experienced my first peak, Goth-
ics, with my sister Andrea, Aunt Glo, Cousin Shannon, and Stan. The climb was
fun and challenging, but I did not feel compelled to climb again until Derek ("D")
and I decided to try Marcy. Tucked in a warm notch on the summit enjoying the
sunshine and the comfort of his arm, we vowed to do all 46 together. With that
vow in 2000, there was no question where I should marry the man I love—on an
Adirondack peak. With aging family members, the only peak suitable for our joyous occasion was Whiteface.

Sixteen family members decided to travel the trail together to reach the
Adirondack altar for our marriage—a very long aisle indeed! Anxious, nervous,
excited, with scattered pieces of climbing gear on each climber, we were off at
6:00 AM Though we traveled with experienced 46ers Andrea, Glo, and Shannon,
and experienced climbers Cliff, Robert, Derek, James, and myself, my heart was
touched by my three children who were willing to walk alongside D and me as
they have throughout our seven-year journey. Jordan, twenty-two, was wearing
canvas shoes wet from fishing the night before and with toes popping out the top.
He has climbed seven peaks, but smokes two packs of cigarettes a day, parties too
much, and sleeps too little. Ben, nineteen, was fresh from Korea on leave from the
Air Force. He was very fit, but exhausted from a nineteen-hour flight grounded
in New York City because of a transformer explosion, a long bus trip home, and
lack of sleep. Kristin, eighteen, despised climbing, had challenged this mountain in 2005 and had been unsuccessful because of heat exhaustion, and hadn't
worked out much since she broke her leg the previous fall. My three sweethearts
were willing and excited to do it for D and me.

We had asthmatic girlfriends, their attire tennis shoes and white shorts, cousins with bad knees, nephews who didn't utter a word, but most inspiring was Lance,
the best man. Though hiking boots were a far cry from the hockey skates that he's
most comfortable in, he had worn a smile as he had come downstairs with a box
of new boots. Much to his surprise, he found two different shoes inside. "Oops, I
guess I should have checked them out before." With his perpetual smile, he tied on

Belinda and Derek on Whiteface Mountain. Photo by Robert L. Wright.

a pair of Derek's sneakers and started his ascent. Near the top of Marble Mountain, Andrea turned and said, "Great climbing. Great time. Looking good, guys." Lance turned around with his wonderful smile and said, "I think that I would rather have another circumcision before I ever do this again," and continued to trudge on in his sneakers. Once over Marble Mountain, the climb was enjoyable, fun, and entertaining, with Jordan up to his usual antics. With jokes and laughter, we reached the summit easily with time to relax.

Predictions for thundershowers, cloud cover, and only a slight possibility of sunshine had almost made us decide not to climb, but sunshine prevailed. There was a parting of the clouds, so Donny the pilot and Kevin the photographer could fly over our rocky altar taking aerial photographs; the belly of Donny's plane announced that "D and Red" had just been married. Jim Rogers stood on the highest point as my father and I walked to meet him arm in arm. Brooke, our daughter, scattered birdseed in front of us. Andrea, Derek, and Lance waited with Jim as fifty-one family and friends stood watching. My father kissed my sweat-covered cheek and put my hand in Derek's. With parents melting to tears at the words they spoke about family, unity, strength, and marital bonds, my four wonderful children recited the Apache Creed with confidence that I would never walk alone again. Noah and Hannah carefully escorted the rings to us on handmade loon pillows as if they were sacred goods. The spectacular view was no more spectacular than the view of all our friends willing to be there with us. The smiles and applause from strangers were exciting, as if we had done something unique. Marriage is common, but the unity of a couple with so much love and happiness from husband/wife, family and friends is rare.

The last two activities were The Cairn and Taylspin's release. Our first date had been a climb up a small northern mountain called Owls Head, from where we brought a rock home. D etched the infinity symbol ∞ with "D & Red" in this rock, and Kristin, Evan, and Lance escorted it up the mountain. Our group of 46ers read the poem "Together We Climb a Mountain," and we placed our rock on the summit cairn together.

Last, but certainly not least, was Taylspin. Legend says that if you capture a butterfly and whisper a wish to it, upon its release it will take your wish up to the heavens to be granted. D and I had found Taylspin as a caterpillar, hence his name, and he had quickly formed a chrysalis before we were prepared. He went through a difficult metamorphosis, and biologists from Up Yonda Farms were skeptical that he would survive. Derek's attempts to get more butterflies fell through, so all was resting on Taylspin. Two days before the wedding, he came to greet us as a beautiful monarch butterfly. Though he was not flying or eating much, we hoped that his strength would prevail.

My brother Craig handed us the box and read the Indian "Legend of the Butterfly." Derek took Taylspin out of the box, but he did not fly. He waved his wings a little, but stood perched on D's hand. With a gentle blow from both of us, he lifted off into a graceful glide as everyone applauded. Much to our surprise Taylspin circled over all of us, friends and family, as if to say goodbye and thank you before he flew down the same direction from which we had come. Taylspin was on his flight to freedom and to transport our wish to the heavens.

That night we looked at Gram, D's ninety-year-old grandmother, and said, "You must be tired." She replied, "Of course I am. I climbed an Adirondack peak today and watched my grandson be married on the summit. It was a good day, and George (D's grandfather and a special person, who passed years ago) would have been proud." My life is blessed with good health, wonderful family, beautiful and loving children, and a man who truly is my soul mate and companion in life, and now is also my husband. A match made in heaven. 🦋

*B*elinda Spinner Taylor: *After years of childrearing and professional advancement, my journey began with the 46ers. I experienced a stroke in 1997 that affected my complete right cerebellum, and I should never have walked or had controlled bodily functions again. Once health was regained, I was fortunate enough to find the love of my life. We married on the Whiteface summit on July 24, 2007.*

29

JOHNS BROOK TRAIL MEMORIES

ADVENTURES OF A HUTBOY
(WHO ALWAYS TELLS THE TRUTH)

Neal Burdick

One of my favorite hikes in the Adirondacks leads not to a peak, pond, or natural phenomenon, but to the Adirondack Mountain Club's Johns Brook Lodge—"JBL"—where, in summer, you can get a bunk and hearty meals. In front of the porch, the main trail continues to the summit of Mt. Marcy. To the left is the Great Range, and right goes to Big Slide or Klondike Pass and Adirondak Loj. You can return to Keene Valley via two trails to The Garden parking area—indeed, once a garden; the Southside Trail, to me not as pleasant a hike, affords more access to the endlessly delightful Johns Brook swimmin' and fishin' holes.

Why do I like the hike to JBL so much? It's gentle, gaining only eight hundred feet of elevation in three and a half miles. One of the toughest hills is within sight of The Garden; once you surmount that ascent, you'll rarely realize you're climbing. It traverses lovely mixed hardwood forest with some conifers for variety. On its last half mile it hugs Johns Brook, one of the most beautiful streams in the Adirondacks. At the end are friendly hosts who will sell you a snack, or if it's rainy you can dry out at the big stone fireplace with an honest-to-gosh moose head presiding over it. Along the trail are three lean-tos and several streams—Deer Brook and its lean-to are especially attractive—and the Johns Brook Interior Outpost. And the Resting Rock.

The Resting Rock—sounds like something out of Harry Potter. It's on the left about halfway along, a glacial erratic left behind some ten or twelve thousand years ago when the ice sheets retreated to Canada, leaving their refuse behind like tourists ever since. The Resting Rock once played a supportive role in my life. In the summers of 1969 and 1970, I was a JBL "hutboy," as the crew was called before gender equity in language came into vogue. Part of our job was to pack in food for the meals we served (with the occasional culinary "Titanic"—hey, we were three college guys on summer jobs; cooking was exploratory at best). We packed in supplies ranging from annoyingly bulky toilet paper to annoyingly heavy bundles of roof shingles. We would rest at this glacial erratic at the end of the other noticeable ascent on the route. The glacier had thoughtfully sculpted the boulder so we could prop our packs in a notch and slip out of them. That was the closest I've ever come to defying gravity; after divesting myself of an especially weighty load, I felt as though I could fly into the treetops.

One time as I wriggled back under my burden, I lost my balance and capsized, boots waving in the air as if I were an upside-down turtle. I realized that 144 eggs for the Labor Day onslaught of guests were now beneath 122 pounds of provisions. I remember simultaneously muttering, "I don't think I can right myself; I hope somebody comes along to help," and, "Man, I hope no one comes along; this is really embarrassing." For better or worse, no one came along, although a chipmunk did laugh its fool head off at me. When I finally got my feet under me, to my great relief not a single egg was broken. To this day I marvel at the design of egg cartons.

Did I mention that cooking was an adventure? Ask any of the members of the Ba-To-Na Hiking Club of Philadelphia who stayed at JBL in 1969. "Ba-To-Na" stood for "Back to Nature," but we called them the "Ba-Lo-Ney" bunch because they seemed to be full of it, at least to a trio of know-it-all college kids. One day, cream of wheat was on the breakfast menu and, bleary-eyed at 6:30 in the morning, I misread the "tsp" instruction for salt as "tbsp." When it all came back to the kitchen uneaten, I took a taste and consigned it to our garbage bin, which was regularly raided by raccoons that fought over the contents. Every night—we could set our watches by them—they'd let loose with the most blood-curdling yowls imaginable; some of our guests would go to bed with dark hair and come out to breakfast with white hair. (Remember, hutboys always tell the truth.) This particular night, they were worse than usual—they weren't screaming at each other, they were screaming at me because I'd ruined their midnight snack. How they got into the bin, when we could barely lift its solid iron cover, I could never figure out.

I had my first encounter with a bear at JBL. We burned what trash was combustible in a cut-open fifty-five-gallon drum, which was dangerous and ecologically insensitive; the practice has long since ceased. One evening while hauling a boxful of refuse up to the drum, I looked into the eyes of a bruin who was contemplating whether the burn barrel might contain anything worth flipping it over for. The bear was as startled as I was; we stared at each other for a few seconds, and then I said, "Stay right there, please; I'm going back to the lodge for my camera." When I returned, the bear was nowhere to be seen—apparently neither my burn barrel nor I were worth any more if its time.

I learned to assemble and carry loads that weighed nearly as much as I did, by getting the weight as high as possible so that most of my slender frame was beneath it. To people coming toward me—a scrawny, mustachioed guy in a jaunty Scottish tam—I must have looked like a stack of roped-up boxes with legs, or a hippie with

The Adirondack Mountain Club's Johns Brook Lodge. Photo contributed by John Kettlewell.

a martyr complex. They'd stop, and since I couldn't be rude to potential paying customers, I'd pause too, no matter how much my body wanted me to keep to my pace. When they'd admire my cargo, I'd say things like, "Well, when I was hired for this job I was nearly seven feet tall, but all these heavy loads have driven me down to five foot eleven, and I'm afraid I'm stuck there for life." I'm still astonished at the number of people who acted as if they believed me. On the other hand, hutboys always tell the truth ...

Only once did my slight build raise a comment. A fellow said, "You're kinda thin to be carrying such a load." I could hear the mockery, but bit my tongue while observing that he—overweight—was puffing mightily while going downhill with a tiny knapsack, while I was heading up under ninety pounds of dinner (a spring scale at the lodge was the arbiter in the crew's friendly competition to see who had the heaviest loads). Seeing a backcountry "teachable moment," I said calmly, "It's all in how you pack it. And in being in shape."

The best part about the hike, under baggage that would have made Sisyphus envious, was getting there. A small pool in the brook awaited, enlarged by means of a rock dam that we constructed. We shared it with brook trout. After lugging food for forty people on a hot and muggy day, nothing felt better than to submerge ourselves into that cold mountain water. It was like a Jacuzzi, just big enough to lie in and let the brook pour itself over our shoulders. I can still feel that relief, forty years later. The dam regularly washed out in cloudbursts, as did the bridge we laid across the brook. The "bridge" was only two planks lashed end-to-end, balanced hopelessly on rocks, and it didn't even reach from bank to bank but, like beavers, we delighted in replacing them each time, trying to engineer new ways to outsmart the relentless current. We never did.

As a hutboy I navigated that trail dozens of times, ruining my back under the accumulated weight of those groceries. I've employed it countless times since those halcyon days, on my way to other points, but sometimes only to the lodge, just because. I've hiked it in terrific thunderstorms, under summer-night heat lightning and through the sad sunlight of fleeting autumn days. I've skied it in swirling snowstorms, slogged it in mud season. If I close my eyes I can see nearly every foot of it, and I never tire of it, either on the ground or in my mind. 🏃

Adapted with permission from an article that first appeared in Adirondack Life *magazine's 2007 Guide to the Great Outdoors (Volume XXXVIII, No. 4).*

~~~~~~

*N*eal Burdick: I am editor-in-chief of Adirondac, *the magazine of the Adirondack Mountain Club, and edited ADK's eight-volume series of hiking guides for over twenty years. A frequent contributor to* Adirondack Explorer *and* Adirondack Life *magazines, I am coeditor of* Living North Country *and of the new edition of ADK's* The Adirondack Reader. *I am on the Steering Committee of the Adirondack Center for Writing and cofounded St. Lawrence University's Young Writers Conference.*

30

SPOTTED MOUNTAIN—TAKE FOUR

AN ELUSIVE (AND SPECTACULAR) ADIRONDACK PEAK

Spencer Morrissey

You wouldn't think that a 3,400-foot mountain could give a hiker so much trouble and in so many different ways. But, yes, it took me four attempts and one reconnaissance trip to finally top off on this bald beauty. The four attempts were spaced out over a few years, because I hate it when Mother Nature beats me and it takes me awhile to forgive and forget.

Recon mission, 1997. I was twenty-four and had been hiking heavily for the past couple of years, but all on trails. I was reading Barbara McMartin's *Discover the Adirondack High Peaks* and fell in love with the idea of climbing this bald peak named Spotted by way of the South Fork of the Bouquet River. Along the route we would visit another bald peak, Elizabethtown #4. My father, Bud, and I had never really bushwhacked before, only a couple of small peaks like Sabattis in Long Lake and Discovery in Lewis—nothing where we were off the beaten path for long. We were a little nervous, but confident. We did a reconnaissance, to be safe, and walked up the path that follows the North Fork of the Bouquet and joins the South Fork on the northwest side of Spotted. It was a most excellent hike, beautiful day, warm—a perfect day for a swim in the river. But we didn't have any swim trunks, and skinny-dipping with my old man just wasn't going to happen.

We were near the base of Elizabethtown #4 and could see it well. On our hike out we heard people playing in the slide waterfall, and it kept getting louder and louder as we got closer. *Sounds like a party*, I thought. Twenty nudists were cooling off and having a great time. Ever slide down bare rock on a bare butt? Me neither, but I can't imagine it's too pleasant. I was actually embarrassed and continued down before they saw me. Was my father behind me? No! He had struck up a conversation with a husband and wife. What the heck do you talk about when you're face-to-face with a naked couple? Nice weather we're having? Care for a towel? Whatever they chatted about didn't faze anyone but me, but it seemed to drag on forever. I only wish I'd hung around for some snapshots but, sorry, no pictures—this is a family book, you know.

Take 1, Summer 1997. A week later we decided to try to find the ridge. I invited a friend, and she was very excited about joining, even though she was aware that a trail would not be available for part of this hike. We used the herd path that follows the South Fork from Route 73 just past Malfunction Junction, rather than the previous one, and it was easy to follow. We got to the end, at a major split in the river, in excellent time. From here we would bushwhack to the summit of Spotted; time to get out the map and compass. I tore apart my entire pack and so did my father—no map! After a snack, we decided to try for the ridge anyhow. If we can make the ridge, we have a line to follow to the summit. It was a clear day; we knew the ridge was pretty open and that there was a trail to the north. How hard could it be? But the canopy was very thick in the hardwoods, and we couldn't see a thing. It felt like we were walking in circles, the temperature was reaching 80° and it was feeling hot. Our patience and confidence were weakening; we retreated, beaten.

Take 2, Winter 1998. It was mid-January, but Old Man Winter was taking the day off with temperatures in the high thirties. My brother-in-law Ferris and I planned to attack the peak from the north via that herd path. The trail wasn't broken, and we were disappointed to have to push through over a foot of snow that at times was very tough to navigate. We lost the trail a couple of times, but we figured, return to the river and cross it. We got twisted onto another herd path that led steeply uphill and overlooked the river, but soon that path disappeared. Rather than retrace, we headed down to the river, but now there was no path along the brook—it must have crossed downstream. "Let's just cross it," we said in unison. We had come to an excellent spot to cross, a nice thick ice heave to walk across.

I was first, as always, and heaviest—as always. I got exactly halfway across before the ice heave buckled and collapsed on my thirty-six-inch snowshoes. I was now sitting on the edge of the ice with my feet almost knee-deep in the river and what felt like a ton of ice and snow resting on my snowshoes. I was stuck; nothing I did freed my feet, and my boots were filled with crisp, clean, river water. I saw the look in Ferris's eyes, more humor than concern, but he still needed to come out to pull me loose. He was a good sport and finally found what he felt was a comfortable route to get to me. It wasn't. We were now sitting side by side in the river just soaking our feet. This might have been a humorous scenario had it not been January. But the good news is his dip in the river cleared away enough ice so that we could pull ourselves out and return to the bank. Need I say more? We followed our track out quickly to avoid a serious cold injury. Back at the car all we could do was laugh, once we got changed, of course.

Take 3, Summer 1999. Third time's a charm, right? I guess not for me, and I'm Irish. This time it was my brother-in-law Brian, brother-in-law Phillip, their cousin Alan, and I. We chose the northern approach via the herd path to the Great Slide of East Dix. It was another gorgeous morning with a slight threat of rain later. The hike was rather easy for most of us; Alan seemed a little tired, but was a great sport in such muggy weather. We found the correct brook crossing, stayed on the right

View from Spotted Mountain to Elizabethtown 4 Mountain. Photo by Spencer Morrissey.

path; everything was going as planned; it looked like I was finally going to get these peaks. The closer we got to the base of the ridge, however, the colder the air was becoming—it had dropped 15° in the last hour. The rain was coming early, and bushwhacking in the rain isn't that much fun. When it started to sprinkle, the tight canopy seemed to stop most of it, however.

We were finally below Elizabethtown #4 and could see open rock. We ate a snack, refilled water and juiced up for a steep climb. Just as we lifted ourselves from our rock "lazy boys," the clouds opened up. It was an instant soaking, and the rain was the coldest I had ever felt. We couldn't traverse the ridge in this weather, so we called it a "wash" and headed back. We weren't pleased about this situation; we were in hypothermic weather, soaked through, and we didn't even get what we had come for. We were happy, however, not to be on the open ridge when the rain started. The hike out was exhausting, with all the added pounds of water we were carrying. Alan was frustrated and tired. He crumpled up his pack of Marlboros and threw them on the ground. "I need to quit!" he muttered out loud. I picked up the soaked pack of butts and shoved them in my pocket, while never losing a step. I only smiled.

Take 4, Summer of 2000, SUCCESS! We watched the forecast, studied the map, and played out a variety of scenarios—we were ready. It was just Brian and me with my new four-legged hiking partner, Sunny. We now owned a GPS and had nearly 150 Adirondack bushwhacks under our belt, so as long as the weather held, we were going to get there. We started along the South Fork herd path and hiked very fast to its end at the river's fork. From there it was a beeline for the ridge. The weather was perfect, albeit muggy. Before we knew it, we were on the huge boulder summit before Elizabethtown #4, an amazing spot—360° views and solid rock. We made excellent time over to Elizabethtown #4, where even more views awaited from an open rock summit with a killer view of the East Dix Bowl and the Great Slide. This is one of the best views in the Adirondacks. The bushwhack over the ridge was a little slower. We hit a couple of smaller patches of thicker stuff, but mostly it was climbing up and over rock slab sections and small cliffy areas. Views kept popping up in all directions, each different in its own way.

Then, the summit of Spotted was finally under my feet. I could have been on Everest, I was so happy to be there, and the wait was well worth it. The views are outstanding, the weather was perfect, and I didn't want to leave. We planned a different descent route. We wanted to find a source of the South Fork of the Bouquet and follow that back to the fork. It was a steep descent with open ridges to follow to the river, and then we were there at the source. It was a pretty cool spot; the water was actually coming out of a section of rocks. It was an easy branch to follow and kept getting easier as we went along. Before long it was a wide river to follow and rock hop. We found it easier to walk the shoreline in most places. This ended up being a perfect day—no situations, no bad weather, and no disorientation. Back at the car, we were planning to summit East Dix by continuing along the ridge—that's a great trip, and another story. 🥾

Spencer Morrissey: I became a 46er in 2003 and Winter 46er, #5320W in 2008, and serve as a correspondent, communicating with aspiring 46ers. In 2004 I achieved certification as a New York State Licensed Guide. I completed climbs of the Adirondack Hundred Highest in 2006, and the following year my book The Other 54 *was released. My wife, Madeline, and I, and Eric, Kole, and Emily reside in Westport.*

31

LOST POND PEAK

LOST AND FOUND

Neil Luckhurst

If you want to experience a bit of all that the Hundred Highest has to offer, you'll find it here. I planned this as a map and compass hike with three waypoints in the GPS—one for our jumping-off point on the Indian Pass Trail, one for a cool set of cliffs, and another for a low point east of Lost Pond. I did map and compass exercises with my wife, Sylvie, and friend Annick, taking advantage of clear views of Street Mountain and Lost Pond Peak. Within minutes we had superlative views of the MacIntyre Range, and these views only got better as we climbed. Following a 270° magnetic bearing, we were on very steep terrain in thicker conditions. Gradually the slope eased and the forest opened up beckoningly. Suddenly we were in deep snow and put snowshoes on; the snow was nice and firm. We dialed new bearings to reach the cliffs I wanted to check out. We had a stiff hundred-foot climb to the final ridge and followed it straight to the summit, where we soaked up the sun and 180° views from the Sawtooths around to Wright Peak.

I had the bright idea that we'd have an easier descent south of our ascent line and led us into a treacherous gully, but it served as a passageway between very impressive cliffs. We tried to leave this gully, but the cliffs kept pushing us back into it. I thought we were going to have to reclimb, but there was one spot where the drop was only ten feet with a sloped apron of snow and trees to hang onto. I went first, on my belly, kicking steps into the icy snow. As I slid under a cedar, my pack got hung up, so I slithered out from under and got onto terra firma. Sylvie and Annick followed. Then we hit a really serious band of high cliffs. Being an excellent teacher, I explained that, because of cliffs like these, it was better not to do bush-whack descents in the dark. Cliffs stretched off into the distance as far as we could see left and right. From my previous hike here, I figured we were better off going to the right. There was a cut in the cliffs just as I thought I was boxed in. We used the low point between Wright and Algonquin as a bearing, contoured around yet other small cliffs and then heard Indian Pass Brook.

My camera was missing! *Groan.* I'd taken so many wonderful pictures today. It had to be where I removed my pack. I thought I could find that spot again, however, because I had a track log. I decided to return another day.

It had been a day that will live on in my mind forever—what excellent, good-humored hiking companions Sylvie and Annick were on such a challenging off-trail excursion. Quebec girls rock! (So do upstate New York girls, Vermont girls and New Hampshire girls.)

On a sunny warm morning soon after, I began climbing toward my camera. I saw our melted footprints, yet the route looked different. Eventually I saw a cliff band and went on visual. It was a much better route, but according to the GPS I was 100 yards too far north. I down-climbed, traversed, and soon recognized where my camera had to be—and there it was under branches, hard to see in its black case! I continued climbing, but today I kept breaking through the snow up to my upper thighs and realized how lucky we'd been. I tried a different way down, and blowdown fields that would have been passable days earlier were now hellish and dangerous with rotten snow. The temperature was in the high 80s. I walked right through the rushing brook and didn't have shorts, so I walked the remaining three and a half miles back in my underwear. Near the Loj museum, a deck offers a great view of Lost Pond Peak; a guy was doing his karate moves on the deck and seemed surprised to see me walk up in my underwear carrying a pair of snowshoes on my back. 🏃

Neil Luckhurst: The 46 (#5706W) served as an excellent introduction to the High Peaks region. Off-trail hiking provides me with the greatest satisfaction—my favorite region is the Sawtooth Range—and my current goal is hiking off-trail the 130 highest peaks in the park and to complete the ADK Hundred Highest peaks in winter. Some non-peak-bagging nature lovers may not believe that peak baggers appreciate nature as much as they do, but the peak baggers I've met are at least as attuned to the wonders of the forests or streams as they are.

32

HIGH PEAKS SURPRISES

K. KONG AND A. WOLFFE IN THE MOUNTAINS

Barbara Bave

Most hikers have a good sense of humor, and never let it be said that the Bave girls don't like a silly stunt from time to time. So when my sister Jacki told me she was leading a hike for the Glens Falls chapter of the Adirondack Mountain Club up Gothics Mountain for Halloween, I began planning. My first costume idea was a bear—after all, we'd be in the Adirondacks—but all I could find was a gorilla costume.

A friend would accompany me, serving as lookout for when to leap out at people. I made an excuse to Jacki about why I couldn't go, and then I went to the trailhead early. We signed in as K. Kong and Harry Aipe, and took the trail between Gothics and Sawteeth to Pyramid, a good leaping out spot. I briefly questioned the wisdom of donning a black fur suit in hunting season, but decided no hunters would be this high up. I had further pause (paws?) when the cold rubber feet slid around on the snow. We imagined Tony Goodwin's accident report, had I actually slipped off the cliff in my rubber feet. But I hadn't dragged the costume this far to back out now! Jumping out at people was fun, and everyone enjoyed the surprise, although one woman actually looked a little scared.

The next year, Jacki and I planned the surprise together. For a trip up Lower Wolf Jaw, I bought a wolf mask and made a costume out of gray fake fur. Another friend came as a vampire, and we signed in as A. Wolffe and Gabe Blood. We left ominous signs along the trail, picked up by my sister as the group found them: "Beware" spelled out in sticks; fake blood on a ripped T-shirt; a bloody knife stuck in the crack of a tree; icicles dripping from a rock made into a leering, toothy grin by a couple of well-placed rocks; and howls called into a fake microphone. These were all supposed to bring fear and dread to the hike participants. They did make one couple a bit nervous. As we stood in the col between the Wolf Jaws howling into the microphone and stabbing a knife into a shirt stained with fake blood, we didn't see this couple coming up from the Johns Brook side. They gave us a wide berth.

Word of the fun began to spread. More people were joining us and bringing their own masks. Jacki decided that it was her turn to be the scarer, and I would lead the group up Giant. I noticed the ominous name, "E. Normous" written in the register. At the Giant's Washbowl, we found a super-sized toothbrush, a beach-towel-sized washcloth and a box decorated to look like a giant cake of Ivory soap, then a fake beanstalk and some beans. Later we found huge reading glasses, a severed hand, and a very large pair of scissors. Tension mounted as we reached the summit. There, right before us, was the GIANT! Jacki was the top of a two-person-tall creature covered in a sheet with a huge pumpkin head.

That was the last of the Halloween hikes, but years later Jungle Jim Mosher was leading his annual June 21 hike up the slide on Nippletop. I still had an old Halloween costume I'd made representing two breasts, and couldn't resist one more surprise. It required two people, since the costume consists of two flesh-covered tunics with what resembles a large, pregnant stomach with a nipple attached. My friend Terry agreed to be the other half; we signed in as "Dee Cupp" and "Meg A. Brest" and hurried to summit before the rest. One of their party had a hard time on the slide, and we sat there in our bulky costumes enjoying the sunny day. Finally we heard voices and lay down and waited to hear our friends' laughter. Silence. Opening our eyes, we were startled to see two perfect strangers staring at us. We explained what we were doing, and we all had a laugh. The party never made it to the summit; we waited in costume in the parking lot, where they finally arrived at dusk. Maybe some day we'll do a reprise. You never know what you might find on the top of a mountain. ⁂

Barbara Bave: It wasn't until I was in my forties that I became an active hiker. Since then I've become an Adirondack 46er and a winter 46er, #3263W, with my twin sister. It's good to have goals, so I'm also working on the Northeast 111 and the Catskill 3500. The Fire Tower Challenge is in the cards, too, since I'm the ADK correspondent for that goal. I have been active in the Adirondack Mountain Club since the start of my hiking addiction, becoming the Glens Falls/Saratoga Chapter outings chairperson for eight years. I have held vice-chair and chapter-chair positions, and am currently an ADK director for my chapter.

33

FOR WANT OF A FLASH

A ROOKIE MISTAKE

Kevin T. Cahill

This is a true tale wherein no one gets hurt except for maybe a bruising of the ego. The story starts out with Tim, who has been released from a drug and alcohol rehab program. He is a lost soul, twenty-five years of age, a young man who had never camped or hiked before entering rehab. This is an account of his early days of self-discovery and soul-searching—his desire for a better life, a life that he thought he could find in the Adirondack Mountains.

The plan was to climb Algonquin Peak, the second-highest mountain in the High Peaks. Still far too green to undertake this trip alone, Tim recruited a work friend, Stew, to join him. Tim meticulously planned the entire trip. The only thing that he did not plan on was karma. They say in rehab that what does not kill you makes you stronger. An old English proverb states that many things are lost for want of asking. All this young man wanted to do was to climb a mountain, which he did, but with a serving of humility.

The road to the Adirondak Loj offers a spectacular view of Algonquin. Camp had been set up, food stashed away, day packs on and plenty of sunlight left—it was all perfect. The excitement was palpable. To think that they were now on the trail to Algonquin! Soon they would be on top of the peak looking out into the vastness of it all. From atop a mountain, it is easy to sense one's place in this world. Up on a peak, you feel at peace. On a summit you know what it is to be free. It is Eden before the fall, the true meaning to sobriety and a drug-free life.

The pace was brisk when Tim heard his friend cry out in pain. Stew was on the ground holding his ankle, grimacing, and said he couldn't go on; they soon decided to separate. Tim was determined to summit. He made it to the top with time to spare, and the descent was uneventful. His soul was set free on the trail. He soaked his head under waterfalls. He marveled at the views. He was lost in the moment.

At the junction back to Marcy Dam, Tim felt invigorated. It was still early, so he made a big mistake—he would hike back to his truck to a cooler of soda on ice. Why would he do that? Suffice it to say that the thought patterns of an addict, new to recovery, are not always clear. His body was craving chemicals. Caffeine is a common replacement drug in early recovery, and there he was, hiking back to the lodge for a fix, a twelve-ounce taste of heaven after a long day's journey. He slugged down two cans of soda. Full of sugar and caffeine, he started back for Marcy Dam, and dusk slowly settled in. The woods grew darker and more sinister. He thought of bears, so prevalent in the Marcy Dam area, but mostly he thought of getting back to the tent for a good night's sleep.

When he arrived at Marcy Dam, the sun was down, everything was dark and … Tim forgot where his tent was! No problem; he knew the general orientation of their campsite and would find it. Over there! No. Wait, there it is. No. There? No. Where was it? He came upon campsite after campsite, each not his. The embarrassment was growing. Each time he disturbed a group of campers, the response never changed: "Don't you have a flashlight? Don't you know you need a flashlight?" And so it went until he approached a tent that he thought was his and disturbed a couple in the throes of passion. It was then that he decided that enough was enough—he would tough out the night on the trail, having no light to find his way back to the truck. More humiliation was to come.

It was getting colder, but he thought he could handle it even though he had heard that it could get really cold in the Adirondacks at night. Hypothermia could become a reality. Tim sat down against a tree, his arms wrapped around his knees to keep warm, lamenting the fact that he had not packed a flashlight. Live and learn was one thing, but freezing to death was another.

He wondered what he would do if he encountered a bear. Then he heard a noise in the dark. A bear? He spotted a light, then another, followed by voices. It was three women heading his way. They nearly tripped over him in the dark. It was humiliation time again—"Yes, I know I should have a flashlight. I do have one, but it's in the tent that I can't find. Yes. I can't find my tent. I know it's not doing me any good there." Tim sucked it up. He had made a big rookie mistake. The women were good-natured, more surprised at finding him on the trail at night than wanting to give him a hard time. One of them offered him a headlamp so that he could hike to the lodge. He was saved. These were not ordinary hikers; they were angels sent to guide him and offer him a second chance. He felt so grateful over this act of kindness and promised to bring the headlamp back. They were okay with that. They trusted him, and he would not let them down, these angels who delivered him out of the darkness.

Tim started down the trail for the third and final time and made it back to the safety of his truck, where he fell asleep listening to Pink Floyd and the heater's hum delivering warmth for his bruised ego. He woke feeling invigorated. Despite his mistakes, he had come out of it all right. He hit the trail; he had to find Stew and let him know that he was okay. After the junction toward Marcy Dam, he spotted Stew talking to a park ranger. "Are you looking for me?" Stew had packed his gear and was hiking out when he happened on the ranger and told him that Tim had not returned to the tent. The ranger left, but not before imparting words of wisdom. Do you know what it was? That is correct: "Don't you know that you need to carry a flashlight with you?" Tim agreed with the ranger and returned the headlamp to the women, thanking them profusely. And, yes, they had one more flashlight reminder left in them. Tim still considers those three older women to be angels.

He learned some big lessons on that trip. He was lucky that little mistakes did not grow to be big ones—there is no room for error in the backcountry. We all know the most important outcome of this little adventure for Tim. He always packed a light, if not two, on all trips thereafter. A little light goes a long way on a dark trail. Tim no longer wants for a flash, only for the thrill of a summit over a rocky peak. 🏃

*K*evin T. Cahill: I am an avid outdoors enthusiast and enjoy hiking the trails of the High Peaks region. I have recently hiked on a volcano on the island of Dominica. I rock and ice climb through Alpine Adventures in Keene. I am a scuba diving instructor with the National Aquatic of Syracuse. Other interests include oil painting and playing guitar.

34

A NEOPHYTE IN HERMIT COUNTRY

TRIAL BY BUSHWHACK

William J. "Jay" O'Hern

Sitting around the fire at camp, my daughter Sue surprised me. Flaming, popping logs and the distant call of a hoot owl as the sun disappeared below the horizon had set a mood. She would try mountain climbing and bushwhacking, and asked me to take her to the site of Noah John Rondeau's hermitage along the Cold River. I didn't foresee problems other than her ability to carry a pack loaded for three days.

I offered basic orienteering when we left the Northville-Placid Trail to Boiling Pond, and we headed toward Ouluska Pass Brook under deep blue sky. At Rondeau's high pond I traced the route we would take—an old lumber camp clearing, a small stream off the south side of the Seward Range, a winding track of old corduroy I wanted to follow, a scoot to a fresh slide we'd have to traverse before ascending to Mount Emmons, then on to Mount Donaldson, Seward Mountain, and down to bivouac along Ward Brook, hopefully at the lean-to. These objectives were all feasible for me. The wild card was Sue's doggedness to bear bushwhacking realities. I considered her a strong teenager who could suck up the tiring hours. But I remembered her clueless choice of food for the outing—a huge bag of cinnamon balls and pretzels. "Enough for three days," she had proudly announced. Going trailless was not going to be the fun, educational opportunity I anticipated.

Investigating logging artifacts, finding parts of old logging roads, perspiring under a heavy pack, enduring endless insects, working up steeply sloping ground— I was in my element. But swarms of June black flies wiped away the pleasures I'd hoped Sue would enjoy. Any exuberance she still maintained ended as we faced a steep ledge of rocks, but a different ascent would eat more time. "Drop your pack, climb on my shoulders, reach up for handholds and scramble up," I offered. "It'll be faster. Once you make it to the narrow ledge, you can lower a rope, haul up the packs and then give me a steady line." The plan worked, and within twenty minutes we came out on the herd path between Emmons and Donaldson. Victory was ours, but there was a downside; on Seward we ran out of daylight. The way off this trailless summit was steep and slippery. The descent stretched down for almost a mile—rivulets, crevices, a jungle of trees, the steepness of the mountainside, sudden cliffs with dire drop-offs. My thoughts were about safety. I imagined one or both of us breaking a bone and lying helpless in the pitch dark with stinging, biting insects complicating the discomfort. If I had an accident, how would Sue get herself off the mountain, down to the trail, and then out to the vehicle fifteen miles distant? Experience taught me not to take risky chances. Ten minutes off the summit we stopped to study the situation and said in unison, "Let's settle down here for the night."

For the first time in my daughter's outdoor life she was in a discomforting situation, without experience to help her weather the stress. In the dark on steeply sloping ground, she was deprived of the shelter of a tent and the ability to cook a warm meal. A rope was looped around her shoulders and tethered to a tree to arrest her sleeping bag and her from slipping down the mountain once she wiggled inside for the night. She felt close kinship with every form of life she could imagine would crawl into her bag. Black bears played on her imagination in the loneliness of the long night. This was largely a psychological experience—mind-induced fantasies. The game was the human being against nature. But bad stuff can become grist for the mill of growth. Adventure, large or small, is exciting not only to our physical selves, but to our imaginative sides—true adventure is a psychological affair and a spiritual matter.

Famous Adirondack hermit, Noah John Rondeau, entertaining guests. Photo courtesy of Richard J. Smith from Noah John Rondeau's Collection.

To keep Sue from searching for imaginary dangerous animals in the darkness, I told her stories that Helen Menz had shared. Helen, now ninety-one, and her sister, Mary Dittmar, climbed Wright and Algonquin in the dark one August night in 1944 to view the sunrise.[1] Whatever inspirational philosophy I thought my yarns might evoke, it failed to motivate Sue to do any further bushwhacking. She has no motivation for overnight trips after a black bear bolted directly in front of her mountain bike as she rode into Remsen Falls lean-to. But it didn't discourage her from enjoying the outdoors.

Now grown, my daughter has joined forces with her brother Mike; she writes children's books, and Mike illustrates cartoon characters based on real woodland animals she encountered on her Adirondack outings. Both have a special connection with the outdoors, and Sue writes each account as a labor of love. Her writing draws attention to damage that humans unconsciously do to our fragile environment. She attributes her motivation to family camping trips and even her first three-day adventure with me! 🏃

[1] See "Algonquin Sunrise—August 1944."

〰️

William J. "Jay" O'Hern: Family vacations introduced me to the Adirondack Mountains. Bushwhacking helped me learn more about remote areas, and conversations with native residents motivated me to record their social history. I take pleasure in researching and writing Adirondack history, preserving the stories, photos, diaries, and history that old-timers have shared. A full biography and my books are featured on www.Adirondack-books.com and www.theforagerpress.com. I am 46er #1830.

35

TO THE SUMMIT

CASCADING EMOTIONS

Darielle Graham

"**I** can do it, I can do it!" The boy's voice, cascading with confidence, contrasted to my own half an hour earlier claiming, "I can't." The ascent of Cascade was suited for someone like me, who likes to climb but dislikes steep pitches prevalent on other peaks. Not once had I thought *I can't manage this*, or *I'm dreading the descent*. I'd had to be careful not to become complacent in case I tripped over my glee the closer the peak approached. Just below the summit I balked like a horse at a water jump as I faced a near-vertical rock slab with a foothold I didn't believe my boot could wedge in without my slipping or freezing like a petroglyph. *If I manage to clamber up*, I thought, *I'll never get back down*. I didn't want to continue. John offered help, but the more I gazed at the rock the more afraid I became, until even Cascade's open face drenched me in a wave of agoraphobia. "I can't," I repeated. "I'm not the woman I once was." Pain shadowed John's face, and a deep snow of silence fell between us.

The woman I once was had snowshoed Cascade and Porter in one day and had gone on to gain many more of the Adirondack High Peaks. That was a woman confident she could handle any challenge and, more importantly, who owned a body strong enough to accommodate. Knee surgery and years of injuries had eroded both. Cascade culminated a camping trip to Rollins Pond during which John and I had hiked Jenkins and St. Regis mountains and explored all the ponds comprising the Floodwood Loop. John chose the easiest of the 4,000-footers, Cascade, confident I could climb it. He couldn't conceal his disappointment at continuing alone and hoped I'd change my mind. Finally I said, "You carry on, I'll eat lunch."

Alone in the mountainous silence of a panorama of peaks, I thought about how I had never let go of the woman I once was, but often imagined her back in my body seducing me into believing it had never broken down. I'd never fully regained her peak of fitness or recouped her confidence. She wouldn't have given the rock that rooted me a second glance—she'd have shinned up in seconds and been on her way to Porter by now. *That was another time*, I told myself. I eased back into the present and removed her presence as if it were a veil preventing me from seeing the view. After three days of hiking—legs still limber, arthritic knees not grating, Achilles tendons and metatarsals uncomplaining—I accepted my good fortune.

A day nothing hurt was something to celebrate! My spirits rose and doubts about my decision to forego summiting Cascade began to disperse like clouds the wind whisked across the sky.

When John returned we were no longer alone; people of all ages had begun descending. There was a girl of about ten taxiing down the runway of Cascade's face like a plane about to lift into the air; her eight-year-old brother rejected their father's assistance when he came to the slab of rock, his insistent "I can do it" lingering long after. Amazing was the toddler, blond curls splashing sunlight against gray rock, each tiny step a source of pride for his parents. The woman with hiking poles convinced me it wasn't too late to claim Cascade. Hunched over, face pinched with concentration, her gait was unsteady, every step hesitant as if she were afraid to trust the traction of her boots. At the rock, she considered the best way down before retreating and letting her husband take the lead. He slid on his backside and instructed her to do the same. Her poles became entangled between her legs and she struggled to extricate them, thrusting them at her husband. "You take them," she commanded. She inched on her backside until, above the foothold, she slowly slid downward until one of her feet reached it. She looked like someone performing a side split and getting stuck midway unable to proceed, yet unable to pull herself back. Her husband grabbed her round the waist and lifted her toward him, the prince rescuing the dying swan.

I thought, *If a woman that shaky can summit Cascade, why can't I?* John must have thought likewise because he said, "Come on, let's try for the summit." He glided up the rock, long, muscular legs leaving no doubt that he was on good footing with his surroundings. Leaving my pack, I followed, a blinkered horse focusing on John's feet. If my eyes wandered left or right or looked upward I'd rein them in, afraid the exposed peak would again induce an agoraphobic wave. The trick was to move sufficiently swiftly that I had no time to reflect upon the lack of tree branches to cling to or that my feet might slip out of the crack. Within seconds I was standing atop Cascade exulting, "I can't believe how easy that was!"

Adirondack peaks rose and fell like waves on a fetal heart monitor. I traced each one with my eyes, as a blind person touches every feature on a person's face so the shape of eyes, nose, and mouth becomes imprinted in the brain. Vermont's Green Mountains seemed to say, "Remember us?" Since the rainy July day that John and I completed the Long Trail, we'd never returned to Vermont. Though its rugged ways wouldn't be kind to my knees, the hope that we'd go back remained curled in my mind's womb. A lazy Lake Champlain lay on her side sunbathing, unruffled by gusts of wind that sporadically swept across Cascade's summit. I remembered another hot, humid July day when we cycled to Champlain's shore and spent a mystical hour lapping its serenity.

My thoughts returned to January 1987 when Cascade and the world around it were cloaked in snow, and John and I had the summit to ourselves before pursuing Porter. The woman then had been so sure of herself, so strong physically and mentally, wearing confidence like a gold medal. Retracing her footsteps had brought me as close to her as I'd ever been. Cascade was again mine. I wore it like a crown. And a wonderful thing happened on the way down. A waterfall of confidence gushed through my body. I skated down rocks and ledges, reveling in a newfound surefootedness. In less time than I imagined possible, I completed the descent. "I'm glad you made it to the top," John said, "you can go home happy." That was an understatement! I changed into sneakers, giddy with joy like a new ship christened with a bottle of champagne. 🚶

*D*arielle Graham: I served on the Publications Committee of the Adirondack *Mountain Club, and enjoy writing articles for Adirondac magazine and writing poetry. I live with my husband, John, in Mount Kisco, New York.*

36

A SAWTOOTH #1 ODYSSEY

IN QUEST OF THE HUNDRED HIGHEST

Michael Patrick McLean

The Sawtooth Range is a series of rugged trailless mountains in the western High Peaks, east of Street and Nye mountains and west of Ampersand Lake and the Seward Mountains. To those nuts out there with dreams of climbing the Adirondack Hundred Highest Peaks, a visit to five of the Sawtooth summits is necessary. Sawtooth #1 is the highest, at 3,877 feet, and near the center of the range. To avoid cuts, scrapes, and loss of flesh and blood, you should choose the approach with the shortest bushwhack—the Ward Brook Truck Trail from Coreys for seven miles to a USGS benchmark past the Number Four lean-tos along a beautiful stream, then bushwhack on an 80° bearing 2.2 miles to the summit. A picturesque unnamed pond with wonderful views of Sawtooth #1 awaits you. I became familiar with it, as I attempted four times to get to the summit.

Indian versus Chief. The Laurentian chapter of the Adirondack Mountain Club scheduled a hike by co-leaders Tom Wheeler and Dick Mooers with aspirations of climbing four of the Sawtooths. I was contemplating climbing the Adirondack Hundred Highest and thought, *Why not?*

Jim Close and I hike in to the lean-tos on a very soggy Friday. Chiefs Tom, Dick, and Jim discuss routes, while I am content to be an innocent Indian bystander. We begin at daybreak, planning to climb Sawtooth #5, #1, and #2. The going is slow and wet, through thick vegetation. We arrive at #5, and the three chiefs consult maps and compasses, then head for what we believe is #1, and the hours roll by. Checking the time, I find my watch is no longer there, the victim of a spruce tree strainer. Dick loses his safety glasses and compass. After a very long, tough time we arrive on #1—but wait, what is that? We actually have climbed Sawtooth #2. The view is magnificent and reveals that #1 is quite distant through more steep ups and downs and thick going. Tom is tired and has hurt his leg. It is very warm and getting late—how about we call it a day? We give a cheer when we reach the trail, and arrive at the lean-to an hour before dark—eleven and a half hours to climb the two peaks. None of us are in a hurry to have anything rub up against arms or legs, let alone do another bushwhack, so we head out at first light.

Postholes and a Sick Dog. On a sunny, unseasonably warm April day, I decide to give #1 a try with my dog Duke. Even with snowshoes the post-holing is deep, and Duke is on the tails of my snowshoes. Sweat is rolling off me and stinging my eyes in the warm temperature, while I have to wear protective nylon pants and shirt. We retreat to enjoy a pleasant day at Duck Hole, wearing shorts and a T-shirt.

That summer, Cindy, Duke, and I pack in to the lean-tos. She had tried smaller bushwhacks, and her brain functions properly, so she is content to explore around the lean-to area. I plan to meet Mark Lowell at the pond at 3,100 feet, and Duke and I head out at first light. An hour into the hike, at a stream crossing at 3,000 feet, suddenly Duke starts vomiting and breathing hard. A third of a mile from the pond, I yell for Mark, get no response, and debate what to do. The day is hot, and with Duke's condition I hesitantly turn around, let him enjoy a long rest at the lean-to, and then we slowly pack out, letting Duke enjoy streams and pools. Mark did wait for me and he climbed #5, but failed to summit #1.

Four is the Magic Number. October the next year proves to be a charm. Hiking in at 4:00 AM, a full moon and headlamp help, but it's difficult to see where and how deep the mud is; in one section the mud goes over my boots. Stumbling over branches, I retrace and find that the trail was rerouted. Barred owls and the rustling of other critters keep me company, and I arrive at the lean-tos at 6:45 AM.

Mark is camped at the 3,100-foot pond between #2 and #5. At the 2,320-foot benchmark south of the lean-tos, I head on an 82° bearing to intersect the stream draining the pond; after twenty minutes I realize I'm following the wrong drainage and nervously head over a steep ridge on my original bearing. Thirty minutes of pushing through balsams gets me to a much larger drainage stream. The grade forces me down into it, where I start rock hopping and waterfall climbing, getting feet wet. Mark is at the beautiful pond, and we take a direct route for the mountain, passing another pretty pond and beautiful grassland before woods envelop us again. Another hour gets us to the base of a steep cliff face—only five hundred more feet of steep up. We find a good but wet way up the cliff face; the moss is a bright red. Spruce and balsam get thicker, and we encounter snow. We admire wonderful views southwest, and then find the prize, a canister with only thirty-one folks who signed in over the last twenty years. We enjoy the stories in the log and the views; it felt so good hanging out here.

For the descent I wore gloves; my hands couldn't take any more cutting or scraping against the vegetation. We get back to the lean-tos by 4:15, and it felt wonderful to get hundreds of balsam needles off my neck, back, and bottom. With a quick pace I make it out just before dark. A most excellent adventure, #83 of my

Adirondack Top 100—but after Sawtooth #1, it's my opinion that finishing the Hundred Highest is all downhill. 🚶

Michael Patrick McLean: I am an environmental engineer with the Department of Environmental Conservation and live in northern New York with my wife, Cindy, and daughter Zoe. I've climbed the High Points of the fifty states and plan on running a marathon in all fifty. My climbing has brought me to the high points of four continents. I'm a Winter Correspondent with the Adirondack 46ers, #3869W, lead hikes, have adopted two lean-tos with the ADK, and am chair of Azure Mountain Friends, which maintains the Fire Tower and Volunteer Interpreter Program on that summit.

37

FOREST BURGLARS

THE WILD—AND THE UNCIVILIZED

Friedel Schunk

On June 30, 1984, I felt the call to experience the Adirondack High Peaks by way of a new challenge—hike the entire Great Range via Rooster Comb to Marcy, including a side trip to Haystack, starting from The Garden parking lot. The tour was beautiful amidst varied weather of haze, fog clouds on and off, drizzle and light rain, and sporadic sunshine. A Boy Scout troop was spread all over the trail of the final ascent from Lower Wolf Jaw's col, interspersed by two families who received more attention from black flies and mosquitoes than they had bargained for. The crowds disappeared until I met up with a proud father who had been on the Range Trail all day with his two young children. It was a memorable way to enjoy eight major peaks in one day. After more than 9,000 feet of elevation gain and loss, and almost a marathon distance of hiking, I returned feeling in fine shape—knees and feet had withstood the formidable challenge of some of the Adirondacks' most rugged trails. Conditioning and willpower had withstood the test.

Another test was waiting, however—my car had been totally cleaned out. I had concealed important belongings, leaving visible only cans of non-gourmet food, fruit, maps, and a small camping cooler. Gone were the pack that had served me well to the summit of Mt. McKinley, the Gore-Tex and down parkas that had shared my winter mountaineering experiences, the reliable MSR backpacking stove, pads, sleeping bag, pots and other camping and personal paraphernalia including a newly acquired larger cooler, several pairs of boots for alternative hiking plans, even mountaineering magazines and Hornbein's book on Everest. After the long hike, I would now have fit better into my reserve pants—now that I didn't have pants to fit into! Nor anything else to switch into and become Mr. Normal after a sweaty hike. The first clue that something might be amiss came at the register, which was open and the register book unfolded—an unusual sight. Thieves might have compared car license plates with registered hometowns and itineraries, and my out-of-state origin convinced them I was ripe for the picking.

At first the episode left me emotionally neutral, stunned in disbelief. Then I became angry at barbarians who had coldly taken away pieces of myself, wiped out pleasant memories, robbed my blanket of security of so many items that had

Summit, 4,736-foot Gothics. Photo by Steve Boheim.

served me well. I must fight now with the insurance company whose policy fine print will try to convince me that none of these items had value. Signs warn the hiker of these occurrences, but I had parked there before for days.

Having become a victim, I can vouch for how personal this audacious crime can be. I hope you are spared a similar experience. This day was my wife's birthday, and she had had to be in Europe. I'd contemplated going with her, but fiscal priorities had prevailed. Little did I know at the time, but I could have flown first class with what I lost in the theft. What a way to finish a marathon! The police did find the thief, who stole to support his drug habit. He had an enormous amount of hikers' and climbers' equipment when he was apprehended. I recovered a third of my items. 🥾

Previously published in the Catskill Canister, *spring 1985.*

F̲riedel Schunk: Growing up in Germany I was always outdoor-oriented, including extended hiking trips staying at youth hostels. I am a 46er, #1468, #30W, completed winter climbs of the Northeast 4,000-footers, New England Hundred Highest, the Hundred Highest Adirondacks and Catskills, and solo summitted Denali. For completing at least ten of fourteen international cross-country-ski marathon races ranging from 26 to 56 miles, I achieved the World Loppet Master award. Other races were the three-day, 100-mile Arctic Circle Race in Greenland and the Rajalta-Rajalla in Finland, 280 miles in seven days. Other interests include rock climbing, sea kayaking, triathlon, and competitive athletics.

38

THE FELONS

CAMPING QUALMS

Arthur Boni

For several years my pal Mike and I took our teenage daughters on an annual spring trip in the Adirondacks. The girls were allowed to take one friend each. Yes, that's right—we volunteered to chaperone four teenaged girls! These experiences gave Mike and me new insight into the Adirondack motto, "Forever wild." This was especially true after the girls had consumed a steady intake of candy during the four-hour car trip.

I had discovered that camping was permitted just south of the base of Roaring Brook Falls and thought it would be a fine location from which Mike and I could introduce the next generation to the joys of hiking. The girls, of course, would have been only too happy to confine their hiking to the main drag in Lake Placid. To their chagrin, shopping was not on our agenda. I had explained to them that we would walk about a quarter of a mile in the dark through the woods to our campsite. Knowing this and actually doing it are two very dissimilar experiences, as they were about to find out. With eyes the size of pie plates, the girls set off into the bush, encouraged by Mike and me and guided by an array of headlamps and flashlights. The shadows cast by our big packs loomed large. The crack of every twig we stepped on sounded like a gunshot. (Was this a harbinger of things to come?)

One must negotiate a crossing of Roaring Brook, which can be tricky even in broad daylight and is definitely unnerving at night during spring runoff. Past this defense you enter an undulating triangle of land, well treed and bound on two sides by fast-running streams. The ambient moisture has created a rain forest type of microenvironment. With the spring melt in full throttle, the running water built a wall of sound. Fumbling, we found a wide, level site on which to erect two tents—one for the girls, and one for Mike and me as far away as we could get and still be in the same state.

The next day, soon after reaching the summit of Noonmark, rain began and did not let up. Returning late in the afternoon, we got busy erecting a tarp shelter. We noticed that during our absence several tents had been pitched well away from us. With the omnipresent sound of running water, however, we were not concerned about noisy neighbors.

Then I was startled by the sudden presence of a stranger. It took me a few seconds to understand exactly what he was telling me: our neighbors were felons—his word—young men from urban centers who were doing jail time. He hastened to add that their crimes were nonviolent. If this revelation was meant to be reassuring, it was not. I noticed his sidearm pistol and a large German shepherd pacing nearby. He explained that a local prison believed strongly in promoting outdoor activity as a rehabilitation tool. It was his duty to tell me these things, he said, so that we could make an informed decision whether to remain or not. "Have a nice evening, sir," he said and returned to his guard duties.

To say that this was a wholly unexpected turn of events would be a gross understatement. As I relayed the information to Mike, there were four additional pairs of ears that were on high alert. The ensuing buzz surpassed that from the sugar high of the previous day. It was late afternoon; everyone was hungry, wet, tired, and Mike and I were responsible for four impressionable teenaged girls. What would you do? We are men, after all, and capable of defending our hearth and home, correct? Well, actually our thoughts were not quite so heroic. The guard had made a point of saying that we had nothing to worry about, and we were inclined to agree with him. We polled our charges. Although the girls were imagining all manner of defense strategies, they were agreeable to staying.

Mike and I were more afraid of what our wives would say about our decision to stay than we were of the felons. We had *chosen* to stay on a campsite with their daughters and their daughters' girlfriends, separated from a gang of felons by nothing more than tent fabric and one hundred feet of open ground! So the girls, of course, were sworn to secrecy.

The rain let up, we had a roaring campfire, told silly stories, and otherwise had an enjoyable evening. The next morning I noticed that I had left a hand impression on the handle of the hatchet tucked under my pillow. 🏃

*A*rthur Boni: *I live in Ottawa, Canada, and made my first trip to the Adirondacks in 1982 to climb Mount Marcy. Whether it is scrambling up the Benny Brook slide, traversing the High Peaks in a one-day marathon, or rambling along the Gill Brook trail during spring runoff, I find deep contentment and relaxation in these mountains. My goal is to stay fit in order to continue to hike, cycle, snowshoe, and cross-country ski until I fall down dead.*

39

IF A TREE FALLS

DOES IT MAKE A SOUND IF NO ONE IS THERE?

Mark Schaefer

Most people have heard the age-old imponderable riddle, *If a tree falls in the forest and no one is there to hear it, does it make a sound?* On a 1976 Adirondack backpacking trip, I learned the answer.

I was hiking alone and returning to Elk Lake after climbing the five Dix Range peaks. It was a sunny, calm summer day, and I heard an unexpected, loud, sustained *whoosh!* An enormous tree was falling in the deep woods about thirty yards off the trail. It certainly made a sound, but I was there. Proves nothing, right?

But before the tumult of that great falling tree had subsided, an even greater cacophony drowned out the sound—birds, squirrels, chipmunks, insects, and other critters within earshot were now raising their voices in response to the crash. They all had heard that tree fall and were talking amongst themselves about it. It was then that I realized the answer to the riddle! There is *never* "no one there." The premise of the riddle is invalid and human-centric. Wildlife exists in all healthy forests, and they hear any tree that falls.

An interesting note on the tree's fall is that it resembled the fall of a high-rise building that had been imploded during demolition—the tree's trunk and branches fell straight down on its own roots. The trunk must have been hollow and rotted, and it decided to give up the ghost on that calm day just as I was passing. I am glad it did. 𝕞

*M*ark Schaefer: I am primarily a three-season hiker in the Catskills, Shawan-gunks, and Hudson Valley. I joined the Catskill 3500 Club in 1975 and the Adirondack 46ers, #3124, in 1992. I'm hiking the Catskill Hundred Highest, but I am in no rush to complete this list because I enjoy hiking in the forest more than on summits. Other outdoor interests include cross-country skiing, road bicycling, observing wildlife, and photography.

Part II:

IN QUEST
OF THE FORTY-SIX
HIGH PEAKS

*A waterfall had turned to ice on these rocks, and it was
extremely treacherous to descend, but I had no other choice—
I was too far down the mountain to turn back. I sat on my butt
on the icy rock and tried to do a controlled drop down to the
next level. As I slid off the rock, I completely lost control and
ended up plummeting face down onto the icy rock below! I
didn't even have a chance to put out my arms or hands to protect my face—I felt my face actually bounce off the ground! And
then I felt myself sliding, but luckily my body stopped before
sliding off the next drop-off*

— Kristin Konchar-Schafer, "Icy Slide off Big Slide"

Summit, Mount Marcy. Photo by David White.

40

AN UNPLANNED OVERNIGHT IN THE DIX RANGE

INJURY MILES FROM NOWHERE IN WINTER

Arlene Heer Stefanko

My sister Doreen and I looked forward to this hike. It would bring our winter peaks to twenty-two, and we were going to hike with our friends Tom and Jane Haskins. The alarm at the Keene Valley Hostel went off at 4:30 AM. At the last minute I grabbed a garbage bag to line my pack to keep extra clothes dry if the light rain continued. Doreen did the same. I pondered carrying a lighter pack since it was going to be a long day, but decided to go with my usual winter gear even if it was a few more pounds.

We spotted Jane's car at the Bouquet River trailhead parking lot, and I drove us back to the Dix/Round Pond trailhead. We were on the trail at 6:30; it was over-cast with temperatures in the twenties. The hike to Dix was beautiful—and very steep. It was fun to look down through our legs to the climber below, but sobering, knowing we needed to be surefooted to avoid tripping and knocking the person below off the trail. We were exhilarated on the summit, whooping and hollering as usual. The skies were beginning to clear, and we were rewarded with a view of the range.

After a small celebration we were off to Hough. Abundant spruce traps kept our pace slower, but we had many laughs at each other struggling to get free. There was an American flag on a spruce tree—a beautiful picture opportunity with Macomb Mountain in the distance. After celebrating on Hough, Tom skirted "Pough" on our way to South Dix. Side-hilling in snowshoes on the steep moun-tainside was a challenge. We arrived at South Dix and knew we would be saving Macomb for another day, as it was getting late and we were tired.

The trail to East Dix was a section we hadn't been on before. The previous summer we had ascended East Dix via the Great Slide to achieve our 46th High Peak, but Tom now recommended descending at the South Dix/East Dix col, rather than down the Great Slide—a relief to Doreen and me. With the snow so icy, we were concerned that the Great Slide was too steep to descend safely. Earlier rain had created a hard, icy crust that you broke through every few steps and jammed into your leg just below the knee. Our legs were sore, and I was trying to ignore the pain and just focus on getting back. But we were all happy to have four more winter peaks under our belt.

We stopped at the base of the East Dix Slide to look at the view—we could almost see the summit. It was 5:00 PM. We came upon a small stream flowing with the start of spring snowmelt. Tom was first to cross on a log, then Jane. Doreen stepped on the log with her snowshoe and slipped, ending up on her back in the stream. The pained look on her face coupled with her immobility spurred me to action. I grabbed her hand and encouraged her to pull herself out. She hesitated and said she had injured her leg. I pulled her out of the water and, after assessing for obvious fractures or external injuries, I wrapped her knee with an ace bandage. She was wearing a Gore-tex jacket and pants that proved to be a lifesaver, keeping her from having gotten thoroughly soaked.

Doreen could only take small, painfully slow steps, and it was clear that we would need help to get her out. Tom suggested we continue as far as we could, and he would run ahead for help. Before he left, Jane had the presence of mind to get items from his pack; he gave her his PrimaLoft jacket and emergency bivy. With great resistance from Doreen, we divided up her pack contents and I carried her pack. This became a bit of a screaming match of wills, since she insisted on carrying her own pack. But even though I am the little sister, I won! Jane was quite entertained by the exchange.

Doreen said that it was easier to take a step with the snowshoes on; it made her more surefooted, and any slips on the snow brought excruciating pain. We devised a three-legged walk to inch along—I supported her injured leg by using my snowshoe to step on hers and thus ensure it did not slip, as she used her other leg to place her next step. Jane led, following Tom's tracks, until we came to a larger stream. We lost his tracks there, and it was getting too dark to proceed safely. We started putting on more clothes right away. Jane put on Tom's PrimaLoft jacket. I gave Doreen my PrimaLoft jacket, and she gave me her lighter-weight fleece jacket. It had stayed dry in her fall because she had wrapped it in a garbage bag inside her pack. I also helped her put on my spare dry socks. My own boot heaters had long ago run out of juice, but I could move about to stay warm—Doreen was nearly immobile.

We had no watch and lost all sense of time. We needed fire and shelter; the skies had cleared, and the temperature was falling into the single digits. We attempted a fire, without success. I carry a small folding saw, and we took turns sawing small branches to make a shelter. We were able to make one big enough for our torsos, and we had Doreen lie down in the emergency blanket while we added more branches. Whenever we adjusted the branches, dried needles fell on Doreen's bare face, and that provided us with some comic relief. Jane and I then climbed in with Doreen, but our feet were getting very cold. Jane had an idea—to put our feet inside our packs for added insulation. My feet were so painfully cold that I was determined to make a fire, but again I was unsuccessful.

Doreen airlifted out of Dix Range. Photo by Arlene Heer Stefanko.

We knew we had to stay in a positive frame of mind and do everything we could to keep moving and keep Doreen warm. We tried isometrics, singing songs, playing word games, anything we could think of to generate heat. I was praying silently. When we looked up at the stars through the trees, then looked down the stream, it was as though we saw lights in the forest. We kept staring down the stream, thinking we saw headlamps coming. But it was an illusion. Since it was St. Patrick's Day, we joked that leprechauns were playing with us, or that Tom was teasing us. (In reality, Tom was at the Keene Valley firehouse assisting with our rescue. Tom had reached a phone by 8:00 PM and called for a rescue.) More than once one of us said, "Look! Here comes someone!" We would blow the whistles and turn on our headlamps, to no avail.

Doreen was kept stationary, but moved her arms to generate heat. She and I tried getting in the bivy sack together, but it didn't seem as warming as moving about, even slightly. Our next attempt at fire was with greater urgency as we were all beyond just cold. Jane and I took turns sawing branches, and Doreen hobbled about collecting dead branches. We had a baby fire going when Doreen called out, "I see headlamps coming, and I see more than one!" Jane and I didn't take Doreen seriously until she said, "There they are, coming right toward us!" We counted five headlamps coming at us, and we were *very* relieved—it was 2:30 AM.

The rescue team identified themselves as Forest Rangers Joe and Chris, and Search and Rescue Volunteers Ron, Lauren, and Charlie. Lauren is a physician assistant at Lake Placid hospital. She attended to Doreen's injury, and then put her into dry, warm clothes. Someone handed me a feather-down coat, for which I was grateful—I felt instantly warm (except for my feet!) We were fed, given hot tea, and a roaring fire was made. As Jane and Doreen drifted off to sleep, I listened to the conversation as the rescuers planned the next steps. They discussed the finer points of making a harness from nylon straps for Doreen. I interjected that Doreen still thought she would be hiking out in the morning with their help. They said that she would be convinced otherwise in the morning. I noticed the first light of morning at 4:30 AM, and was relieved that this night was ending.

When Doreen woke up, the rescuers explained that a chopper was coming for her at 8:00 AM. They would explain exactly what she was to do and how it would feel to be lifted into the helicopter. The rest of us divided up Doreen's stuff, because she couldn't take anything with her. Nothing could be left on the ground to be blown about by the helicopter. The call came that the chopper was delayed, so again we sat by the fire; Doreen was harnessed up and ready. I gave her a hug and, with tears in my eyes, ran behind the rock that would shield us from the turbulence from the chopper. When we heard it coming up the valley, the rescuers put boughs on the fire to signal our location. We were instructed to stay behind the rock and not look, or we would risk getting embers blown into our eyes. I just couldn't resist a picture, however. Weeks later I surprised Doreen with an eight-by-ten photo of her on the cable being lifted into the helicopter.

With Doreen safely on her way to Lake Placid Hospital, we began our five-mile hike to the Bouquet trailhead. I enjoyed the beauty along the path, even though I hadn't slept for twenty-four hours. We put our crampons on, as the last mile near the Bouquet River was very icy. Charlie was the only one without crampons and nearly ended up in the river after slipping on an icy section. Quickly grabbing a branch, he prevented another disaster.

Many Department of Environmental Conservation vehicles were at the trail-head with "behind the scenes" people. After a stop at the Keene Valley firehouse, we headed to Lake Placid to pick up Doreen. We then went back to the hostel to pick up our belongings. Everyone there was anxious to hear about our adventure and rescue. After a much-needed shower and change of clothes, we started our four-hour drive home. It was 4:00 PM. I wasn't sure how I was going to stay awake after the long hike and with no sleep for nearly thirty-two hours, but after a good meal I felt alert, refreshed, and blessed with reserves I didn't know were in me. We thoroughly discussed how differently we would pack for future hikes after this misadventure.

Doreen had surgery for a torn ACL and meniscus, and recovered even stronger than before. We went on to complete the Winter 46 in January 2006, having climbed the High Peaks as day hikes in the winter. All were climbed with my sister, my best friend. 🏃

*A*rleen Heer Stefanko: *I thought climbing a mountain was reserved for those with great athletic ability. A coworker introduced me to the High Peaks in 1992, and I was hooked! My sister Doreen was my climbing partner for the first 46er round, and we climbed the Winter 46 together (#4855W). My kids boast about their Mountain Climbing Mom, but I'm just an ordinary person doing some extraordinary things (Matthew 19:26).*

41

ALGONQUIN AND IROQUOIS IN WINTER

PERSEVERING THROUGH EXTREME CONDITIONS

Andrea V. Wright

When setting out on a hiking trip, I have confidence both in my abilities and in those of my experienced fellow hikers. After all, I have climbed the 46 peaks above 4,000 feet in the summer and more than twenty of them in the winter as well. We check weather conditions and previous trip reports on the Web, have checklists for essential gear, review trail descriptions and map, and load the GPS with our route. Three of my regular hiking companions—my husband Robert, my aunt Glo, our friend Bill—and I attended the ADK winter hiking school and can efficiently "glissade," "self-arrest," use an ice axe, crampons, snowshoes, and build three different kinds of shelters with a shovel, trekking poles, and a small piece of plastic. Despite the best preparation, however, Mother Nature reminds us occasionally that she is a force to be reckoned with and commands our respect. Our winter hike over to Iroquois in March 2007 was one of those times.

Leaving at 7:00 AM, we immediately had technical difficulties—my trekking poles wouldn't latch to stay extended, and my sister Belinda ripped the binding out of her snowshoes. Luckily my husband is "MacGyver" and can fix anything with a paper clip and a piece of duct tape. Out came his trusty Leatherman, and in a few minutes all repairs were completed and we were back in business. The temperature was very warm for March 14—a balmy 50° in the early morning, and warmer as the day went on. During the mile to the Marcy Dam–Algonquin Trail junction, we shed layers until we were down to T-shirts. The snow conditions were soft, with snowshoes sinking up to four inches on the packed trail and deeper as we started up the Algonquin Trail toward Whale's Tail. It felt different than walking in fresh granular snow—more like walking on sand. We made it to the birches before it started to rain. Because it was so warm, we used light ponchos instead of our typical rain gear. This kept us relatively dry and allowed for the breeze to cool our body cores. At the falls, water had started to trickle and snow was melting around it, a hint of things to come.

As the grade increased, Belinda, who never complains and usually leaves me in her dust, said she was feeling low on energy and didn't think she would be able to make the summit. Robert taught her to use the resting step we learned in winter hiking school—a simple variation in pace that allows for a second of rest between steps. She mastered the pace change quickly, and it made a huge difference—her heart rate decreased and her breathing normalized. Just below tree line the wind picked up. We changed into our heavier gear and headed up to the open rock. What a contrast from the conditions at the beginning of our hike! Winds were 60 MPH with heavier gusts, and the rain turned to ice balls. The yellow poncho Belinda wore was quickly getting shorter as pieces were torn away by the wind, so we stopped to remove what was left of it before continuing on. Robert, always ahead, took our picture and a video clip so that we could relive this moment—ideally, over a cup of hot chocolate in front of a warm fire. Standing on the geological marker on Algonquin's summit, we decided to continue to Iroquois, my goal. The strong winds continued on the back side of the mountain as we descended into the cloud that had settled in the col between Algonquin and Boundary.

Another group had completed this hike a few days before, so I thought the trail would be easy to find. We found no sign of it, however, as we hiked through a minefield of huge spruce traps. Derek was the first of many casualties—he ventured too close to a spruce tree, and its snow-laden branches gave way under his weight. He dropped into a hole so deep that we could barely see the top of his head! None of us were spared. A few GPS readings and much digging out later, we climbed over the top of Boundary. The vague remains of the trail were quickly lost, so we proceeded in the general direction of Iroquois, exiting the woods a little farther down the mountain than we should have.

After a quick picture on the summit, we found the established trail on the way back; we had missed it by fifteen feet. The snow continued to soften, and the spruce trap minefield was even more dangerous—Belinda went down to her armpits, and the snow filled the hole, burying her waist-deep. She struggled for a few minutes, not making any headway. We offered help, but she eventually wiggled her way out of the snow cocoon on her own. At the base of Algonquin, we found a walking stick—apparently that of a very large man, because it was almost seven feet tall and quite heavy. Derek reminded us that on a previous hike he had left his snowshoes hanging in a tree on the top of Blake Peak, and some thoughtful hiker had carried them down from there. We decided to return the favor and carry the walking stick down to the information center.

We pushed back up to the summit of Algonquin, the wind's impressive gusts throwing us off balance. The descent on the other side was even more treacherous. What had been ice on the way up had turned to slush over water—more difficult to negotiate and much more slippery. A few bruises, but we made it off the rocks and caught only a few good glissades. The brooks that had been iced over on the way up were open on the way down. I stopped at the brook above MacIntyre and listened to the roar of the water beneath the snow bridge. There was a three-foot swath of open water, and I told Derek that I didn't like the looks of this crossing. Derek thought that if he walked lightly and quickly, he could make it across the now-raging stream. As he crossed, the snow bridge collapsed underneath him, enlarging the crossing to a six-foot swath of rushing water. He went in waist-deep. Because of the current and the weight of the slush, he was pinned to the bank on the opposite side of the brook for what seemed an eternity but, in reality, was only a few minutes. Standing on the opposite bank from him (and without a rubber dinghy), we watched, but couldn't help. Derek finally struggled free and pulled himself out of the cold water. We used the tall walking stick to gauge the depth of the stream; the stick was almost entirely submerged, meaning seven feet of raging water. Robert climbed higher upstream and found another crossing. It held under his weight and only his feet got wet, but the crossing was unstable and the opening was growing rapidly. Belinda and I searched both upstream and downstream. No other crossing looked safe, so we crossed where Robert had while he stabilized our jump with the tall stick.

We were all soaked from the rain, from glissading, and from falling in the stream. Derek was carrying the most water. His boots made that little gushing sound as he walked. Had the temperature been colder we would have changed

Summit Algonquin. Photo by Neil Luckhurst.

into dry clothes, but there was another brook to cross and a few more glissades ahead in the slushy snow. We decided to wait and change clothes at the information center. Trail conditions continued to deteriorate—even wearing snowshoes, we post-holed over a foot on the packed trail, significantly decreasing our speed of descent.

We certainly had not anticipated that this beautiful spring-like day would bring so many challenges. Regardless of our drenched boots, tattered ponchos, and bruised egos, however, we all appreciated our time together and our great accomplishment. Can't wait to get out there next winter! 🚶

Andrea V. Wright: In 1992, after standing on top of Mount Marcy inhaling that fresh, misty air, I traded in my high heels and painted fingernails for hiking boots and a backpack. Then I added snowshoes, crampons, and an ice ax. Climbing provides adventure, treasured memories with family and dear friends, and valuable life lessons. May it continue for many more years. I am 46er #4982.

42

MISADVENTURES ON THE WAY TO A WINTER PATCH

EXPERIENCE: THE BEST TEACHER (IF YOU SURVIVE)

John B. Graham

When I first began winter climbing, I wondered how I'd avoid the pitfalls. The answer was simple—I wouldn't; the winter mountains would teach me. Over the last fifteen years I've learned by making mistakes, and I'm still learning.

My first winter climb was Big Slide from Grace Camp in 1980, chasing after Sam Steen and determined not to let someone old enough to be my grandfather outpace me. I panted behind, overdressed and overheated, too intent on keeping up to stop and remove some layers of clothing. As Sam stepped lightly up the steep pitch to the summit of Big Slide, I flailed my way up, slipping backward two steps for each step forward, finally hauling myself up from tree to tree. On top I sat shivering in my wet clothes. Sam ate gorp and drank hot cocoa while I sipped icy water and tried to eat my frozen sandwiches. Only after becoming thoroughly chilled did I put on my down jacket, though by then I had no warmth left to conserve. Luckily I had a heated cabin to return to.

I concluded that it would be far easier to complete my peaks in the other three seasons, and it wasn't until I had done so, in 1984, that I returned with Pete Ricci and Charlie Goodrich to resume my winter climbing over the Christmas holiday. I could hardly have picked a worse time. Temperatures rose to the fifties, and it rained torrentially. As seasoned 46ers, however, we were not going to be deterred by a "little rain." The fact that others were bailing out made us feel fortunate—there would be space for us at Grace Camp. But we were about to learn how treacherous a winter thaw could be.

We climbed Big Slide without snowshoes, but as the downpour continued, we had trouble crossing the small stream at the base of the mountain to get back to camp. That night Johns Brook roared as two feet of snow washed out. The floodwaters swirled over the island on which Grace Camp is situated and threatened to wash out the bridge. Trapped, we could only hope that the cabin would not be swept away. By morning the rain had stopped and we found that the bridge had survived. We had to retreat, as any stream crossing could be fatal. Every little gully was now a raging torrent. All the small log bridges were underwater; on our way out we were obliged to wade through water up to our thighs.

After drying out in a motel, we decided to climb Colvin and Blake. It was a long way, but now all the snow had washed out (we thought) and we wouldn't need to carry snowshoes. Halfway up Colvin we hit snow; luckily, a large party had preceded us and the trail was packed. We caught up with them after passing over Colvin. The leader warned us that we'd have trouble climbing Blake without snowshoes—it wouldn't be broken out—but we could take a shortcut out by descending to the Carry Trail and coming out over the ice of Lower Ausable Lake. He mentioned that if the ice wasn't safe, we should follow the north shore out. We insisted we'd have no problem. How much snow could there be?

We went up the north-facing slope, and the snow was two to three feet deep. At first I tried staying on top of the crust, but I plunged through with every other step, so I just stomped through. I could hear Pete and Charlie cursing as they sank even deeper in what were thigh-deep postholes for me. It took us an hour to go half a mile to the summit, and it was two o'clock before we headed down. We were back at the col in twenty minutes, and it was there that our judgment failed. If we'd retraced over Colvin, we would've easily been on Ausable Road before dark. But the allure of that downhill trail and the easy walk across the ice was too strong, so we went merrily plunging down the trail. At the bottom our misjudgment became apparent; the river between the lakes was in full flood and the ice was gone or broken up as far as we could see.

Then we made our second error. We had been advised to go around the north shore, but it looked very rocky and a good deal longer, so we took the south shore. At first the going was easy, but more and more frequently we were forced to detour over and around big rock faces that went right down to the water. As night fell we found ourselves clambering by the light of headlamps over house-sized boulders covered in snow. Eventually we resigned ourselves to an unplanned bivouac, and we were fortunate enough to find a cave under some giant fallen rocks. Dead wood filled the crevices of the rocks, and there was enough draft that we could build a fire without smoking ourselves out. In fact, we built two fires and made a spruce bough bed between them.

The temperature dropped drastically that night, and we didn't get much sleep. Pete and Charlie had Sorel pack boots on, but I just had leather boots, which were soaked. I put plastic bags over my socks, which probably saved me from frostbite. Pete and Charlie wore wool, but all I had on was lightweight polypro under a Gore-tex jacket and pants and a lightweight fleece jacket. All night I thought about what I would bring next time—and I've packed plenty of extra clothes ever since.

In the morning we made our way down to the lakeshore and found that the lake had refrozen. Large blocks of ice had rejoined. When we could proceed no farther along the shore, I volunteered to test the ice, tethered by a nine-millimeter rope Charlie had brought. The ice seemed very solid, so we roped up and shuffled across to the boathouse, and the adventure was over.

New Year's Day I started up Marcy alone in heavy snow. A couple of guys named Howard and Gary joined me at Marcy Dam. By then the snow had turned to rain. At Indian Falls, footsteps led across the frozen stream, but as I walked across, the ice gave way under me and I plunged face first into the water. The water wasn't very deep and I leapt out quickly. I decided to continue on—I was already wet from the rain anyway—but Howard was not in very good shape and

The Trap Dike. Photo by Carol White.

we had to nurse him along. Just below the summit cone we stopped to put on crampons, as all the rocks were covered in a thick glaze. The ice cracked off of us as we bent to put on our crampons. Howard was a little out of it, so I put his crampons on for him. We made it to the summit and then quickly started down at four o'clock.

I'd thought to gain safety by climbing with others, but climbing with strangers can be risky, and once you accept someone as a companion, you must stick with them. Gary and I had to half-carry Howard down after he sat and said that he was going to rest and we should go on ahead without him. It was eight o'clock before we got back to Marcy Dam.

Later that week I was climbing Algonquin alone. The entire mountain was a sheet of ice, and I wore crampons all day. As I bent at my tripod to set up my camera for a summit shot, I heard a ping and I winced as I realized that one of my crampons had broken. I was wearing soft-soled Sorel boots, and they were too flexible for crampons. I hadn't brought an ice axe, so I had a harrowing descent down five hundred feet to the tree line wearing just instep crampons.

At winter school the following year, I learned a unique method of self-arrest. Descending Yard Mountain, I heard a crazy airborne ranger, Bruce Gafner, wildly glissading behind me and I stepped aside to avoid being run over as he demonstrated his snowshoe telemark technique. No sooner had he passed me than he tumbled down a ledge, rolled at the bottom and crashed into a tree. As we gazed on in concern, he looked up and said, "Whew! Sure glad that tree was there."

But the worst accident during that winter school happened not outside, but inside. We were celebrating New Year's Eve on the last night of winter school when we suddenly heard a loud bang. Mike Douglas, one of the section leaders, called out my name, thinking I had let off a firecracker—but for once, I wasn't guilty. Guy Hughes, the other section leader, carried a homemade lithium lantern and the battery had shorted out and exploded in his shirt pocket, badly burning his face.

After winter school, Bruce, Eric, and I set off to backpack the Ausable range in light snow. By the time we'd come over Bear Den, we were engulfed in a full blizzard and found ourselves lost on the side of Dial. There was no flat ground on which to pitch a tent, but we had to stop, so we used our snowshoes as shovels to construct a platform and managed to get the tent up. It was fortunate we had spent the whole week practicing making camp, or we never would have gotten one up in such a howling storm. It snowed two feet that night, and we had to repeatedly shake the snow off the tent to prevent its collapse. We set up our stove on a snowshoe and found later that it had melted some of the webbing, which we replaced with cord. It was quite an adventure.

In March of 1987, Mike Douglas, Bruce Gafner, and I were ski camping at Flowed Lands. We packed snowshoes and skied to Avalanche Lake and started climbing the Trap Dike up Mount Colden. We had planned to use our snowshoes, but it was too icy, so we switched to crampons. Mike and Bruce had more rigid ski boots, but my boots were quite flexible and, at the second waterfall, one of my crampons popped off. Panic gripped me as I hung by an ice axe and one crampon, but I managed to work myself onto a ledge. Mike lowered a rope to me and hauled up my snowshoe-laden pack. Thus freed, I was able to reattach the crampon. Mike then belayed me up the last pitch, as I was shaking badly. I was happy to get back into snowshoes and declined to follow the others up the rockslide to the summit, preferring the safety of the gully. (The following year I declined to join another party that planned to climb the Trap Dike, as it was even icier that year. That group successfully negotiated the waterfall, but as they raced up the slide to the summit, Linda stumbled and slid several hundred feet down the slope, striking her head a fatal blow against a tree in front of my horrified friend Mike. The Trap Dike has me fully spooked now, and I've never been back.)

The following day, Mike and I skied up the Opalescent River and the old Twin Brooks trail as far as the height of land between Cliff and Redfield. There we changed into snowshoes and descended the washed-out trail to the slide that comes off the summit of Cliff. Ascending this slide, it was a short hop to the canister. As we signed in and were having a snack, a pine marten appeared, boldly looking for scraps; we were amazed to have this lunch guest! That night we had another visit from a pine marten, but he ignored my food bag, preferring Mike's home-baked goodies that hung in the tree alongside my bag. As we came down the slide from Cliff, I had a terrific ride down, but lost control of my slide and was fortunate to avoid the rocks at the bottom, only tearing my Gore-tex pants on brush at the bottom. Mike made a much more sensible, if slower, descent, which elicited my derision. 🏃

Originally published in the Spring/Summer 1996 edition of Adirondack Peeks *magazine, the magazine of the Adirondack Forty-Sixers, Inc. This abridged version is reprinted with permission of the Adirondack Forty-Sixers, www.adk46R.org.*

*J*ohn B. Graham: *I am an Adirondack 46er, #2027W, regular and winter, and especially enjoy employing my route-finding skills to explore and map new areas and trails. For several years I served as outings chairman for the Catskill 3500 Club, whose members lead hikes on weekends all year-round.*

43

A NIGHT ON THE TRAIL

AN "UNFORGIVABLE" LAPSE

Thomas D. Pinkerton

Over the years I have developed and refined lists of equipment, food, and clothing for any type of outdoor activity, so I was not inexperienced when I decided to become a 46er. It was a beautiful day, sunny and warm, when I left the trailhead at Coreys for a Labor Day weekend backpack in 1988. I had pored over maps, my *Adirondack Trails: High Peaks Region*, and was prepared to spend several nights on the trail. I wanted to climb the Seward and Santanoni Ranges, with MacNaughton Mountain thrown in if all went well. Arriving at the occupied Ward Brook lean-to, I hung a bear bag and switched to a daypack for climbing Seward, Donaldson, and Emmons; it was too late to climb Seymour and still hike to Duck Hole, hang a bear bag, pitch a tent, and eat before dark.

I started my evening meal at 7:45 at Duck Hole and got into my sleeping bag after cleaning up. I wanted to get an early start the next morning. The following day, the wet trail to Bradley Pond was more a herd path than a blazed trail, poorly maintained at best, and this would play a big part in my experience this day. It was sprinkling when I arrived at the Bradley Pond lean-to. On the herd path to the Santanoni-Panther col, it was beginning to rain in earnest. I summitted Santanoni, and now it was raining hard. The wind had picked up, making my hands shiver as I signed the register. At Panther's summit I couldn't read the time because rain had seeped into my watch and clouded the crystal. The wind was now so strong that it seemed to be coming at me horizontally. Two hikers said it was an easy hike to Couchsachraga and I decided that I had plenty of time.

The trail back to Duck Hole was even wetter, and I hadn't anticipated that it would be darker now than in the morning. I had recorded sunset times so I'd know when I needed to turn around. Now, I had three problems: I couldn't determine the time, the stormy weather was darkening the sky, and I had made the unforgivable mistake of forgetting to put a flashlight in my daypack—I had two flashlights back at Duck Hole! This very wet trail was little better than a herd path with trail markers, and was so overgrown in places that bushes had to be pushed aside to find it. It soon became too dark to see either markers or any slight path. If I continued, I risked losing the trail and ending up lost. My only safe choice was to stop where I was, stay on the trail, and spend the night.

Cold and wet, with no tent, no flashlight, and only trail mix for food, I lay down across the trail to spend the night, using my daypack for a pillow. Although the rain had stopped, the wind was blowing water off the trees and occasionally spraying it into my face. Later, there were several short showers during the night. Lying down and still, I began to cool off and shiver. I discovered that if I bent my knees and waved them back and forth, I could increase my circulation enough to warm up and fall asleep. But when I fell asleep, I would soon cool off and wake up. All night I cycled between wakefulness and moving my legs, and being asleep and still. I could see stars, so I was hopeful that it was clearing.

When it was light enough to see, I got up and continued toward Duck Hole, where the other campers hadn't stirred. I changed, crawled into my sleeping bag, and pried the back off my watch with my knife. I dried off the crystal, took out the battery to dry, and quickly fell asleep.

I moved later to the empty lean-to, hung a clothesline, wrung out my clothes and hung them up, and enjoyed my first meal since yesterday's trail snacks. It rained intermittently, so I decided to remain at the lean-to. Still tired, I climbed back into my sleeping bag and took a long midday nap, then built a fire to help dry out my boots. Several hours of slow drying took most of the water out of them. I put my watch back together and it now ran, but I had no idea what time it was. (I found out later that my guess was off by only nine minutes.) I held my damp clothes close to the fire, and nearly everything dried.

On Tuesday, unable to locate the herd path to MacNaughton, I headed back to the lean-to and now felt hot spots—the start of blisters. Seymour would have to wait. No matter how prepared I think I am, or how much experience I've gained, I still learn more with every trip into the mountains. I know to expect the unexpected, prepare for most problems, and not take unnecessary chances—but one can never be ready for every eventuality. All one can do is hope that nothing will occur that one can't handle.

Both lean-tos have been relocated, and the trail between Duck Hole and Bradley Pond was greatly improved in 2000–2001; I was glad to be a part of that trail crew. 🚶🚶

Thomas D. Pinkerton: I became involved in scouting after having children, and took my Explorer Scouts to the Adirondacks where I had scouted as a youth. I fell in love with the region all over again. I'm a 46er, #2732W, and was the third to climb all high peaks in all four seasons. To give back to the mountains and to other climbers the great pleasure I've enjoyed, I've volunteered over 800 hours of trail work with the 46ers.

44

STREET WALKING

INTO INDIAN PASS BROOK IN WINTER

Leonard H. Grubbs

When my daughter Wende and I first began climbing in winter, we ventured out on our own. We soon realized, however, that we could learn the trade more quickly and safely by hiking with seasoned winter mountaineers. The Albany chapter of the Adirondack Mountain Club (ADK) had an active group of winter enthusiasts who were climbing every weekend, and I noted that Bob was leading a hike to Street and Nye in mid-February.

That weekend nine participants met at the Adirondak Loj. The preceding week had been unusually mild for February, with periods of rain, even in the High Peaks. Bob expressed concern that Indian Pass Brook, a stream that we had to cross, would be ice-free and running deep because of the rain and mild temperatures. Streams that time of year are usually covered with thick ice that provides a bridge to the other side. So we decided to take the Indian Pass Trail to Rocky Falls and cross the brook there. If we could cross, we would bushwhack west for two miles up a ridge to the summit of Street. The usual route crossed Indian Pass Brook more than a mile north of Rocky Falls to a col between Street and Nye, also a bushwhack.

At Rocky Falls, only a narrow ribbon of ice spanned the water below the falls. The temperature had dropped to more normal February readings, so it would not be healthy to go swimming today! Bob stated that if anyone got wet, we'd return to the Loj. A volunteer removed his pack and gingerly stepped onto the ice to test its strength. He slowly crossed without incident. Then the rest of us crossed, and we set our compasses to work our way up the mountain. We caught glimpses of the MacIntyre Range, its summits capped with billowy, white clouds on this ideal winter day. We found the Street canister at one o'clock, ate and discussed the advisability of going to Nye. We had five hours of daylight left and Nye was only a mile away. We had plenty of people to break trail, and snow conditions were pretty decent. Bob made the decision to go on, and we were at the summit of Nye in less than an hour.

We signed the logbook on Nye and celebrated getting both peaks, something that is not always possible in winter. Now we discussed our exit strategy. We could return the way we came, or we could head off Nye on an easterly heading to Indian Pass Brook; once across, we'd take the Old Nye Ski Trail back to the Indian Pass

Trail and the Adirondak Loj. The second route would be shorter and quicker. The only question was would we find ice spanning the stream at our intended crossing? We decided to take the chance, set our compasses and began our descent. We came to the top of the valley and followed it down, making good time. Then someone raised an alarm—glancing at his compass, he'd noticed that our direction was shifting more to the northeast than east. We took out a map, evaluated the situation, and our dilemma became apparent. A short distance below Nye's summit is a valley that runs generally northeast; farther southeast, at a lower elevation, a second valley—the one we wanted—begins. We had descended toward the wrong valley. We had three options: retrace our path to pick up the correct route; climb south over the high, steep ridge that separated us from our intended route; or continue down this valley to Indian Pass Brook, reaching it more than a mile north of our intended crossing. Not wanting to retrace our descent and not knowing how difficult the climb over the ridge would be left us with option three—we continued our descent down into the valley.

We reached the brook at five o'clock, with daylight waning. All we saw was open water. We began a search up- and downstream for suitable ice for a crossing. To the south the search party found a small sheet of ice spanning the brook. We went immediately to the spot, because we wanted to complete the crossing before dark. Bob took off his pack and began a slow step-by-step crossing, testing the ice. He was about ten feet from the bank, in the middle of the stream, when we heard a loud crack and the ice beneath him gave away. As if in slow motion, he tilted slightly to his left and slid into the water up to his chest. His ice axe slipped from his grip and plunged to the bottom of the stream. Most of us charged onto the ice like lemmings. Bob motioned for us to get back as he struggled onto safe ice and made his way back to shore. It was zero degrees, so time was critical. Bob stripped while others pulled spare clothes from his pack. He replaced everything that was wet except his boots. While Bob was changing, another brave soul ventured onto the ice only feet from where Bob had taken his plunge, and found a safe way across. The final person crossed as the last glow of day faded from the western sky.

With headlamps we followed the stream south, stopping frequently to warm Bob's freezing feet on a willing volunteer's stomach. Other than his wet feet—forced to coexist with his soaked boots—Bob was doing okay. Our progress was slowed by the dark and by significant blowdown. Finally we reached a sharp bend in the stream, a spot that I knew was very close to the summer route. In the dark, however, we couldn't locate the path that would take us to the ski trail and the Loj. Some wanted to stay with the stream and continue bushwhacking south to Rocky Falls, where the Indian Pass Trail closely paralleled the stream and could easily be located. That approach would add three more miles to the trip. Others wanted to plot a heading to the closest point where we could intercept that trail.

I took out my map and compass and did the calculations: an easterly heading would get us there in less than a mile. Bob made the decision; we'd bushwhack east to the trail. Off we went through heavy undergrowth, slowed by frequent blow-down. Surrounded by inky blackness, our world was limited to the tiny area illuminated by our puny headlamps. In the lead, I climbed a small embankment and there was the trail! It was nine o'clock—thirteen hours since our departure. We sat next to the roaring fireplace reliving our adventure and accomplishment. Bob had proven to be an effective leader. He had listened to the opinions of the group, but when it counted, he had decided on the proper course of action. Nine went out, and nine returned. But somewhere on the bottom of Indian Pass Brook rests a perfectly good ice axe. 🐾

Leonard H. Grubbs: I'm an avid outdoor person who hikes year-round, canoes, and skis both Nordic and Alpine. I am trailmaster for the Adirondack Forty-Sixers, running their trail maintenance programs for fourteen years, and was an instructor at the Adirondack Mountain Club's Winter Mountaineering School for seven years. I completed the Winter 46, #2541W, with my daughter, Wende,[1] and winter ascents of the 53 Vermont and New Hampshire peaks exceeding 4,000 feet. I'm a Northeast 111er, completed the 35 Catskill 3,500-footers, and now live in New Hampshire with my wife Betty.

[1] Wende Grubbs Hokirk is featured in *Women with Altitude: Challenging the Adirondack High Peaks in Winter*, compiled by Carol S. White.

45

OCTOGENARIAN ADVENTURES

AGE IS ONLY A NUMBER

Al Laubinger

April 18, 1998, age seventy-six. My daughter Jennifer and son-in-law Mike Stelzer offered to take me up Cascade Mountain. We summitted in three hours. I quote from my hiking journal: "Much steeper and took longer than anticipated; sat in back seat going home with legs stretched out on seat because of cramps; legs so sore the next few days that it hurt to walk *downstairs*; took a week for legs to get better—so much for being in shape." And this was the easiest of the 46! However, incompetence has never deterred me from the enthusiastic pursuit of hopeless goals. Onward and upward! Jennifer accompanied me to Porter on May 30. Only forty-four to go—you can see the optimism building. Little did I dream what I was in for. But eight years later, I climbed Porter in two hours.

Notes from climb of 5,114-foot Algonquin Peak with Jennifer and Mike: "Boots do not fit properly—had to moleskin heel. Will try two pairs of socks next time. Summit in 4 ½ hours." In 2002, I climbed Algonquin in three hours. "My backpack is inadequate—bought new pack after trip." July 13: "Gale winds on summit of Wright with Jennifer. Two pairs of socks did not work and I must buy new boots. Lesson learned: "Never buy mail-order hiking boots." That year I climbed twelve peaks, including Giant and Rocky Peak Ridge solo in October—about 4,300 feet of vertical ascent. My legs were so tired climbing the 800 feet back up Giant that I almost didn't make it. A scary experience—all alone on the mountain and not sure I could make it to the trailhead.

In 1999 I climbed thirteen more high peaks, including an August bushwhack of Seward, Donaldson, and Emmons with Mike and mountaineering friend Brian. It was my first experience with headlamps, descending to Blueberry Pond lean-to at 8:30 PM. We had a tent pitched at the lean-to and planned to climb Seymour the next day, but Mike and I weren't able to climb another mountain. Of note that year was climbing Marshall two days after Hurricane Floyd. The Opalescent River looked like the Hudson River. The usual two hours to Flowed Lands took three hours, and some in this ADK group led by Jay McCullough were reluctant to continue. A vote was taken and we continued—I was one of the idiots who voted to press on. Herd paths on the lower two-thirds of the peak were running brooks, with fifty- and sixty-foot blowdowns to climb over and around. It was a horrendously difficult hike until we reached the upper part of the mountain. We descended through Indian Pass by Wallface Mountain. I was slowing down the group, so Jay sent the rest ahead. At 8:30 we were using headlamps and fighting blowdown when we reached Henderson lean-to, where we decided to hole up for the night rather than fight these conditions in the dark. It was impossible to communicate with my family, who went into panic mode and came close to calling out the National Guard. As we hiked into the parking area at 9:00 AM, a DEC ranger asked if I was Al Laubinger. He probably recognized me from my white hair and haggard look.

In 2000, because of family trips, working for the census, and taking a course in cultural anthropology at Adirondack Community College, I climbed only four more peaks—Seymour and a day trip up Sawteeth, Gothics, and Armstrong, after which I was so tired that I had to lift my legs into the car. Not in very good shape. After Seymour my journal notes: "decided to abort quest for 46 peaks. Resolved to pursue as many as possible and not worry about getting all 46."

In 2001 I climbed only Haystack. I ran for political office as town supervisor in the Town of Moreau, which blew the entire summer and fall. The only consolation was that, running as a Democrat and outnumbered two and a half to one by registered Republicans, I nevertheless received 45 percent of the vote. I was seventy-nine and didn't want the job in the first place—another example of my deranged state of mind. I worked out strenuously during the winter to get back in shape.

The year 2002 was a banner year. I climbed fifty-two mountains and nine high peaks—one for the second time. That year our current hiking group came together. Tim Kupetz, Frank Pusateri, and Jim McCauley were determined that I finish the 46. They hiked with me throughout the year and were a driving force in keeping me on track. Later we added Gail Epstein and the legendary Gretchen Stark, and we continue to hike as a group. I tried a solo hike of Marcy, but was turned back at Marcy Brook because of torrential rains the night before. Marcy Brook was a roaring river; I was alone and wasn't about to take a chance of being washed over Indian Falls, never to be heard from again. The worst trip of the year was a washout on the Santanoni Range in June. It rained from parking lot to parking lot. We summitted Panther in horizontal rain and sleet and opted to forego Couchsachraga. Soaked to the skin, boots, backpack, everything. In case you are keeping score, I was now up to thirty-eight mountains, my peak year in physical conditioning.

At my annual physical in early 2003, I told my doctor, "I cannot claim to have reversed the aging process, but I sure as hell have brought it to a screeching halt." That year was dismal, however, starting with another aborted trip to the Santanoni Range in mid-May where we post-holed up to our hips in ice and snow just beyond

Al Laubinger at 4,120-foot Seymour Mountain canister, July 8, 2000. Photo by Jim McCauley.

Panther Brook. On Fathers' Day we did MacNaughton from the Duck Hole trail, and MacNaughton was a bear. Fighting through heavy brush, no trails, blowdown all over—for those with masochistic inclinations, I recommend MacNaughton from the Duck Hole trail and firmly believe that those who complete this mountain should have an Oak Leaf cluster or a Purple Heart added to their 46er certificate. On the way I had a bad fall and banged up my right hip and knee. The pain wore off enough to complete the climb, but I hiked only a few more times and had a knee operation in October to repair the medial meniscus on my right knee. My orthopedic surgeon was a 46er. He showed me the surgical pictures and told me that only 10 percent of the problem was the fall. The other 90 percent was eighty-one years of wear and tear, and probably my other knee was in the same condition. I should back off the high peaks and do only smaller mountains—advice he knew was going to be ignored.

I worked hard and came out of the winter of 2003–2004 in great shape. Only eight remaining peaks, but of course I saved the worst for last. I reckoned the eight must be completed that year. How much longer would my knees hold up? First, I climbed Marcy with Jim, Frank, Gretchen, and Darrin Youker, a reporter for the *Post Star* newspaper. Darrin was doing an article on people completing the 46, and he picked me because of my age and the likelihood of being the old-est to complete all the peaks. It was a beautiful day for eight hours of climbing plus summit time. Next came Allen, a twelve-and-a-half-hour day. A journal note says, "They don't call it the Big Nasty without reason." Then on to the San-tanoni Range for the third time. On the trail at 5:00 AM, Times Square at 9:30. We waited for thirty minutes for Jim and Frank to do Panther, and then got lost for another half hour taking the wrong path out of a swamp on the way to Couch. This mountain is not a trip you are eager to rush back to. I left my pack at Times Square for the two-hour round-trip to Santanoni. Back at the car at 9:30 PM; this was the longest and toughest day so far.

On July 26, with Frank and Jim, our climb of Cliff started out with the lon-gest and deepest stretch of mud yet encountered. Then came the blowdown from Hurricane Floyd. Finally, the steep pitches, straight up, hand over hand to the first summit. My workout routine had thankfully provided the upper body strength necessary for this trip. I left my pack and carried only water to the final summit; we were back at Uphill lean-to at 3:00 PM. If we had attempted Redfield, we would have spent hours coming out by headlamp. On August 2 we went back, and Red-field was an enjoyable climb. Now, I was up to forty-four!

Five days later all five hiking companions—Tim, Frank, Jim, Gretchen, and Gail, whom I met for the first time—accompanied me on Esther and Whiteface. It was overcast, intermittent rain, no views, but nothing short of a hurricane would have deterred us. Esther is one of the easiest trailless peaks—one and three-quarter hours round-trip from the Whiteface trail. At eighty-two, I summitted Whiteface at 12:42 PM, August 7, 2004—in just five hours and twenty-two minutes, including Esther. As I came over the stone wall at the summit, I was met by Monty Calvert, the photographer for the *Post Star*. We went to the restaurant for a stupendous feast prepared by Mike, who harbors a desire to become a great chef—and he outdid himself. Jennifer, Mike, my wife Diane, another daughter, Judy Green, Frank's wife Rosemary, and friends Carol and Jim Smith drove up Whiteface for the celebration.

Even our dog Byron was there. The final report to my 46er correspondent, Carol Reese, was simply, "The dastardly deed is done."

My only claim to fame is my age. I am the oldest person to complete the 46—#5404—having started the quest at age seventy-six. My hope is that my accomplishment will inspire others to pursue similar feats and realize that age doesn't have to keep you out of the game. Extensive research has proven that exercise and physical fitness is the fountain of youth. New studies suggest healthy older adults can reverse skeletal aging and generate muscle tissue that is genetically similar to much younger muscle. The more extreme the exercise—within limits—the greater the benefit. The only requirement is motivation. It is never too late to start. The rest is lifestyle, which is under your complete control. Only 25 to 30 percent of what you accomplish in life can be credited to genetics. My greatest wish is that someone will break my record. 🏃

Al Laubinger: At age 74, I walked up two flights of stairs and my leg muscles ached; I was out of breath. I started a six-day-a-week regimen of weight training and aerobics, and in six months my physical conditioning dramatically improved. I felt like my old self, an avid outdoorsman who enjoyed tennis, badminton, fly-fishing for trout, skiing, gardening, and now, hiking.

46

THE DAY I ALMOST DIED

HYPOTHERMIA—SOLO

Dean Gletsos

On October 19, 1991, I decided to hike alone. October can be very cold, with snow and ice on the High Peaks. It was just such a day—cloudy, cold, and windy—as I started up the Algonquin Trail. I joined an Australian fellow and his girlfriend, and together we climbed Algonquin to Iroquois and retraced to climb Wright, my twentieth mountain. My fellow hikers continued down—high winds had picked up; sleet and fine hail was falling. The steep, rocky trail to the summit of Wright Peak was icy and slippery. The trail reaches bare rock, marked with cairns. After steep scrambling, I reached the foggy summit exhausted and wet. I had a strong headache, was nauseated and started shivering. The wind was very strong above the tree line, and the sleet and hail continued. I was feeling dizzy, disoriented, and just horrible.

I'd heard and read about hypothermia and knew that these were its symptoms. I never thought that I would become one of its victims! Thanks to what I had learned about hypothermia, I am alive today. I wanted to descend, but

Plaque at site of plane crash, Wright Peak. Photo by David White.

could not move my extremities. I could not drink or eat. I started convulsing, so I curled in a rock crevice to protect myself from the wintry elements, trying to preserve any strength I had left and stop convulsing. Most of all I wanted to keep myself alert and prevent myself from going to sleep or into a coma. That would have been the end of me. I was only yards away from the wreckage of the B-47 bomber that went down in 1962—a grim vision. The plane had been returning to Plattsburg Air Force Base from a training mission. All aboard perished, and a bronze plaque near the summit commemorates the tragedy. Pieces of the plane are scattered over the area.

After an hour I stopped convulsing. I was still shivering, but had a little strength now. Very slowly I walked down the steep trail to the junction and down the rocky Algonquin Trail as it was getting dark. This life-threatening experience taught me a lot. First, read articles about the hiking experiences of others to learn how they handled difficult situations and, most of all, how to be prepared. Second, never give up. Evaluate the situation calmly and logically, and don't panic. Fight with all available resources to get out of the predicament. I've climbed Wright Peak three more times since, and the views are terrific from its rocky summit—it is one of the best Adirondack peaks to climb! 🏃

Dean Gletsos: Born in Greece, I began hiking seriously in 1989 when I was transferred to Plattsburgh and joined the Algonquin Chapter of the Adirondack Mountain Club at the tender age of fifty-five. Learning of a 46ers club and being goal-oriented, I got the bug—I hiked them in all seasons, #3082W. I also got the downhill and cross-country skiing bug and became an expert. I've been a hike leader since 1990. After joining ADK's Ramapo Chapter I discovered the Catskills, climbed those peaks in all seasons, and the 115 4,000-foot peaks in the Northeast. With our four children we traveled by camper from Florida to Newfoundland, from Maine to Vancouver Island.

47

A BAD DAY IN THE MOUNTAINS
BEATS A GOOD DAY ANYWHERE ELSE

HUMBLED BY NATURE'S RAW POWER

Tom Rankin

This seemed like an easy hike—six miles gets you two peaks, Cascade and Porter. Piece of cake? I'd been planning this hike and when the day came, it was a driving rain with the temperature in the forties; no one else was willing or able to go. Although the trail was well packed, I wore snowshoes to keep from post-holing in the soft snow. The wind would whip up into a loud, roaring gale that raced through the trees. Half a tree cracked off and fell to the ground one hundred feet from the trail.

I decided to do Cascade first. I was damp, but not too cold. When I got to the open top of the mountain, the wind was raging across the summit from right to left. I dropped my pack and started up the rocky slope. The wind was incred-

Summit of Cascade Mountain. Photo by David White.

ibly strong. Water was flowing *up* the slope! For that matter, *I* was being carried up the slope! I was knocked down twice before I got to the summit, sometimes crouching, sometimes crawling, sometimes flitting from boulder to boulder during calmer periods. At the very top the wind was so strong that I had to lie down and hang on to the rocks to avoid being blown off. I realized with some alarm that my snowshoes had turned into sails! I was being pummeled by blasts of wind, and rain stung my face. I didn't dare move for fear of being tossed around on the rocks, but I knew I had to get off the summit as soon as possible. When the wind abated slightly, I made my way down to the trees, humbled by the raw power of nature on lowly Cascade.

I braced myself for the summit of Porter, but only the last few feet of the summit area are exposed and I laughed aloud at how easy it was in comparison. I saw Cascade across the way and could almost feel the beating it had given me. Heading down, I came upon a very large tree that had just fallen across the trail near the giant boulder. It had missed me by only a few minutes! Soaked from head to toe, it was great to change into warm dry clothes, and even better to enjoy a 46er IPA at Lake Placid Brewery. Yup, I'm a peak bagger, the only idiot climbing those peaks that day. But in a strange sort of way, it was a good day. 🐾

Tom Rankin: I completed the 46 in August 2004 and the Winter 46 in 2007, #5444W, and have also climbed the hundred highest peaks in the Catskills and the 115 4,000-foot peaks in the Northeast. I enjoy many sports and am an amateur astronomer, active in the Mid-Hudson Astronomical Association. On June 23, 2007, I married Laurie Moore on the summit of Whiteface Mountain.

48

THE AGONY AND THE ECSTASY

NO SECRETS NEAR GOTHICS

Tom Rankin

Having completed the Wolf Jaws and Armstrong yesterday, Harry needed Sawteeth, I needed Gothics, and Nancy needed both. After a late-night celebration with a wide variety of "propellants," the three of us headed again to the Great Range. I was *sooo* tired from a cold and the late night that I almost bagged the hike. Hiking up to the saddle between Sawteeth and Gothics was torture! I was feeling very weak and my heart was racing; I had to keep taking short breaks. Why are we doing this again today? I was keeping track of my progress, noting that I was climbing one hundred vertical feet every five minutes—slow for me—but if I could keep up this pace, I would eventually get to Gothics and be back down before dark. This gave me hope.

View from Pyramid Peak. Photo by Neil Luckhurst.

Getting to the saddle earlier than I thought we would encouraged me, but the trail to Gothics was not broken. My heart sank. I almost gave up again. Harry and Nancy decided to summit Sawteeth, which was broken; I'd start up Gothics, 1,200 feet more of ascent. They would follow my trail and, if I turned around, they would too. Now the hike hung on my shoulders! Great. Just what I needed.

The first one hundred yards of the trail were the toughest mentally. With six to ten inches of powder to break, it wasn't too bad, but progress was slow over many steep, icy sections. Hiking alone, I was extremely cautious. I was very tired and stopped frequently. I was about to turn around several times, but willed myself to continue. I didn't want to let the others down. Eventually I could see Pyramid ahead and was getting a second wind! As I got there, however, clouds rolled in—a bummer—but I kept going. I was feeling better and better. I drew "I CAN" in the snow beyond the summit, and descended the steep slope to the saddle between Pyramid and Gothics. There was no turning back.

Clouds raced by, below me now, and higher summits were revealed in their snow-capped splendor—Marcy, Skylight, Haystack, Whiteface, and other peaks in all directions. The wind was almost calm on Gothics. Three thousand feet below, I could see the boathouse at the edge of Lower Ausable Lake. The feeling of accomplishment was great—a moment of exultation. I drew "C U @ JCT" in the snow and continued down to the saddle between Armstrong and Gothics, where I ate lunch, rested, and changed clothes. All of a sudden I heard Harry and Nancy talking! Had they caught up with me? I yelled out and they yelled back, but we could not understand each other. They were in the Pyramid-Gothics saddle, a long way away. How could voices speaking in a normal tone carry for such a distance? Perhaps the great vertical wall of Gothics' east face, spread out between us, caused this phenomenon. Whatever the cause, one thing is clear: don't tell any secrets in the High Peaks! 🥾

For biography of Tom Rankin, see "A Bad Day in the Mountains Beats a Good Day Anywhere Else."

49

HAVING AN ICE DAY

INTO UPHILL BROOK

J. Michael Forsyth

I put this climb of Cliff and Redfield on the Rochester Winter Mountaineering Society schedule; I would climb my 46th winter peak on this February 2001 trip. The party consisted of Frank Cabron, Sabina Hodgson, Peter Howard, Paul Sheneman, and me. On the trail by 7:30 AM, we established camp at Uphill lean-to and reached the Cliff canister at 3:30. We were enjoying Frank's hearty cooking back at camp when we heard an explosion from the lean-to followed by the sound of ricocheting cookware. Peter and Paul had tried a recipe calling for a butane lighter, braised or broiled.

The temperature was zero when I arose to face my 46th winter peak. We enjoyed a leisurely breakfast and were on the trail by 8:20. Uphill Brook was well frozen, so we followed it to avoid blowdown. The stream narrowed at a chute a few feet high whose sides were close enough to allow one to chimney up, so I tried it to avoid a detour up and out of the streambed. There were two layers of thin ice over the pool at the bottom of the chute, with air space below each, and water below that. I discovered this by going through the ice and into water above my knees— I did not find bottom. The stream level had dropped during a hard freeze before creation of a thick layer of ice, leaving two thin ones, so the ice around the hole was not strong enough to support me. My snowshoes had toggled under the ice, so I could not easily lift out either foot.

This small pool may have been ten feet deep for all I knew, and I realized that I was in serious danger of going under the ice and drowning or getting soaked from head to foot in icy water on a near-zero day. One of the party took out a camera to shoot pictures. I figured that if I went under, he'd alert the rest of the party, who might try to extricate me. I needed to get out. I slipped off my pack and threw it as far as I could reach, holding onto the straps. This spread my weight over a greater area and gave me purchase on ice away from the crumbling edges. I wiggled my feet to get my snowshoes lined up with the opening, shifted my weight to my arms and the pack, and propelled myself up and out. Someone said I looked like a walrus coming up out of a hole onto the ice.

I considered Frank's suggestion that we go back; then I put on Gore-tex boot liners and heavy liner socks, and then put the wrung-out woolen socks over that and was back in my boots before they could freeze. To summit might be worth a toenail or two (I would lose two), but not a toe—at the first sign of numbness, I'd attend to my feet and turn around. My toes did get painfully cold, but that was reassuring. With mental discipline I treated the pain as useful information that I still had circulation, and it soon lost its character as pain.

We followed the stream, then the tributary, and took a rough compass heading for the summit ridge. Occasional ankle-high surveyor's tape gave us assurance that we were climbing in the right direction, but with five feet of snow there was no discernible herd path. I like to see flagging when I'm trying to find or follow a herd path. Cataclysmic storms and blowdown are on the increase, making it more important to find a known usable route. We followed the summit ridge south. I was behind, looking for the canister on a knob, when I saw it behind Frank's knees! I signed us in, noting acknowledgment to Maria Hosmer-Briggs, 46er #3872, a frequent climbing companion who shared her years of Nordic ski patrol and winter backcountry experience with me. I put a "W" after my climbing number for the first time. We didn't tarry, with winds gusting above 30 MPH at near zero degrees. 🚶🚶

J. Michael Forsyth: I'm a Staten Island native and an Upstater by choice. I completed the 46 on Fathers' Day 1996 with my two teenage daughters, and the Winter 46, #3873W, five years later with fellow climbers of the Adirondack Mountain Club Onondaga Chapter and the Rochester Winter Mountaineering Society. A friend said, "Sunday, we'll worship in the Church of the Pines." That sums it up—in the forests and on the mountains I find spiritual regeneration. One beautifully clear day on Gothics, I thought, This is the view from God's front porch.

50

PURSUING THE 46: THE DARWIN AWARD METHOD

TALES FROM THE CLUELESS HIKER GENE POOL

Steve Boheim

Earned Discount. In June 1968 we decided to bag as many peaks as we could. State Range Trail seemed to go over a lot of peaks, so let's do that—Lower Wolf Jaw to Haystack! Off we went from John's Brook Lodge at dawn, equipped with jelly sandwiches and Twinkies with milk in a glass thermos, wearing insulated high-top work boots (at least they didn't have steel toes), cotton chinos, cotton shirt, Kodak box camera (with the blue flash cubes!), a nylon windbreaker, a canteen of water, a DEC flyer mentioning the State Range Trail, a dim idea that the color of the trail marker indicated the trail's general direction, and a fifteen-minute USGS topographic map (but no idea what all those closely-spaced lines would really feel like).

The list of what we didn't have easily surpassed what we did have—no matches, flashlight, first-aid kit or emergency gear, hiking boots, or backpack. Youth combined with climbing on one of the longest days of the year would ultimately mean we didn't hurt ourselves, and we would have time … barely. We found we couldn't tarry—bug spray only partially worked against black flies when we were standing still. The only defense was to keep moving. Ascending Gothics, we thought this trail wasn't too bad, and if we'd only spotted a second car we could've gotten Marcy and Skylight and Colden on the way out to Heart Lake! This notion would change dramatically when we experienced all those topo lines from Gothics to Haystack.

At 4:30 PM we were dragging at Sno-Bird lean-to. Backpackers asked us where we were going. "You haven't time," they said. "Stay with us. We have a fire and room in the lean-to." "No, no," we said cluelessly, and continued on. We hit the proverbial energy wall going up Little Haystack, but persevered. On Haystack, viewing the snowy east slope of Marcy across Panther Gorge, we finally decided that we couldn't do Marcy. Heading back, we encountered a flooded trail and guessed directions based on trail colors and that DEC flyer. Fourteen hours after we started, as we sat on the hood of the car to untie boots, our legs were charley-horsing so badly that they wouldn't stay still. At a motel, a room was $10. "What did you do today?" "Range Trail from the Garden." "Which peaks?" "All but Marcy." "You're kidding—uh, make that $9." For years we were quite full of ourselves for having done the Great Range in a day, then we read about what Herb Clark and the Marshalls did in the 1920s on the Range in one day, *trailless*, and we were suitably humbled.

Polio Hike. In October 1983 our *bad* hike leader—me—was too focused on getting the view. I had set up a combination beginners' hike to Fish Hawk Cliffs and an intermediate hike to Nippletop—I'd had no view there before. We hoped that lots of people would come and we'd split up, but it was at the end of Tropical Storm Dean, drizzling, and many folks cancelled. We met at 1:00 AM to drive up.

At the Gill Brook Trail junction, two in the group thought we should go on and see how the weather developed. Anne (victim) wanted to do just Fish Hawk Cliffs, so I hypnotized her into thinking that Nippletop's view would be worth it. In Elk Pass, Anne stepped on a hollow log and was stung by bees. She gamely struggled up the trail, and at the ridge announced she could go no farther. I tried "only fifty more feet," but she knew that ruse. I offered to carry her pack. No joy. So I offered to carry *her*, swearing that it really was only fifty more feet; she reluctantly agreed, and for once it was true. We arrived on a viewless Nippletop; then, abruptly the clouds opened up briefly on one side then another, and we scrambled to catch quick views. Then, with a whoosh, all the clouds cleared off and we got the magnificent view. Anne was only extremely annoyed with me, and things started to look up.

"Okay," I said, "let's go back over Dial, and Anne—you'll get another peak!" Anne asked, "Is there any more *up*?" "No … well a bit of bump over Dial and Bear Den, but nothing major." This elicited a reluctant "okay"—Anne cursing and limping, but persistent. All was well until we got to what I'd forgotten—the 320 feet up over a shoulder of Noonmark. Anne stopped, in pain. We would carry her pack, take her out and feed her frozen strawberry daiquiris. She was moving *very* slowly, and it was well past dark when we got out. In Lake Placid a convention was in town. It was also Columbus Day weekend and Canadian Thanksgiving, plus the height of fall tourists, so instead of frozen strawberry daiquiris and surf and turf, Anne got McDonald's. Oh yes, and nowhere to stay.

As we're driving down Route 9, a man is lying in the road. Anne is an intensive-care nurse, and she leaps out of the car (she can barely walk) to help. We flag someone down and they determine that it's "old drunk Bill"—he walks to the local bar and later staggers home. It took Anne a week to walk normally, hence the name, Polio Hike. She still hikes with me, but never lets me forget this trip.

Lost. How many people have you lost on the trail … none, eh? I lost a party of nineteen. The sordid tale:

We arrive in too many cars at the Garden and park all but mine. Everyone else is ready, so I give them directions for Big Slide via the Brothers: "turn right just beyond the trailhead." I follow twenty minutes later after squeezing the car into a non-space.

Summit, 4,620-foot Nippletop. Photo by Steve Boheim.

As I ascend the Brothers trail, I see no footprints in the snow, but muddy spots, so maybe they sloshed through. In twenty minutes I meet two hikers who haven't seen anyone. I run up another ten minutes, then give up and return to the Johns Brook Trail, eventually finding a furious member of the group who is wondering where I am. They are three miles up the Johns Brook Trail having a grand time and only sometimes wondering where the junction is. Ranger Spence advises the group to be cautious because of iffy weather, spitting snow. He's dubious since the group has lost its "leader" and is not looking for him. Some eventually do climb Big Slide.

The Fist of Ghod. We climbed the MacIntyres on a windy, unsettled day. On Algonquin, the wind was so strong you couldn't rock hop, but rather rock crawl. The wind would suddenly stop, the bugs would come out, and you'd hop/ walk normally, and then the bugs would dive to the ground and the wind would abruptly start again with a roar and throw you around. To take pictures with a box camera, I had to sit, and my two hiking buddies had to sit on each side sta- bilizing my arms—the wind was that strong and buffeting. We went on to Iro- quois and back over Algonquin. On Wright, somebody said that the pounding wind wasn't *that* bad, which apparently angered the mountain ghods—in our pantheon, that would be "Queen Mother" Marcy and her son "Topo"—for we see the top of Algonquin disappear as black-gray clouds crowned with lightning come in fast. We made a mad dash down, reaching tree line even as trees off-trail were puffing up like a cat's tail and taking major lightning strikes; the thunder was unbelievably loud. After ten minutes things settled down to a hard driving rain. We didn't care—alive and wet was just fine. We've never again said the weather's "not too bad."

You Decide. On October 1, 1972, our *Guide to Adirondack Trails* included this comment on Panther: "An alternative route is to climb Santanoni first and then to traverse the ridge to Panther, but this is a longer and more difficult trip than a look at the map would suggest."

What this really meant, for us, was: "After enjoying the gorgeous height-of-autumn view on Santanoni, you will have to crawl for extended distances under (surprise) snow-covered blowdown that you thought was just dead blowdown to descend and traverse said ridge, and the easy, easterly exit off the ridge towards Bradley Pond that you thought you saw en route to Panther you won't find again, so instead you must re-crawl the heinous ridge back up Santanoni, then not find any trace of the old Tahawus Club trail that you had extreme difficulty ascending in the first place, except for an old, rotten, fixed rope on a cliff with a single paint blaze, none of which you saw on the way up, so follow it anyway, even though it isn't the way you came up, and slip/slide down the treacherous, mossy, slippery, log-clogged Easterly Brook and then, once you are completely soaked and banged up from falling a million times, triumphantly find the Bradley Pond trail, but it's now dark and you won't have brought a flashlight or matches, so you will then miss a key trail turn and instead spend the night sitting on a log and freezing with your friends, since you will have lost your jacket in the blowdown you encountered during the descent."

Fast-forward, September 2006: I'm alone, it's raining and foggy, and nobody in their right mind should be trying to do the Santanonis—but the register says a group is doing just that. I encounter the bedraggled group on the Bradley Pond trail. They had done Panther and then turned back, since there was nothing up there but rain and fog and mud. I thought they were crazy for even trying the three peaks, but then they asked what I was up to. "Oh, I'm just looking for a log I spent the night on over thirty years ago. I want to take its picture." (And I found the right area, too!). The look on their faces was priceless. You, dear reader, get to decide who was crazier. 🏃

*S*teve Boheim: *This New England Hundred Highest, 46er #1481, and Catskill 3500 Club member is also a chagrined charter member of the FAS, Flaming A**hole Society, founded after surviving three hikes by sheer luck in spite of blatantly stupid decisions—like using trash-bag-as-poncho in heavy blowdown during freezing rain. He offers feeble apologies to Bob, Charlie, Joe, Bill, Ross, John, Anne, and Hans, scarred veterans of way too much "carwash" (wet blowdown) and cripplebush "cedar" inoculations. He lives disguised more or less as a normal person with his wife and daughter in Boxboro, Massachusetts.*

51

ICY SLIDE OFF BIG SLIDE

SOLO DANGER

Kristin Konchar-Schafer

On January 5, 2005, I headed to the Adirondacks for a solo hike to the summit of Big Slide Mountain via The Brothers. The hike up was treacherous with snow-covered ice on rock faces, so I decided to follow a different trail down and went over Yard Mountain, thinking it might be less dangerous. It turned out to be a bad choice. Partway down I encountered trail that had a steep cliff to the left and a steep drop-off to the right, and the only way was down the snow-over-ice-over-rock-covered trail. A rock dropped about four feet down to another rock. A waterfall had turned to ice on these rocks, and it was extremely treacherous to descend, but I had no other choice—I was too far down the mountain to turn back. I sat on my butt on the icy rock and tried to do a controlled drop down to the next level. As I slid off the rock, I completely lost control and ended up plummeting face down onto the icy rock below! I didn't even have a chance to put out my arms or hands to protect my face—I felt my face actually bounce off the ground! And then I felt myself sliding, but luckily my body stopped before sliding off the next drop-off.

As my slide stopped I ended up facedown, suspended on some branches that were over a small, icy stream. I was looking down into the stream and saw my car keys, which had been in the inside chest pocket of my parka, drop down onto the ice over the stream. They just missed falling into a crack between the ice and rock, where I would have been unable to reach them! After a moment of lying there in stunned disbelief, I was able to retrieve my keys and gingerly sit up. I assessed my condition—my nose was bleeding, but not too badly. Probably it helped that my nose was partially numb from the coldness of the day. Nothing else felt broken, sprained, or badly damaged. Shaken, I continued on the trail as darkness started to fall. I still had at least five miles left to the Garden parking lot. Having no choice but to continue, I plodded along, eventually needing to turn on my headlamp.

I remember relaying my experience to family and friends and their horrified reactions. It was an extremely humbling experience, and one that made me realize that anything can happen on the trail. If you are alone when it happens, you are in serious trouble! I remember saying, "That mountain kicked my butt." I now have more respect for the dangers of the trail, especially in winter, and approach hikes with more caution, more people, and more gear. A rope and full crampons probably could have prevented my face plant, but I only had my snowshoes and instep crampons with me. I'm just glad I got out of the experience alive and, except for scratches and bruises, relatively unscathed. My ego and self-confidence got bruised more than anything else! 🏃🏃

Kristin Konchar-Schafer: I joined a hike with Binghamton's Triple Cities Hiking Club and soon became hooked on hiking in the Catskill and Adirondack mountains and on the Finger Lakes Trail. The Catskill 3500 Club helped me summit some trailless Catskill high peaks, and I finished my Catskill 35 in 2005. I enjoy camping, kayaking, swimming, bicycling, and cross-country skiing. Playing in The Great Outdoors keeps me happy and healthy.

52

FAMILIES RULE, BUT STUPIDITY REIGNS

NOT YOUR TYPICAL BACKPACKING TRIP

Shannon (Willies) Holt

"**Y**ou're pregnant," Dr. Sawyers states with little emotion. I remain neutral, staring at the floor and shuffling my feet. She is trying to gauge my reaction. "Is this a good thing?" she asks, trying to figure out how to proceed. "Yes, yes, this is wonderful news," I respond, a little overdramatically, trying to make up for my hesitation. All I'm thinking is, *I haven't finished my 46 peaks yet!* I had four left to climb and only nine months to complete them—it was crunch time. I called up my best hiking companions to share the great news, but also to beg for their assistance in completing my 46 peaks. My mom, Glo, and my cousin, Andrea—46ers themselves—readily agreed to help. Hiking together since 1990, we are a high-functioning unit and get along famously. Being family is a bonus! One thing to know is that the women in my family are self-sufficient, competent, and proud—or as my husband calls it, stubborn. You'll see what I mean …

Both Glo and Andrea stated, "I will never climb Allen Mountain *again*!" But on the afternoon of August 1, 2005, we all met in Upper Works to start the two-day backpack. We'd hike in, spend the night, climb Allen and hike out that day. We had done these types of trips numerous times. Doing last minute packing of our backpacks, we divided up the meals, the stove, and the pots to make sure nobody's load was too heavy. Being concerned about the weight of her backpack, Glo decided not to pack the extra supper we usually carry "just in case." Seems like an insignificant detail, except we would soon learn that this was not going to be a typical backpacking trip.

Walking along, catching up with each other, and snacking on abundant raspberries, we heard a crack of thunder and picked up our pace to set up camp before rain started, but a downpour began. We fished out the tarp and set up a makeshift shelter for an hour to keep our bags and ourselves as dry as possible. Like clockwork, camp was set up, dinner cooked, and all food put in the bear barrel. Andrea and I unpacked our sleeping bags and inflated our Therm-a-rests. Glo was ready for bed, lying on a tiny piece of insulated foam with a thin, very small fleece blanket that was strategically covering three-fourths of her body. It was a blue blanket with white fuzzy sheep on it, meant for a child.

"Where is your sleeping bag!" exclaimed Andrea.

"I thought it would be too heavy to carry, so I brought a blanket instead," replied Glo. "I'll be fine," she assured us.

We were speechless. We could not believe that she did not pack a sleeping bag. There was no way she would be warm enough with a "fuzzy sheep" blanket. I awoke in the night to hear *CRINKLE CRINKLE CRINKLE.* I couldn't see much, but the sound was coming from *inside* the tent. *CRINKLE CRINKLE CRINKLE.* A headlamp came on—Glo had retrieved the small silver emergency blanket and was unfolding it carefully to ensure that she did not rip it. Andrea was awake, too.

"I'll be fine," Glo reassured us as she noisily wrapped the blanket around her. Every time Glo moved, or breathed, all that could be heard was *CRINKLE CRIN-KLE CRINKLE.* None of us got a very good sleep that night, but we had a laugh about it in the morning (mostly at Glo's expense).

I wasn't laughing when I put on my hiking boots, however—those hotspots on my feet from yesterday had turned into blisters! I had bought a new pair of hiking boots last month, and my feet were paying the price. Amazing how your feet swell and change shape when you are six months pregnant. I did not say a word. I dressed my heels with moleskin and painfully slipped my feet into my boots. I was determined to climb Allen Mountain, blisters and all.

It was typical Adirondack conditions, wet and muddy with water continuously flowing over the rocks. It made for tricky ascents, but overall it was an uneventful climb. When we summited, I was in great pain, my feet throbbing. I finally admitted to Glo and Andrea that I had blisters. I patched up my feet again, but knew it was going to be a tough walk out. They offered me painkillers, but I didn't want to take anything that might harm the baby. I hobbled down the mountain, really holding the others up, but I just could not go any faster. Back at our campsite, Andrea wanted to get back as planned. We were already several hours past our projected return time, but I knew that I could not do it. The only thing I wanted to do was take off my boots. We agreed that we would stay the extra night. Andrea told me to soak my feet in cold water, and it felt heavenly on my abused feet. I had a blister on top of a blister, and then a blister on top of that—I have never experienced anything like it.

It was dinnertime, but the extra meal was in the car. We needed to divide up enough food for dinner and breakfast. We had half a bag of gorp, one Power Bar, a small bag of jujubes, three Swedish berries, two granola bars, and one baby carrot. Andrea and I split the Power Bar, and Glo had a granola bar. We ate our meager meal slowly and quietly.

Again we had a good laugh as we were getting ready for bed. Glo had put on every piece of clothing she'd brought, and then covered herself with the "fuzzy sheep" blanket and the noisy silver blanket. *CRINKLE CRINKLE CRINKLE.* I had a fitful sleep complete with fever and shivers. My feet were searing with pain. The constant throbbing was becoming unbearable, and I was dreading having to put my feet back into my boots.

We decided to skip a breakfast of jujubes and gorp, and break camp instead. I could barely walk; every step I took was excruciating, and I was not even wearing my hiking boots. I decided to perform minor surgery. A massive fluid-filled bubble had tightly formed overnight over the top of all the blisters. This was causing the extreme pain, and I had to pop it if I was going to walk out. I got a safety pin and matches from the first-aid kit, heated the safety pin until it was red hot and touched it to the pulsing bubble. The bubble exploded, sending fluid and puss flying all over the ground. It was instant relief! I did the same thing to the other foot, dressed my feet in the remaining moleskin and second skin, and slid my feet into my boots. There was a little pressure, but I could walk. At the parking lot I exclaimed, "I am *never* climbing Allen again!" Andrea and Glo rolled their eyes. "Where have we heard *that* before?" 👣

Shannon (Willies) Holt: I learned to love the outdoors when canoeing, windsurfing, and sailing at camp. I cross-country skied from our back door. As a camp counselor I led overnight trips and joined my high school's Outer's Club, climbing my first Adirondack peak in 1991. I climbed my 46th peak while eight months pregnant! I'm a member of GORP, Gals on Rugged Peaks, five friends who have been climbing in the Adirondacks for years. I live in Ottawa, Canada, with my husband, Trevor, daughter Darcy, and a menagerie of pets.

53

THE CURSE OF THE DIXES

THE MOUNTAINS WILL DECIDE

Tom Wheeler

Near the end of my second winter of hiking, I began to envision becoming a Winter 46er. During the first winter, my attitude had been to extend the season and do some hiking in winter on mountains with trails or short trailless sections, and this limited experience taught me much about the difficulties I would face. I turned back on the summit of Pyramid without doing Gothics, because I had become chilled to the bone by wet snow. I separated my shoulder while returning from an ascent of Colvin and Blake. I seemed an unlikely candidate to complete all of the peaks in winter.

The second winter had gone reasonably well. We ascended Marshall in a daylong assault, despite losing the way. Street and Nye finally succumbed to our persistence despite our following a meandering route in the lower reaches. Amid this success the mountains still sent cautionary signals. The last trip of the winter was a marathon ascent of Haystack, Basin, and Saddleback. I hit an energy low on the ascent of Basin from Haystack; toward Saddleback, my crampons sheered off the icy trail and I whooshed down the steep path, coming to a stop some seventy-five feet down, unscathed. I had climbed sixteen new peaks for a total of twenty-one. Ignoring the difficulties I'd encountered, I began seriously to contemplate becoming a Winter 46er. I thought that the main difficulties would be the Sewards and the Santanonis, and gave little thought to the Dix Range. I calculated that it would take me two trips to complete the five peaks in the Dix Range. I now know that the mountains were listening. They thought me too arrogant and decided to teach me a lesson.

January 28, 1996, was a cold, crisp day. Dick Mooers and I decided that we would go in and knock off the southern Dixes—Macomb, and South and East Dix. Dave and Carol White, who had hiked with us a number of times, joined us. The trip in was pleasant as we headed up the herd path near Slide Brook toward Macomb. The Whites had scouted the brook route before and decided to climb through the woods instead of up the slide. Dick and I came equipped with crampons and ice axes, ready to climb the slide, so we split up.

The slide was covered with rock-hard ice and coated with a half-inch of fluffy snow. The higher we went, the more nervous I became—the crampons were not biting in well; the ice axe was providing only a limited anchor. When I looked down the slide, I envisioned myself as a snowball at the bottom. Any slip could be dangerous. About a third of the way up I called, "Dick, I am not having any fun. I think we should get off the slide." Dick responded, "Okay, I'll come down and we'll talk about it." As he descended, he slipped and started sliding; he executed a nice ice axe self-arrest.

We decided to ascend through the scrub in the woods, a slow and difficult route. The snow was soft, requiring snowshoes in dense thickets of scrubby trees, but in open areas it had a hard crust that required crampons on the steep slope; changing back and forth was time-consuming. We were constantly blocked by thick scrub, and I fell into innumerable spruce traps. While climbing a section with a hard surface in my snowshoes, one of the snowshoes slipped off my foot and slid down the mountain out of sight. It hid from my searching eyes for well over fifteen minutes.

We finally reached Macomb's summit at two o'clock and found a note from the Whites at the canister: "Found a wonderful route up. Arrived a little after noon. Waited forty-five minutes and went back." Our faces defined chagrin. Of course, South and East Dix were out of the question. We followed their path down—a wonderful route descending a ridge through mostly open woods.

On Saturday, March 16, 1996, I was unable to hike (ECAC hockey playoffs), but planned to meet Dave and Carol on the 17th. They were hiking the Santanonis on the 16th and would need just Dix and Hough to finish the Winter 46. I arrived at the Clear Pond parking area and soon was ready to go. The day was bright and sunny; perfect weather for the attempt! When the Whites arrived, they had bad news. On the previous day's hike, Dave had broken through the ice on Panther Brook, neglected to change his socks, and developed a serious case of frostbite. He could hardly walk, much less hike. They must head home to a doctor. Having promised not to hike alone in the winter, I left the Dixes to another day. Yet, I finished the winter of 1996 feeling that achieving the Winter 46 was just a matter of time. I had ascended Couchie and Santanoni in a day trip. I had ascended Seward, Donaldson, and Emmons in a single day. I had but eight peaks to go, and four of them were in the Dixes. I could get those four in a single day!

January 12, 1997: What a great idea—we will climb East Dix from the east, a wonderful route with opportunities for a traverse across to South Dix, Hough, and Dix if everything goes quickly. We explored the route this summer and loved it. The east side of the Dix Range also has less snowfall. With these optimistic thoughts, we headed out. An easily discernible herd path in the summer was invisible beneath the snow, and we spent much time route-finding. At last we crossed the East Dix slide and headed up. Those of us in the lead were making reasonable progress when we received the bad news. When planting his ski poles, Dick felt

View to the Beckhorn on Dix Mountain summit. Photo by David White.

something pull in his back with significant pain. He wisely decided he had better turn around; with his approval, the rest of us proceeded to the summit of East Dix—we were near the top. But there was no thought of going on.

January 19, 1997: It's a cold day, but we are ready to do Dix, hopeful that if we make good time we will go on to do Hough. We lined up a strong party of hikers, missing only Dick (still injured) and the Whites from our hiking cadre. We left Potsdam, rendezvoused with the Omohundros and Spencers, and headed down. With a party of eight we proceeded in two vehicles. We arrived at the trailhead, but where was John's vehicle? Finally realizing that they weren't coming, we retraced and found their abandoned vehicle above Cascade pass. After we made contact, John reported that the Jeep just suddenly stopped. Attempting to restart it was futile, and a tow was on the way. Oddly, when John now tried to start the Jeep, it started up. By now we no longer had enough time for the hike. As you can plainly see, it was not paranoia that caused me to recognize that the Dix Range, resenting my hubris, had placed a hex on me. It was clear that I was a victim of the curse of the Dixes.

January 20: The Omohundros and Eileen and I had Monday off from work and we could attempt Dix, but with a smaller party. We caught up with Barb Harris, Sally Hoy, and Ellen Ohnmacht, but the going was slow. The steep portion of the trail by the slide presented an interesting barrier, with ice walls we somehow had to ascend. We reached the intersection with Hunter's Pass Trail by 1:40 and met a new problem. Persistent winds had erected an obstacle course along the summit ridge—snow formed four-foot-high drifts behind each small balsam, and behind each was a trough. The wind-sculpted crust of their surfaces was too thin and weak to support someone on snowshoes, yet the drifts were too high and firm to kick through. The only way to make progress was by the leader kicking into the drift, smashing the snow down and going through it to reach the trough, only to start over with the next drift. We were exposed to a chilling crosswind that froze those waiting behind the leader. It took us over an hour to do the last four-tenths of a mile! We did not reach the summit until three o'clock. This had been the most difficult of the trailed peaks I had climbed in winter.

February 1: The hiking group (without Mooers and the Whites) went into Slide Brook for an attempt of Macomb, South Dix, and possibly Hough. During the past days there had been repeated snowfalls. We planned on avoiding the slide because of my experience of the year before, and instead attempted to repeat the route taken by the Whites. But because of the conditions, this was probably exactly the wrong decision, for the slide was covered with snow, not ice, and the snow on the ridge was deeper and mined with spruce traps. The snow on the ridge was not just deep, it was also unconsolidated—no melted or compressed layers to provide a base for the snowshoes. Whoever was in the lead had to work very hard to break trail. My snowshoes were too small for these conditions, and I fell into countless spruce traps. Since everyone else had not climbed Macomb, the decision was made to head for that summit first. When we reached it, fatigue had set in. Although I tried to convince the others that we still had time to do South Dix, I was already resigned to leave it for another day. I had spent the entire weekend reclimbing Macomb. Amazingly, I still had two summits to go, after six trips to the Dixes.

February 15: The Whites had successfully climbed Dix with Dick Mooers and David Meeker, and now needed only Hough. We would all make a determined effort to reach this summit. There was talk of going to South Dix, but I had learned to discount such optimistic blather. We had a large group, and all but Dave and Carol trekked in the previous evening to camp at Slide Brook so that we could get the earliest possible start. Although the snow was deep, we made steady progress as we headed into the Lillian Brook valley. We took a compass bearing toward the south side of Hough and headed up. Our charted course was steep, as we discovered we had headed more directly dead-on to Hough. On occasion we seemed to be trapped between slides. Progress was so difficult that some began to speak of turning back. With deep snow and steep slopes, the leader was sometimes forced to attempt to make progress with a whole body lunge up into the snow. The ones behind the leader could only wait their turn to force a way upward. We made very slow progress, but at last we broke up onto the summit ridge high up on the side of Hough and reached the summit at three o'clock. It was Dave and Carol's 46th, and they had brought 46 shrimp, with sauce, to celebrate. Of course, South Dix was out of the question. Yet there was a sense of satisfaction in being the first group in a month to reach the summit of Hough.

February 23: I have now been to the Dixes seven times, reaching a summit five times, but still have not summitted South Dix. But this weekend we would get this last mountain. In midweek there was a warm spell with rain, followed by a hard freeze and temperatures below zero. The soft snow of previous weeks now had a crust like bedrock. The trail we created up the Lillian Brook valley was firm and crusted. From the valley, a well-established herd path went into the col between Macomb and South Dix and then ascended the open rock of South Dix to within a hundred feet of the summit. I was savoring the day. It was effortless to walk on top of the crust. Some celebrate finishing the Winter 46; I would celebrate finishing the Dix Range with as much enthusiasm. My ebullience was such that I suggested that, rather than continue on the herd path, we simply make for the summit. The new route went well, and then we hit steep terrain with ledges and dense thickets of cripplebush. There was a sharp, exhilaratingly cold breeze. Working our way through took much time and effort, but I was in a good mood, enjoying the challenges, and eventually we broke out onto the open rock.

My enthusiasm was less than universal. To my surprise, a solid majority expressed belated skepticism toward my leadership. The drift of it was (omitting the expletives) that when there was a plain herd path, to go up a much steeper, wind-exposed, clothes-ripping route was lunacy. But I was immune to the criticism, for I had finally finished the Dixes. I could only smile. The curse was lifted. The return back to the car went swiftly, and I waved cheerfully as David Meeker drove off. We got in my car. I turned the key. Nothing. The battery was dead. I was three miles from an isolated highway, in the winter, who knows how many miles from a telephone, who knows how long before others would come out, and my car wouldn't start. The curse of the Dixes had struck one last time. 🐾

Originally published in the Fall/Winter 1998–99 edition of Adirondack Peeks *magazine, Vol. xxxv, No. 2, the magazine of the Adirondack Forty-Sixers, Inc., David and Suzanne Lance, editors. This abridged version is reprinted with permission of the Adirondack Forty-Sixers, www.adk.org.*

*T*om Wheeler: *I first climbed a high peak in 1993 and immediately became an avid hiker. I completed the 46 five months later, became a Winter 46er, #3356W, in 1997, and a Northeast 111er. I have been active in the Adirondack Mountain Club, served as its president for three years and will assume the presidency of the Adirondack 46ers in 2009. My wife, Eileen, and I are avid amateur birders, and I collect rare books about the Adirondacks and the mountains of the Northeast. I believe in the transforming nature of the wilderness experience and value the opportunity it provides for introspection and appreciation of life and nature.*

54

FROSTBITE!

NATURE IS UNFORGIVING

Carol White & David White

We met John and Susan Omohundro and Eileen Wheeler for dinner at their snow kitchen near Bradley Pond on March 15. The next morning Dick Mooers joined us for the climb of the Santanoni Range. The ascent up Panther Brook was spectacular amidst icy cliffs, but suddenly Dave fell through the ice up to his knees. Because the forecast had been for warming temperatures, he believed his feet would stay warm if he hiked fast, so he didn't change into dry socks with plastic bags.

Back at camp by five, after a gorgeous day on the three peaks, we decided to pack out. After four miles, Dave's toes felt like they had blisters on top, and he could not remove his boots at the car. At Dun Roamin Motel, he stayed in the bathroom a long time. "Should I bring in something for dinner?" I asked through the door. "That would be a good idea" was his response. Now I'm nervous—he had wanted to go out for a big dinner. He was in bed when I returned, and he said, "We're not going to finish this year—I've got frostbite." We had only three more days of winter and had been planning to meet Tom Wheeler to climb Dix and Hough. We must catch Tom before he left for Slide Brook lean-to! Dave was discussing his frostbite at the trailhead when Tom tapped him on the shoulder. "I was on my way in—and turned around when I heard your car," he grinned.

The doctor said Dave was fortunate—he has good circulation and would be okay. Dave wouldn't let me see his feet for two weeks, and then one night he pulled off his socks—his toes looked like black, cracked plastic. At our ADK Open House, we manned the winter equipment table. Dave decided that one look is worth a thousand words and showed his feet to some mothers with kids, who were duly awed. "See, when I tell you it's too cold, you should listen!" The next weekend Dave hiked Mt. Tremper, a 2,000-foot ascent. His feet bother him only when it is very cold and we're out for many hours. 🏃

Carol White: On our first climb of Mt. Marcy, in 1989, David and I both experienced an overwhelming desire to continue exploring this vast wild land, and we completed the 46 the following year, #2880W & #2879W. We then pursued Catskill 3500 Club membership, which requires four winter climbs, and we went on to

Carol climbing Panther Brook, Santanoni Range. Photo by David White.

complete winter climbs of Catskill, Adirondack and White mountains high peaks. We wrote ADK's Catskill Day Hikes for All Seasons *and we edit ADK's* Catskill Trails. *My books are* Women with Altitude: Challenging the Adirondack High Peaks in Winter *and* Catskill Peak Experiences: Mountaineering Tales of Endurance, Survival, Exploration and Adventure from the Catskill 3500 Club.

55

NATURE RULES

THE GOOD OLD SNOW DAYS

Wally Herrod

It was March 1970, "back in the old days" when snow really blanketed the Adirondack High Peaks. You had to dig down to even *find* a lean-to, let alone negotiate a chute to get in and out of it. We were Hamilton College outing club chums who spent winter weekends climbing mountains and exploring new routes in the High Peaks. Tom was the only one with a car, and when we weren't backpacking, we would do day trips from Tom's family's cabin on the west side of Nye Mountain, near Lake Placid.

One Saturday morning Tom decided to cut firewood, while Craig and I had our sights on Mt. Colvin and Blake Peak. Tom drove us to the trailhead near the Ausable Club, and the plan was that we would snowshoe six miles up Lake Road and the length of Lower Ausable Lake to approach the two peaks from the Carry Trail. Tom promised to ski in later to meet us, to be sure that everything was all right. He'd be our backup. We'd forgotten that "nature rules" in the backcountry.

As we started out on the lake, snow began falling steadily. When we reached the trail, it was snowing hard. After fifteen minutes of breaking trail in chest-deep snow, we knew we were in for a really tough day. Ascending 2,000 feet from the lake, the 1.7-mile trail was relentlessly steep to Blake's summit. For most of the day, we kicked and clawed our way up Blake, the trail camouflaged by the heavily falling snow. It was reassuring to know that Tom was going to meet us later. Our headlamps would function at least part of the way back, and then we could rely on Tom's light.

Finally, we reached the summit and descended immediately before our tracks were obliterated with new snow. It was dark shortly after we reached the lake. We were wet, tired, and facing six miles of breaking through eight inches of new snow with our wooden bear paws. Every step was a chore. Where was Tom? We kept anticipating that welcome sight, hoping he might have warm drinks and have carried in some gear. It continued to snow heavily. As we reached Lake Road, with four miles to go, still no Tom. Having only day packs, all we could do was keep plodding into the night. Our headlamps had gone out.

We had no way of knowing that the highway was closed through Cascade Pass because of the snowstorm, and there was no way Tom could get through. We were exhausted from breaking trail when we finally reached the dark Ausable Club after 8:00 PM. There were no cars on Route 73. There was no phone at Tom's cabin, even if we had had access to one ourselves. What do we do now? We were on our last legs in terms of strength. We had no money, no sleeping bag, little food and nowhere to go. We needed to warm up and dry out! Somehow we had to get through this night, and we were on our own.

Tom and I were friends with Carolyn Schafer, proprietor of Skyline Outfitters in Keene. Maybe we could borrow money from her for a motel and bus fare. She might have some clue about what happened to Tom.

It was still snowing heavily as we trudged along Route 73 to Keene, seven miles distant. Someone eventually came along and saw us in spite of near-zero visibility, and gave us a ride. We were lucky that Carolyn was at her weekend apartment. She told us that all roads toward Lake Placid were impassable, which explained why we had been stranded. She loaned us money for a motel and for bus tickets.

On Sunday night Tom told us he'd been helpless—it was all he could do to get out of his cabin and back to campus himself on Sunday. To this day I feel fortunate that neither of us were injured or became hypothermic—for nature had surely had her way. 🚶

_W_ally Herrod: _My interest in hiking began in the Boy Scouts, in Massena, New York. My mentor in college was Tom Kensler, an ADK-AMC Winter Mountaineering School instructor; I attended advanced courses, including a winter ascent of Mt. Katahdin in Maine. I led trips year-round for ADK, served as director of the 46er Outdoor Leadership Workshop and as 46er president, and am 46er #750. I'm now chapter chair of the Mohawk-Hudson Chapter of the Appalachian Mountain Club._

56

THE WATER HIKE

WEATHERWISE OR OTHERWISE?

Ann West

Okay, I admit it. My plans were grandiose. It may be time for me to join Overzealous Anonymous: "Hi, my name is Ann, and I'm overzealous." I had planned The Big Hike: six of us would hike in Friday night and camp at the Calamity Brook lean-to; on Saturday we'd hike Marshall with an ADK day trip led by Don Berens; on Sunday we'd get up early, hike Redfield, descend in time to meet another ADK day trip led by Tim Kase, and hike Cliff, my 46th peak! I purchased three half-liter boxes of wine and plastic stemware to serve my friends on top of Cliff. I figured I'd raise the bar—or at least *have* the bar—for celebrating a final peak.

It rained the week before, and the forecast called for rain the entire weekend with temperatures in the forties, so four of our companions declined the trip. Mike Davis and I were the only brave (or foolish) ones still willing to go. Roman Laba then decided to join us, despite the forecast (which leaves me wondering if he's as brilliant as I'd supposed him to be). Ralph Keating had hiked with me the weekend before The Big Hike and became ensnared in the intricacies of our plan. So Mike, Roman, and I drove up in the pouring rain.

We were surprised to find numerous cars at the trailhead. We set off in the pouring rain for the four-and-a-half-mile trek to the Calamity Brook lean-to. It might sound like an exaggeration, but the trails were so waterlogged that hiking them was akin to crossing a brook. It was so bad that in the darkness (and pouring rain) we crossed only two of the three bridges on our trail, apparently thinking that the brook we crossed was just more deep water on the trails. By eight o'clock we huddled around my GPS as we tried to reconcile not yet crossing the third bridge with the irrefutable logic of the GPS mapping software. Ten steps later we found ourselves at Flowed Lands.

The prime-real-estate lean-to was taken, but we gratefully clambered over to the "other side of the tracks"—to our dirt floor, leaking ceiling, mouse-inhabited lean-to. It's curious how social mores become irrelevant when you're soaked and cold; in the lean-to we stripped down and changed into warm dry clothes. After a meal and hot drink, we crawled into our sleeping bags. I'm not sure why it never occurred to me that since I had a forty-degree sleeping bag, and the daytime temperature was a sopping forty-five degrees, it would probably be inadequate. And it was. I spent a restless night, too cold to sleep well and too cold to get out of my sleeping bag to get more clothes and figure out how to get the leaking roof to stop dripping on my ground cloth.

We awoke at seven o'clock to pouring rain. We moved our gear to the better lean-to, where more space would be available, giggling as we walked past the large blue tent floating in a temporary pond between the good lean-to and the privies. We waited for Don's planned eight o'clock arrival with ten day hikers. He arrived with one hiker, Liz, whom he introduced as being lionhearted. Together we set off for Marshall.

In Don's words, "Soon we five (fool)hardy souls were on the herd path along Herbert Brook, which pounded and foamed over rocky chutes and slabs." At one wide, shallow, but swift steep stretch, Don's feet were swept from under him—but on toes, knees, and hands he crossed. The others found a better, flatter crossing upstream.

Higher up the rain eased and the brook grew smaller and quieter. We had a glimpse of Iroquois Peak, and lingered at the summit for a half hour as mists blew in and out of the valleys and patches of blue appeared. On the descent I fell on one of my hiking poles, breaking it. Ten minutes later the second pole inexplicably came apart. Mike graciously shared a pole, knowing my need to spare my knees, and I proceeded with his one good pole and my constantly separating pole. At our lean-to we filled Don and Liz with hot drinks for their return.

Mike and I settled down for the afternoon's entertainment—a deck of cards and watching Roman occupy himself gathering all extraneous objects left in each lean-to. Ralph arrived, having suffered a lapse in judgment as evidenced by his driving up to the Adirondacks (in the pouring rain), hiking Mt. Adams (in the pouring rain), and hiking in to join us for the rest of The Big Hike (which would be in the pouring rain).

A showerless interlude followed, and we rejoiced until Mike, Ralph, and I went to the lake to pump water, at which time it started raining again. We hurriedly pumped and filled, squished back and changed into our dwindling supply of dry clothes. I took steps to ensure a warmer night's sleep, including the right to sleep up against the person next to me. I couldn't bear another cold, sleepless night. I wonder if the companions on either side of me were there because they were the ones who drew the short straws. I dozed several times, although howling winds blew. Maybe the front was passing through, because it had stopped raining ... until it was time to get up.

Mike's alarm went off at 5:30. It was dark. It was cold. It was pouring rain. Ralph succinctly observed, "Dark out," and we all fell back asleep. We finally realized, however, that we had a schedule to keep and a group to meet. We hiked—rather, *waded*—to the Uphill Brook lean-to. Somehow we lost Roman along the way. First we thought maybe he had taken a brief rest stop and would catch up. Then we thought that he might have passed the lean-to and headed up Redfield, so, being mind-numbingly cold, wet, and tired, we proceeded to climb Redfield.

Could the weather get worse? Of course. It started snowing near the summit. There was no way that I could also hike Cliff. I was exhausted from two nights of not sleeping, from a weekend of damp cold, and from what Mike called "our complete failure of rain gear." Roman had not continued to Redfield, and we fretted, but we were confident in his strong abilities and joked about being banned from hiking with the Albany ADK because we were the ones who had misplaced Roman Laba. On the descent my uncomfortably cold hands rapidly became stiff, and I was unable to move my fingers. Ralph rescued me with hand warmers, but exhaustion had the better of me—I felt teary each time Mike and Ralph moved ahead out of my sight.

At Uphill lean-to we encountered a group of hikers. One woman hugged me. Was this Liz from yesterday's hike? Then I foggily recognized my good friend, Janice Joyce, along with the ADK group, all of whom I knew. They had hiked in the pouring rain through at times knee-deep water, and had decided to forgo hiking Cliff and head out. Cold and tired, we all knew that we had to keep moving, so we set out on the seven-and-a-half-mile trip out. I soon found myself absolutely unable to pick up my legs and keep moving. Ralph talked with me and realized that I hadn't eaten or drunk anything for hours; after a quick snack and water break, I was able to continue on.

We were the last ones to wade through the knee-deep water on the trail to Flowed Lands lean-to, where we found Roman comfortably ensconced in his sleeping bag. Someone poured a bottle of yellow lake water laden with pine needles into a pot for cooking Asian noodles. Another person contributed Gatorade to flavor the mixture, which was poured into a mug that held cold morning coffee. The eight of us passed the cup around, eager to hold the warm cup and drink the warm liquid. As we clamored for the unsavory mixture, we laughed, thinking, *If our friends could see us now, they'd never understand why we hike!*

I thought it ironic in retrospect that the only "unsuccessful" High Peaks trip was the one that would have allowed me to finish the 46, but I didn't regret turning back; it was clearly the right decision. Enduring the physical and mental challenges of what was affectionately dubbed "The Water Hike" was a life-changing experience for me, and I resolved to return the next weekend to hike Cliff and finish the 46. 🥾

*A*nn West: *Lower Wolf Jaw bewitched me, and I realized on that summit that I had to climb all 46 (#5737). I love everything about hiking in the Adirondacks—the inspiration it gives for my creative endeavors, the truly wonderful people I've met, and the physical challenges. The way I feel when I look at my backpack makes me understand how a dog feels when he sees his leash.*

57

COLD WATER

STAVING OFF FROSTBITE

Thomas D. Pinkerton

Our goal was to enjoy a pleasant winter hike in the High Peaks region on President's Day weekend, 1996. Marta Bolton knew that Vic Pomerville, Mike Bush, Mike Lonegan, and Joe Ryan would be interested in a hike and made the contacts. Mike Bush and Vic were interested in climbing Cliff, while Mike Lonegan, Joe, Marta, and I wanted to do Redfield. We decided to hike to Uphill Brook lean-to together, then "divide and conquer" and meet up again later.

Those who have climbed Redfield know that it can be a tough bushwhack above Uphill Brook, and even more difficult on snowshoes, so we opted to ascend up the frozen brook as far as we could. The ice covering the brook was solid as I took the lead. After I tired, Marta volunteered to take over. We were about one hundred yards below the waterfall that is so pretty in summer. In winter it was well hidden underneath a blanket of snow and ice, and it just looked like a difficult and steep climb that we had to overcome. Suddenly, the ice that Marta was standing on gave way. There was no time for her to react, especially with snowshoes on; she was unable to avoid sinking into the water. I was the closest to Marta, and my immediate reaction was to grab her coat and pull her out, but I was also afraid that I'd end up in the water with her if more ice gave way. I did get close enough to get a grip on her coat, but at such an angle that I couldn't pull her up and could only keep her from going in any deeper. By then Joe and Mike had returned and together, by surrounding Marta to distribute our weight and get better leverage, we got her out of the water and back on firm ice. Even though Marta's feet never touched the bottom of the brook, she didn't get wet above the waist and insisted that she was able to continue the hike.

We climbed out of the brook, and Marta put on a pair of dry socks covered by plastic bags to keep them dry. She again claimed that she was fine, and we continued our climb with a great deal of difficulty trying to find a good route. We kept asking Marta about her condition. I'm sure she was trying to make the day a success for everyone without concern for herself, while hoping for the best. We'd left the brook maybe ten or fifteen minutes when she finally admitted that it wasn't working; the fresh socks were already wet, and her feet were getting cold again.

We descended to the lean-to as quickly as possible to get Marta warm, especially her feet. We had her lie down and removed her snowshoes, boots, and socks, and wrapped her in a space blanket. While Mike and I held Marta's ice-cold bare feet up under our jackets against our chests, Joe gathered firewood. As Marta's feet warmed up, her general body temperature was dropping from inactivity and the consequent slowing of blood circulation. Before Joe was able to get a fire going, we agreed that Marta had to get moving to increase her circulation. We put more dry socks on her feet, and I carried her snowshoes while she continued to carry her backpack. Mike and Joe stayed at the lean-to to meet Vic and Mike Bush or leave them a note.

I've done a lot of hiking with Marta and she moves right along, but that day I had a hard time keeping up. Her speed up to Lake Arnold and back down to Avalanche lean-to was just short of a run. We were both tired, so we took a break there in the sun. But her feet were quickly getting cold again—the socks were wet.

At Marcy Dam, Marta met a friend and obtained another pair of dry socks. The friend joined us, and the three of us continued at a very rapid pace. Half a mile from the Loj, Marta and her friend pulled away from me as I was becoming exhausted. The men arrived not long after.

Marta is courageous—anyone else would have stayed home the next day, but she and I climbed Phelps the next morning on a beautiful sunny day, enjoyed spectacular views, and ended the weekend on a very positive note. 🏃

[Editor's Note: Dave and I camped at Lake Colden and climbed Redfield up Uphill Brook the next day, not knowing this story. We didn't see a hole in the ice, and we were fortunate; the weather was so cold that the ice was thoroughly frozen. With just the two of us, a similar accident would have been dire. This is why a minimum of four people are recommended for a winter hike. That day, we did see their tracks beyond the brook and saw where they stopped, and we wondered why they hadn't continued.]

For biography of Thomas D. Pinkerton, see "A Night on the Trail."

58

THE MACINTYRE RANGE VIA THE WRIGHT SLIDE

THE GOOD, THE BAD, AND THE UGLY

Neil Luckhurst

I had been studying the map to determine how Dominic and I would do our remaining peaks. In the MacIntyre Range we still had Wright and Marshall to do. I heard about the Wright Slide—not the Angel Slide visible from Marcy Dam, but the one best seen from the summit of Colden. I decided that we'd combine the slide with a complete traverse of the range.

We met Doug Hillman at South Meadow Road. The early October day dawned crisp and clear, the mountains etched sharply against deep blue sky. We missed the Kagel lean-to, crossed Marcy Brook at the next lean-to and bushwhacked back to where Wright Brook empties into Marcy Brook. At Wright Brook I didn't know whether to follow the right or left bank; left was a good choice, as we were on a well-defined tote road. We encountered a tributary coming in from the southwest. You could get caught dozing here and think this tributary was the main brook. You have to cross it to the right; otherwise, you'll be off to perdition—the western flanks and cripple bush-covered slopes of Algonquin. We were no longer on the tote road, but the bushwhack was due west, so we just followed our shadows once the morning sun was on us.

The streambed became wide and flat. We stepped onto it into brilliant sunshine and had an open view to the east. Steam rose thickly off us. We ascended the streambed where possible, because bushwhacking was thick and more strenuous as the grade steepened, but progress was good. Cutting away at a 90° angle to the right, away from the creek, we went up a tiny rubble-filled drainage that petered out. We turned west and found ourselves in *extremely* thick bush. Snow fence stuff! We thrashed around, working hard for every foot of progress, and experienced our first moments of doubt, but what's a bushwhack without that feeling of "maybe we're totally lost"? We hadn't caught even a glimpse of the mountain, let alone the slide—had we followed the wrong creek? Doc McPeak's story about the Wright Slide six-timer who got lost and spent hours in thick cripple bush kept echoing in my head. We fantasized how nice it would be to just pop out onto the slide.

We angled back down to the creek, noted we were still going west and concluded that we were on course. Considering the thirty minutes we'd wasted bush thrashing, we should be within fifteen minutes of the mythical cairn where we should turn right and climb to the base of the slide. Farther upstream, Dominic and I clambered up the south bank where it was particularly high and I cried out, "I can see the summit!" Ten seconds later Dominic echoed, "I can see the slide!" Then Doug chimed in, "There's the cairn!" Now extremely happy, we took off up the narrow rocky drainage, which was dry that day. Doug remembered that we had no water, so back down we went to filter water from the lightly trickling creek. It was a ten-minute climb to where we broke out onto the slide and got hit by the sun's full blast. The valley was a kaleidoscope of reds, greens, and yellows on that cloudless, windless morning. Our time to there from the (wrong) lean-to, including the detour bushwhack, was two and a half hours. Figure on two hours if all goes perfectly well. (Does it ever?)

I rate the slide as "moderate"—a little steeper than the Great Slide on East Dix/Grace, and much easier than Colden's 1992 southeast slide. It's not a very long slide, and soon we were near the top and had to cross a band of cripple bush. We split up and took three different routes—each proved to be the toughest route possible! Be prepared for those ten minutes of rough going. I found a misshapen piece of heavy metal, probably from the wrecked plane. Dominic and Doug looked for more wreckage, but were unsuccessful.

It was strange to be on a crowded summit after our last hours in the bush. The busy trail to Algonquin was like taking part in a pilgrimage. Soaking up Algonquin's summit sun, Doug observed that the conversation around us was like being at a cocktail party. Reluctantly we peeled our carcasses off the summit after a good hour's rest. Poor Doug went back because he had to work, while Dominic and I cruised over to Iroquois. The best place to relax in privacy on busy weekends there is on Boundary Peak, off the trail.

Before descending from Iroquois to Marshall, I put on bush-proof clothing—hot and sweaty, but protective—and we dropped down to Shepherd's Tooth. The bush got very thick and heavy, but right after the Tooth, on the Wallface side, a faint herd path leads all the way down. We knew there were cliffs, but by veering east to a gentle ramp or chimney, we avoided them. From Iroquois to the col took an hour; there was water on the route. That little path made a big difference cutting through the brush, but some people might want to wear protective eyewear.

After hiking to Marshall, the long hike out remained. The Iroquois Pass Trail as it nears the Indian Pass Trail is as nice as any I've ever hiked on. The trail runs along the side of a deep gorge with a creek far below. The pools were covered with multicolored leaves swirling in the current. On the Indian Pass Trail we had five miles to go. When it became pitch dark, with fatigue and only having a little circle of light[1] to follow, I kept hallucinating that we were walking in place like on a treadmill. It was great to finally see the lights across Heart Lake.🚶🚶

[1] I always night hiked with a super-bright halogen headlamp running off a 4.5V flat battery, but on this trip I used a triple LED to save weight. I'm going back to the bulky unit, because the LEDs didn't project well and gave an anemic little circle of light at our feet. Had there been any ambiguities to the trail, I would have felt quite insecure.

Neil Luckhurst: I was fortunate enough to hike each of the 46 high peaks with my son Dominic. Dominic's experiences in the Adirondacks kindled a flame that we thought could never be extinguished. His passion for mountaineering led him to Lake Louise, Alberta, in the Canadian Rockies, where he pursued his burning ambition to spend his life in the mountains and become a guide. He was a tireless hiker, a gifted climber and an inspiration for all who knew him, especially for me, his father. On January 7, 2008, at the young age of nineteen, Dominic was swept to his death in an avalanche while learning his chosen profession. May his death serve as a reminder to us all: We may love the mountains but they don't love us. [For biography of Neil Luckhurst, see "Lost Pond Peak."]

Dominic bouldering on Basin. Photo by Neil Luckhurst.

59

IN QUEST OF HIGH PEAK SLIDES

THE SADDLEBACK SLIDE IN JANUARY

Neil Luckhurst

The Adirondacks hold a dazzling array of spectacular places within its famous Blue Line. A great many of them remain almost unknown and unvisited in spite of being minutes from some of the most popular trails and routes. A couple of years ago my friend Glen had mentioned that there is a slide on the south side of Saddleback and that he had been on it. I was planning on a solo winter bushwhack of Averill Mountain 's south peak this winter, when Glen e-mailed me asking if the Saddleback slide and the "basin" of Basin interested me.

They interested me very much, which is why we were standing on top of Saddleback rapidly losing core temperature at 9:30 AM on January 31, 2009. Our hike up John's Brook Valley and the Orebed Brook trail had been uneventful, with the exception of being served hot coffee (sweet heaven!) by Peggy McKellar and Rich Preis at the ADK's warming hut.

There was a lull in the wind just as we arrived at the clearing above the cliffs, so we removed our packs and proceeded to get organized for the drop to the Saddle-back-Basin col. Suddenly, the wind tore at us, and after losing too much precious body heat we beat a retreat to a sun-drenched opening down the trail out of the wind. We ran up and down a steep section of trail several times until we were warm again, and then we sat down and put our crampons on.

We looped a fifty-foot length of climber's webbing around a yellow birch and tossed all of our gear down to the landing below. We were now committed to making the descent. We went back down the trail 100 feet for one more vigorous climb just to get ourselves 100 percent warm and fully functional. We didn't want to be shivering and uncoordinated while executing the rappel. Back at the "belay," I went first and lowered myself very slowly down over the lip, whipped out my camera (note to self: get skin-tight gloves for manipulating metal in subzero wind chills), and got some pictures of Glen using proper rappelling technique.

Instead of continuing directly down the fall line—the winter route that avoids the cliffs of Saddleback—we erroneously made a right turn and followed the cliff wall, which brought us out to the trail marked with yellow paint on the open rock. What the heck, down we went. I more or less butt-slithered, facing Basin and taking great care to place my crampon points onto the rock and lift them straight off again until I got down to where we put our snowshoes back on.

The views were amazing. The sky was cobalt blue, and snow was pluming off of the big summits and swirling across the treetops on the flanks of Basin.

The trip down to the col was very steep and in deep, unconsolidated snow. Rather than attempt to leave a staircase of horizontal steps for the return trip, we snowshoe-skied and/or butt-slid down to flatter ground. Close to the lowest point in the col, we made a hard left turn and entered thicker woods. What a pleasant surprise! Not only did we not sink in very deeply, but the woods were quite open. Within ten minutes we were out on the slide in the blazing sun with no wind.

All around us were spectacular views—back up to Saddleback along the slide and cliffs, Dix, Nippletop, Pinnacle Ridge and, of course, Basin, the star of the show.

We had previously agreed upon making a slow descent of the slide in order to create a staircase-like series of horizontal steps in the deep, unconsolidated snow, which we could then use to climb back up the slide. This was easier said than done, however, because the follower had less snow resisting his descent than the leader and tended to slide, wiping out the steps. The technique that worked best was to rotate one shoe outward and place it halfway out of the two-foot-deep furrow.

The base of Basin seemed to be right in our faces, but it was still quite far away, so we brought up the question of a turnaround time as were leaving the slide and traversing toward the slides of Basin. After some quick calculations and leaving plenty of margin for error in order to at least arrive back on top of Saddleback before sunset, we agreed upon one o'clock.

We traversed some woods and found ourselves below "Big Pink," which is a massive slab of pink granite (readily visible from Pinnacle Ridge). Big Pink was very white and smooth under a mantle of snow on this January day. After traversing along the base of Big Pink, it was clear that the base of the Basin slides was beyond our turnaround time, so we stood and marvelled at the surrounding mountains so stunningly beautiful, so rugged, and so cruelly hostile to puny humans.

With deep satisfaction we turned around and continued our adventure by down-shifting into stump-pulling gear and slowly climbing back up our "staircase." This proved to be very physically demanding. One ten-foot pitch took me no less than five minutes to get up because of the repeated collapsing of the weakly structured snow.

Glen had led the upper two-thirds of the slide, so I took over the lead before reentering the woods. This short section was very easy, but from there to the cliffs we experienced Adirondack winter conditions that neither of us will forget for a long time. The wind had really picked up and swept across our path from left to right, driving snow crystals into our faces. Neither of us had brought goggles or

*The great slides on
Basin Mountain.
Photo by Glen E.
Bladholm.*

facemasks, but I doubt that we would have stopped to put them on at that point anyway. Ascending the steep pitch was not a technical problem. All we had to do was firmly kick one snowshoe into the snow, plant the ice axe to the hilt in the center of the trail above us, push up with one leg while pulling upwards with both arms on the axe, kick in the other shoe and repeat this as many times as was required to get to the cliffs. We didn't rest often, because it was very cold and the wind was relentless, but I did pause a few times and gazed over at the big peaks. They had great plumes of snow blowing off of them, just like Everest!

I spied the webbing flapping in the wind above us, and a few dozen more steps brought us up to it. Like machines we switched over to crampons. Glen went up first. I passed him all the gear, which he carefully stowed. Then, poor Glen stood there in the chilly blast while I figured out how to get myself up. Once I was finally, safely up, Glen immediately took off up the snow chute with the packs. I grabbed the webbing and bunched it up under the front of my jacket, picked up both pairs of snowshoes and the axes, and met Glen, who was returning for more gear. He smiled ear to ear when he saw I had everything with me, and we quickly entered the protective cover of the forest.

After switching back to our hiking gear, we had a very pleasant trip back to the warming hut, where Peggy and Rich plied us with hot chocolate. We chatted with them for half an hour as darkness enveloped the Johns Brook Valley. Just as we were leaving, we met up with MtnHiker and Britdog, whom we had met in the Garden Parking Lot at 5:30 AM. They regaled us with tales of "knock-em-down" winds on Little Haystack.

A sliver of a moon was just bright enough at our backs for us to be able to hike without headlamps. The graceful Bennys Brook slide was glowing faintly on Lower Wolf Jaw. When we arrived at the car, Glen looked at his watch and said, "Thirteen hours, fifteen minutes." What a great and memorable day it had been!

For biography of Neil Luckhurst, see "Lost Pond Peak."

60

TRIUMPHS AND TROUBLES IN THE SANTANONI RANGE

DON'T TEMPT THE ELEMENTS

Donna Tabor

I have a love/hate relationship with the Santanoni Range, north of Newcomb. Yes, they're high peaks, but the allure for us was not goal-oriented; the wild ruggedness of the area is what appealed to us, plus a less crowded trail system. Camping at Lake Harris accentuates the pleasure.

Our first trip was in May 1995 to climb both Panther and Santanoni. Bob and I were in good shape, hiking every weekend and on every vacation. On the trail, we encountered lots of mud accumulated from a rainy week, and a couple of heavy downpours slowed our progress. We donned raincoats and continued, meeting an elderly, disoriented man, separated from his party. He insisted he was traveling to his lean-to, when in fact he was heading down to the trailhead. He was very resistant to our help, so we left a note at the lean-to and searched out his fellow campers. They turned out to be his sons, who stated, "He does this all time. Not to worry. He'll be fine." We continued our ascent, but not convinced that he'd be "fine."

We scurried to "Times Square," aptly called since it diverges into many paths. Having lost much time with the elderly man and his sons, we had to choose only one peak, so it was 4,442-foot Panther—a good choice. Views from Times Square and, later, Panther were breathtaking, despite clouds rolling in and out. We reached the summit of Panther to be drenched once more, but as quickly as it rained, the sun broke through to make it all worthwhile. The trail itself is fascinating from start to finish. Panther Brook from Bradley Pond is abundant with small falls and lush plant life. The woods are vibrant and deep, with an ethereal beauty. It is a challenging hike of twelve miles round-trip; we were determined to return at another time to "finish."

July 1998. A perfect day weather-wise, so we were able to enjoy the beauty much more. The trail is long, strenuous, and rugged, but unique and beautiful. At the beaver dam, a path into the Santanoni Range offers the wonderful diversity we remembered—from waterfalls to rocks, gradual to steep climbs, deep forest with breaks of sun. At Times Square we headed toward Santanoni Peak following a narrow path with dense growth all the way to the 4,607-foot summit. A small open area on top offered a fabulous view, cool breezes, lots of sun, no bugs—and all to ourselves. This is the "love" part of the relationship, where this thirteen-mile trek felt just fine. Now, just one more peak from Times Square.

July 1999. Camping again at Lake Harris, our goal was 3,820-foot Couchsachraga Mountain. We're supposed to get wiser as we get older, but our faculties were failing this day. It was the hottest week of the summer, with intense humidity, but we foolishly decided to tempt the elements. A long vigorous hike into Times Square nearly did us in, however. We headed back down after seriously wondering if we'd make it without critical consequences. A severe thunderstorm moved in with a torrential downpour, hail, and lightning. Foolishly we didn't don our rain gear, thinking we'd relish the coolness. It did cool us off, but it also drenched everything we had on and turned the trail into a river. By the time we reached the trailhead, we were freezing and exhausted. From blistering heat to intense cold, the Adirondacks once again showed its fickleness and we humans proved our foolishness. Needless to say, we're not finished yet, either of us! 🏃

Donna Tabor: My husband, Bob, and I both grew up on dairy farms, so exploring and adventures were a daily occurrence. Our kids were introduced to the great outdoors at an early age—fishing, hiking, swimming, and making new friends around campfires. As the empty-nest syndrome overtook us by surprise, so did hiking—with a passion! Our wonderful extended family still likes to spend time with us. What more could you ask?

61

A (N)ICE SERIES OF ADIRONDACK TALES

EVERYTHING YOU WANTED TO KNOW ABOUT ICE, SNOW, COLD, AND MORE

Donald P. Berens Jr.

Water is a liquid oxide of hydrogen that appears bluish in thick layers, freezes at 32° Fahrenheit, boils at 212° F, has a maximum density at 39° F and a high specific heat. It takes many forms other than streams and ponds—fog, rain, hail, sleet, snow of various densities and firmness, ice in white, blue, green, yellow, or clear (sometimes misnamed "black") hues, and exotically named hoar, rime, graupel, and frazil. The physical chemistry of water, ice, and snow is of more than academic concern, however, to Adirondack skiers, snowshoers, and climbers. Its microscopic properties, multiplied on a mountainous scale, variously attract, enable, and resist our efforts. Adirondack water, especially frozen water, has been the basis for many adventures described here.

Deer Brook and Hedgehog Mountain, 34°F–39°F, April 2006. In a temperature inversion, rain falling from warmer atmospheric layers can be transformed to clear, hard, rime ice when it meets subfreezing surfaces near the ground. I sometimes hike in the rain to see streams and waterfalls at high flow. This rainy day, I found a foaming white waterfall less than a mile from the Deer Brook trailhead, reason enough to count it as a good day in the woods. I visited Snow Mountain for the first time, imagining views from its foggy summit, and then climbed to the notch between Lower Wolf Jaw and Hedgehog. Above 3,000 feet the temperature must have been below freezing overnight, because tree limbs were wrapped in see-through ice. My boots slipped on slick rollers of broken twigs encased in clear ice—imagine thick-crust cannoli of transparent ice with thin dark birch or spruce filling. Near the Hedgehog summit the breeze increased, the forest clinked like wind chimes, and more cannoli fell from above. They were not big enough to do me damage, but they stung. I used my hat and hood for protection, but a helmet would have been more comfortable!

"The Year of the Spruce Traps," Santanoni Range, 27°F–33°F, February 2002. Snow consists of small white crystals of frozen water formed directly from water vapor at less than 32°. Justin Vliestra organized an RWMS (Rochester Winter Mountaineering Society) overnight trip where five of us hoped to visit Santanoni, Panther, and Couchsachraga peaks. Three months of snowfall covered the rocks

and notorious mud. Snow falls as individual flakes, no one of which would support much, but on the ground those flakes begin to fuse when, after partially melting under the pressure of their own weight and the slight warming of solar radiation, they refreeze. Over the winter the snow pack consolidates, approaching half the density of water. In one of nature's ironies, snowshoers cannot walk on deep liquid water but can walk on top of snow that is less dense than water because of the rigid, but brittle, crystal structure of individual snowflakes and the snow pack they form. But if the snow pack is interrupted by pockets of air around the boughs of a spruce tree, the snow may not support the weight of a snowshoer. In the legendary Adirondack spruce trap, one descends into porous snow, and sideways escape is hampered by firmer snow around the hole; upward motion is thwarted by the downward-pointing branches that cause snowshoes to ratchet down more than they can wriggle up. A hole is often too narrow for the snowshoer to reach the snowshoes to maneuver them manually or remove them, and sometimes escape is impossible without help.

As we approached Times Square the snow got deeper, bending trees and obscuring the herd path. By two o'clock we set up two tents near the ridge crest and started with lighter packs toward Couchie, the farthest. Despite fog and falling snow we found the herd path, but soon lost it; we tried Santanoni and again lost the path. What looked like open meadows were actually thickly treed areas completely blanketed by snow. While leading, I went into a chest-deep spruce trap on a slope, but was able to knock the snow away on the downhill side to escape. Catching my breath at the back of the line, I fell into a second trap up to my nose; with Craig's help, I eventually crawled out. Then I entered a hole over my head! Justin later wrote, "I distinctly remember catching up to the group at a rest break and wondered why Don Berens was not there. I saw a pair of mittens poke out of a hole in the snow—he was in an eight-foot-deep spruce hole and fighting for dear life to avoid falling down another four feet."

Having traveled only a quarter-mile in an hour and a half, we would not get to Santanoni, so we picked nearby Panther. Most substances, including hikers' brains, get denser as it gets colder. But the depth of spruce holes expands as temperatures approach freezing, or over time. By morning the prospect of spruce traps loomed large and we chose to save Santanoni and Couchie for another year.

Mount Redfield, 24°F–31°F, November 2005. Close to 32°F, atmospheric water can become hoar frost (spicules of ice growing from air-chilled surfaces) or soft, rime ice (fog droplets freezing in white, air-bubble-filled crystals on cold surfaces), and liquid surface water can become clear ice (drips or splashes in cold air). November features any kind of weather, including the kind most folks consider miserable, but such conditions can produce astonishing varieties of beauty. One cold, wet, gray November, on an Albany ADK chapter day trip from Upper Works to Redfield, we saw *eight* kinds of snow and ice. We hit the trail wearing headlamps in 24° snow flurries at 6:10 AM.

The snow in the air, type #1, was composed of individual flakes—crystals of frozen water vapor. Underfoot we saw #2, day-old snow the flakes of which had begun to fuse under the pressure of gravity and the slight heat of yesterday's solar radiation, but which could be further deformed by the pressure of a passing boot. Old snow lay atop older snow that had melted and refrozen into harder ice, #3, which resisted our boots' pressure and caused us occasionally to slip. Where steep, eroded banks of the trail were not snow-covered, we saw feathery hoar frost, #4, growing from the cold mud. The trail along the Opalescent River was uniquely beautiful. White, yellow, and blue icicles—#5—hung from overhanging rocks and over the river. In the Flume the river has carved a small, steep-sided rock canyon about twelve feet wide and thirty feet deep; pancake ice bobbed in the eddies where the alternation of temperatures just above and below freezing in moving water had created hand-sized platelets, each thicker at the edges and thinner in the middle—#6. Our progress slowed on the icy herd path to Redfield. Where it follows the major tributary of Uphill Brook, we saw splash water frozen into clusters of clear globules of ice, like Waterford crystal grapes, #7. As we climbed into the clouds, rime—frozen fog, #8—whitened the trees up to the summit. A pine marten visited the Uphill lean-to clearing, but we were too hungry to share our food. We returned to Upper Works in the dark, wet and cold at 31°, but hardly miserable.

Blake Peak, 22°F–28°F, February 1977. Bob Collin led a RWMS overnight trip to Blake Peak. We approached the range on skis over Elk Lake, up the West Inlet toward Elk Pass, and bushwhacked on snowshoes up the East Ridge in light snow and mid-twenty-degree temperatures. This was possible because water freezes and ice floats. Even if it is not cold enough long enough for the depth of the lake to freeze solid, the surface freezes. The frozen top insulates lower depths from further heat loss and they remain liquid, and so can support aquatic life until the spring thaw. Cold water lay only inches below the snow-covered ice that supported us, heavy with backpacks. This novice skier with an active imagination was only too glad to let others lead the way over the lake and find whatever holes or cracks there might be.

Cascade Gully, 10°F–15°F, February 1982. To freeze at 32° F, water needs nucleation sites at which crystallization can begin; otherwise it must be super cooled to as low as –43° F to freeze. Nucleation sites can be supplied by water impurities or by irregularities in the container or channel holding it. Gary Noyes and I were teaching Bob Fuss how to climb ice on the 225-foot waterfall on Cascade Mountain that descends toward Cascade Lakes. Gary and I took turns leading and belaying, and were tied into opposite ends of a 150-foot climbing rope, while Bob was tied into the middle. We wore helmets and crampons and carried one or two ice axes tethered to our wrists to grip the ice when we were moving our feet. Gary and I carried ice screws, carabiners (metal snap-links), and nylon slings so that the leader could attach anchors to the ice or to trees. I anchored myself near the bottom of the waterfall while Gary climbed the first of what would be four pitches, each no more than the length of the rope between the leader and the middleman.

In early winter, flatter parts of the waterfall freeze first, thaw, refreeze, and mix with snow, forming ice of varying firmness, usually full of air and therefore white. Steeper slopes and small overhangs that remain free of snow and allow water to fall freely are the last to freeze. As winter gets colder, the steep fast-falling water begins to freeze. Starting at the edges of the channel, clear or bluish-white ice forms next to the main, but diminishing, channel of water. Sometimes a skin of thickening ice forms around a vertical column of falling water; sometimes the waterfall freezes solid. After freezing solid, new meltwater flows over or under the ice, either forming a new, thicker skin of ice or a new liquid center under a thinning skin. This makes ice climbing suspenseful, because the surface does not tell the whole structural story.

Gary led the first and third pitches, and I led the second and fourth. We had solid anchors, both in the ice and on nearby trees, so even the steep pitches were exciting but not terrifying. Still, we placed the points of our crampons and ice axes carefully, preferring not to fall. At my last pitch the ice was nearly vertical, glistening, and just the right temperature for climbing. It was a Goldilocks moment— not so hard that steel couldn't penetrate to grip, not so brittle that it would shatter the ice, not so mushy that ice wouldn't hold the steel after penetration. It was just right! I could tell by the feel and sound as my crampons and ice tools struck the ice. Left foot, up, *thunk*. Right foot, up, *thunk*. Left axe, up, *thunk*. Right axe, up, *thoonk*. Whoa! A different sound, and I heard the muffled sound of running water. But the ice felt firm, I had good anchors below me, I was close to the top, so I continued. I saw that I'd been climbing on a half-foot thick, but hollow, semicircular column of ice frozen to the edges of the channel, but separated at the center from the underlying rock by a foot and a half of air and running water wide enough to swallow a man and deep enough to keep him there awhile. It was awesome, but not immobilizing. I climbed up and around the hole, anchored myself to the trees, and belayed Bob and Gary up the same pitch. It was as close to climbing on air as I ever expect to get.

The Great Range, −20°F to +2°F, February 1979. Charlie Clough led a three-day, two-night RWMS trip of nine strong climbers to the Great Range from the Garden

Mount Haystack. Photo by Neil Luckhurst.

in Keene Valley. Saturday began at −15° and got colder. We reached Saddleback on snowshoes by early afternoon. A 25 MPH wind blew in our faces as we contemplated the trail down the cliffs of Saddleback. Some noses and cheeks were nipped white. We chose a detour through the trees with less exposure to wind and steep slopes. The top of Basin, where Jack Freeman finished his Winter 46, was even windier than Saddleback, so we descended into the bigger trees and camped at the site of the former Sno-Bird lean-to, where it went to −25° overnight.

Sunday was calm and clear, and it soon warmed to zero, ideal weather for winter fun. We snowshoed to the Haystack trail junction, where we switched to crampons. There are spots where the trail going up and down the steep rocks of Little Haystack and up to Haystack can be awkward, especially when they are wet, or icy, or when the wind staggers one. But on this day the rough spots were made smooth—though no less steep—by a white plate of shiny ice-encrusted snow. We could put our cramponed feet anywhere—the icy snow was soft enough to allow not just the crampon tips, but half a boot to penetrate, and firm enough to support a climber, even with his heels cantilevered over space. We *choonk-choonked* up the ice castle under a dome of windless, uninterrupted blue. Later, we sunbathed on Marcy's summit for forty-five minutes, though the temperature never went above +2°. For the sheer joyous harmony of rock, snow, sun, sky, and climber, I have never had a better thirty minutes than that winter climb of Haystack.

Mts. Donaldson and Emmons, –34°F to 0°F, January 2004. The specific heat of water is 4.184 joules per gram-Kelvin—it takes one calorie of heat energy to raise the temperature of one gram of liquid water by one Kelvin (1.8F). But the transition from ice to water at 32° F takes as much energy as to heat water to eighty Kelvin (144°F). Neal Andrews led five RWMS hikers on an overnight trip to the Seward Range. Saturday morning before dawn, we left the car at the Stony Creek Bridge to walk the unplowed road to the trailhead. It was –31°. Although we snowshoed briskly with full backpacks and multiple layers of clothing, it took time to reach a comfortable temperature. During breaks, thickly insulated mittens had to come off to manipulate zippers, stuff sacks, and water bottles.

On the herd path, snow-covered trees leaned in closer—we got very cold snow on the shells protecting our heads and hands. In the upper reaches, snow-covered blown-down trees caused us to lose the path altogether. We bushwhacked toward the ridge, but had to wallow in snow to do so. We set up two tents near Donaldson, and that also required contact with the snow. As we set off with day packs to climb Donaldson and Emmons, my fingers ached from the cold, but soon the pain eased. At 2:30, on Emmons, we had the high temperature of the day, –15° F. Back in tents, I was shivering and clumsy as I changed out of wet clothes. It took longer than usual for the cooks to melt the super-chilled snow to water hot enough for supper. Even with long underwear, in a pile suit, with two balaclavas, in a sleeping bag, inside a bivouac sack, on two Ensolite pads, next to two other sleepers, in a two-layered tent, it was a long night. It went back down to –34° in Saranac Lake that night.

After sunrise it was –20°, so we all agreed that we would skip Seward, eat breakfast, break camp, and descend. It was zero when we got back to the cars. I put the heat on full blast, but never felt warm enough to take off my balaclava or glove liners during the three-hour drive home. When I removed my liners, I had unfamiliar red, white and purple fingertips with blisters on three of them. All ten fingers had first- or second-degree frostbite. My winter hiking season was over. Two of the other four hikers had frostbite on fingers or noses. The real mechanism of the frostbite was the contact with cold snow, especially when we put our gloved and mittened hands into it to brush away deep snow or to pull up on a tree. In the microclimate around insulated fingers, there is a temperature gradient from body temperature of 98.6° down to the ambient temperature. On a subfreezing day, there is a point along that gradient where the temperature is 32°. One hopes that that point is farther, rather than closer, to the skin. But on an extreme subzero day, that point is likely to be somewhere inside the outermost layer of clothing. Even if the point in dry conditions is outside the clothing, the presence of snow near a source of body heat is likely to draw heat energy out of the body into the transformation of 32° snow into 32° water, and smaller but considerable quantities into the transformation of 32° water into 33° water and warmer.

I made a good recovery from my frostbite without permanent tissue loss. But my fingers still ache in cold weather, a reminder of the high specific heat of water and the remarkably high energy absorbed by the phase change of solid ice to liquid water. Experienced Adirondack hikers know, though sometimes not scientifically or quantitatively, that the peculiar characteristics of water, especially around the points at which it freezes and melts, have fascinating effects, for better or worse, on mountain travel and even on survival. Although none can compare with the "brain-freeze" that follows a gulped milkshake upon one's return from the woods, it is wise as well as intriguing to understand, at least intuitively, how water, snow, and ice work their magic. 🏃

For biography of Donald P. Berens Jr., see "Good Grief! Nineteen Years of Halloween Hiking."

62

THE DIX RANGE

FIVE PEAKS IN A TWENTY-SQUARE-FOOT WORLD

Laurie Rankin

On my first round of the 46, I was often solo, so I prepared well for a long hike such as the entire Dix Range. I read trail guides, maps, Internet sites, and spoke with fellow hikers. My choice was to do these five peaks in one day, beginning from Elk Lake and climbing the Beckhorn Trail to the summit of Dix. The highest peak would be climbed when my legs were fresh. I'd reach the farthest point more quickly on the marked trail, and then could hike to the other summits using less physical effort and more navigational skills. It was 6.6 miles to the Dix summit, and I hoped that the fog would burn off. I carefully marked compass bearings on my maps from summit to summit and noted where cairns mark trail junctions. This trip was on September 5, my dad's birthday.

Daylight was just breaking as I headed up the trail. Everyone was still sleeping in the lean-tos. The serious climbing began on the rough, eroded Beckhorn Trail. Up, up, up it went, and I turned around often to catch my breath and look for a break in the mist. The forest smelled great in the damp air. There was no wind. As I was pulling myself up onto the Beckhorn, my pack's waist belt buckle snapped and broke. I was carrying plenty of extra water, and now no waist belt! I tried to fix it with safety pins, to no avail. A swirl of fog surrounded me, keeping me within my own little twenty-yard world as I proceeded over to Dix's 4,857-foot summit with a greater weight on my shoulders.

I touched top and headed back to the Beckhorn, quickly finding the herd path to Hough—a deep plunge into the forest and the unknown over four trailless summits. I was thinking of my dad, who had instilled in me a love of the mountains as well as of maps, and who had taught me the freedom of the compass, which allowed me the confidence of trying this trek. Up, down, up, down. I didn't recall this up and down stuff in my research. My twenty-yard view of fog prevented me from gauging progress. The herd path was obvious, and my compass seemed okay. Finally, a summit sign, but so high that I couldn't read it! There was open rock and a cairn. My notes said a cairn would be on South Dix—could I have missed Hough? I plunged down and came to an obvious col, fire ring, and heavily traveled herd paths. I took out maps, compass points, notes—I'd written that there was a campsite between South Dix and Macomb.

A family with three children between six and ten emerged from the fog. They all seemed well prepared, except that they had neither a map nor a compass! I explained my quandary. The father said that they'd come from Macomb and South Dix and were going to Hough. The marked summit had to be Hough! With great relief, I headed toward South Dix and they followed. "I thought you were going to Hough," I said. "This is the way you came." I had confused him, and here he was with three children, no map and no compass!

Over another high point, down into a col, and up to what must be South Dix. The herd path continued, and the compass direction slightly changed. Had I missed another summit? I backtracked, but the fog offered no help. Only my feet and brain told me that I'd reached South Dix. A hiker emerged, and I asked where he was coming from. "I don't know about you," he stated in an exasperated tone, "but I'm coming from East Dix." "Did I somehow miss the summit of South Dix?" I asked. "You went over it not fifty yards back," he said irritably, "right by the rock cairn." I said that I hadn't been near a cairn. "Yes, you were, just a short distance behind you—when you came from Macomb." I explained that I had not come over Macomb. "Oh yes you did," he said. I said that no, I'd come from Dix. "That would be impossible at this hour!" he replied.

A family passed, heading for East Dix. Their map was a newspaper clipping with the Dix Range roughly sketched on it, and they put star stickers on the summits as they achieved them! They proudly added East Dix to their Macomb and South Dix stars. No other form of navigation, and they had a twelve-year-old with them. They seemed in good shape and happy in their navigation oblivion, so why should I, with my compass, map, and homework, be concerned? We retraced, with me in the rear, and once we'd gotten back to where I'd first encountered them, we continued downhill fast. I called out that we'd gone over South Dix and were heading for Hough, which they weren't planning on. Retracing, I said, "This sure felt like the summit to me, but all I saw was toilet paper in a tree." There were shouts of happiness. "This is where you turn—we put that there on our way over so we'd remember to turn back here." My goodness—navigating by toilet paper and newspaper clippings! Sure enough, if one parted the thick fir trees there, you'd find a herd path to an open rock area with a cairn—the true summit of South Dix. Cairns led us down to the col between South Dix and Macomb, complete with a campsite as my research had said there would be.

The four-hundred-foot climb to Macomb ensued. From the summit, a herd path down to the slide had side paths blocked with logs, another navigational custom my friends hadn't heard of. It was eerie on the slide. You could see very little in the dense fog, and yet sound carried—voices and sounds of falling rocks. The loose character of the slide sent lots of rock rolling downhill, and you wanted to shout,

4,857-foot Dix Mountain summit from the Beckhorn. Photo by David White.

"Look out below!" A child cried loudly, and a parent could be heard comforting the child; had I set loose a rock that had hurt the child? At the bottom of the slide, I came upon the family that I'd met below Hough. The smallest child was sporting a large Band-Aid on his cheek where he'd fallen. Not to worry—he was all smiles around that Band-Aid!

The family that I had met on East Dix had gotten separated from me in the fog. I was concerned, as they seemed like novices. I waited at length for them near the base of the slide. Then, the family from Hough and I traveled through a maze of herd paths—left and right, into and above the streambed. At the trail we waited for the other family to arrive. Traveling with a group, the rule is to wait at a junction (in this case, at the trail) if you get separated. The family with me was tired and sure that the others had gone on, so we headed out. As darkness increased, I became more concerned. "Silly feet"—as I call those stumbling legs at the end of a long hike—were really taking over the feet of one of them. Suddenly, there was the other family at the trailhead.

This was a memorable day, with miles of wilderness, thoughts of Dad, fears that I'd made navigation errors, that disagreement with the lone hiker, and then meeting two families who were unprepared for what they were undertaking. But despite navigating without compass or map, and even using toilet paper to guide themselves back, all were thankfully safe. I looked forward to returning in winter when I could enjoy views.

Part 2. Three of us headed for Macomb on a February day that called for rain. A newly flagged route to Macomb's slide is a magnificent improvement over the myriad herd paths I'd experienced before. At the slide we caught up with trail-breakers practicing ice axe and crampon techniques. On this clear, sunny day I stopped often to enjoy the views; the summit views were the most incredible sur-prise that I've found in the Adirondacks—you could see forever. Then, off we went to the fabulous views from South and East Dix that I had no idea existed when I climbed them in the fog.

One Year Later. Dix and Hough are still waiting. Near 0°, we hike with head-lamps up to Round Pond. Would the day be clear? We viewed a blood-red sunrise following us. Red sky in the morning, sailors take warning. At 5.7 miles, at the base of the Dix slide, we broke into the open and the wind caught up with us. I remem-bered this very steep mile of trail from my first trip. We started up, me second. My snowshoes were not getting traction. I'd go up one step and slide back, each time worrying that I was going to take out those behind me. My telescopic poles col-lapsed as I leaned hard on them, trying to keep uphill progress going. I was becom-ing exhausted, so I let others pass; it became easier then as their "steps" gave me a better purchase.

From Hunters Pass junction on, the trail was often completely blown over. Blowing snow obscured views from the summit, and at the Beckhorn we saw that the path to Hough was not broken. Should we proceed? The other two turned back. Tom and I decided to make a twenty-minute go of it and then reevaluate.

The snow was mid-thigh in depth, but we felt some firmness below our feet where others had made the trek. They'd broken through ice layers that froze trees together. The herd path was usually obvious, so we decided to continue. A battle ensued! We were poked, prodded, had our boots sucked off in spruce traps, lost and found the herd path several times, and bathed in new snow. We took turns in the lead. At the base of Hough, we dropped packs and I started up, facing a wall of snow chest-high. I could make no forward progress, so I went to the right, made progress, then to the left, then chest-high snow. I thanked my teammate and partner for doing this god-awful trip with me—he had already climbed Hough for his Winter 46.

The 800-foot climb back up the Beckhorn was going to be a killer. I was losing energy and began to simply count steps as I struggled with the uphill in completely soaked gloves and very cold hands. My partner insisted that we stop and I change gloves. The break revived me because … here we were, back on the Beckhorn! The descent on our backsides was exhilarating and quick.

At the lean-to by 5 PM, hot tea tasted like a $100 bottle of champagne. We donned headlamps at the trail junction at 6 PM; then, I remembered the *uphill* from Round Pond out! My partner quietly said, "Start looking along the sides of the trail." What was he talking about? "Something that I wrote backwards and discreetly on the way in." Then I saw it—every several hundred feet there would be another number or letter. When put together it read, *6-23-07 Whiteface, Tom loves Laurie*—the date of our wedding on the summit of Whiteface. A message planned hours earlier! It was a great return to the Dix range, most importantly because now it was with a partner rather than solo.

P.S. I discovered the next morning that both of my snowshoe crampons had snapped off! 🚶🚶

L aurie Rankin: I grew up in the Catskills, where my parents instilled a love of those mountains in me, teaching me how to read a map and use a compass. I shared this love with my two sons, and one invited me to climb a high peak; I had a new goal—the 46! I completed the Winter 46, #5525W, with the wonderful company of the man who was soon to be my husband. We maintain trails and lean-tos, work on new trail-building projects, volunteer on hiking club boards and at Balsam Lake fire tower, and have helped restore other towers.

63

A LONG WINTER'S DAY IN THE SANTANONI RANGE

PAY ATTENTION TO YOUR BODY

Alan M. Via

With a good weekend weather forecast, my partners Rich, Steve, Nola, and I headed north on a bright Saturday morning. Laden with heavy packs and optimistic spirits, we snowshoed up to the Bradley Pond area and set up tents for our next day's trip to Panther and Couchsachraga. It was mid-February and cold. After stomping platforms and setting up tents, we started melting snow for dinner and breakfast.

At 4:30 AM our party was excited about the clear, starry skies. After a hot breakfast, we were on the way at 6:15. The sun started touching the peaks, and headlamps came off. The footing was excellent, with fresh powder over a hard crust. We departed the herd path when it neared Panther Brook and bushwhacked straight for the summit of Panther, summitting at 9:00 AM under gorgeous, photogenic skies. The summit had six feet of snow with a good wind slab and protruding treetops. We didn't have to excavate the canister this time, as a previous party had already dug it out. Buttoned up against the cold temperatures and wind, we attended to canister duties. While my friends snacked and drank, I kept shooting film; it was a spectacular day.

We had bearings drawn to and from Couchie but, given the good visibility, map and compass were not necessary. We quartered down the Panther-Couch ridge and right up to the canister by noon, happy to find the canister bottom sitting on the snow. After snacks, we followed our tracks back over the summit of Panther. Our group knew each other well, and everyone was in excellent condition; they would assume I was shooting pictures as I lagged behind. As we descended off Panther's summit, I told them not to wait for me because the white clouds and deep blue skies made for fantastic mountain photography. None of us—including me—was aware that I was in real trouble.

I made some basic mistakes and was now about to pay for them. Distracted by my photography, I'd eaten little and did not drink much during the day, and the shivering had already begun in Panther's lonely, late-afternoon breeze. Like my friends, I headed off Panther's summit in our tracks. The upper portion was very steep, and after two or three flailing falls, I realized that my lack of coordination was advancing hypothermia. The slips were pretty dramatic, head downhill, and my clothing was soaked from snow getting inside. The shivering became more pronounced. I was getting colder and stumbling and falling often. I was aware of what was happening, but it was like I was observing myself from a distance. I was still in fairly steep terrain, and I was in real trouble now. My friends, nearing our tents, surely thought I must be right behind them taking pictures. After many more slips, falls, and soakings, the terrain began to moderate, but I was still a long way from our camp and still repeating the routine of snowshoe, fall, get up, snowshoe some more, fall again ...

By now heavy fatigue had set in. I was taking standing breaks, but then I started to sit. I'd close my eyes and think, *Just rest two minutes more.* Then I'd stand up and start moving again. Two things were keeping me going—excellent physical conditioning and willpower. I visualized the faces of my wife and young daughter, and thought about the coming birth of our second child in a few months. That propelled me back to my feet, and I gathered myself and refused to sit down or close my eyes until I was back in the tent.

Later, Nola told me that they had started to worry some time earlier, but assumed I had fallen behind taking pictures. They had already eaten dinner when I loomed out of the gloom around 6:00 PM. The next day they told me that I looked like a ghost as I stumbled into the light of the headlamps. My friends stripped off my wet clothes, redressed me in every spare bit of clothing I had, bundled me into my parka and Steve's expedition parka, put me in the sleeping bag and huddled close to warm me. I remember being so nauseous that I could not swallow hot beverages or food for hours. The shivering continued into the evening, but after a few hours I could get down some hot Jell-O and tea. By midnight I finally could eat solid food, and the scope of what was happening hit me. The next morning I was ravenous. We packed up and hiked out. I could feel the effects of the hypothermia for days, but was back out with my friends breaking trail on Street and Nye a few days later.

I'm convinced that my physical conditioning helped get me back to the tents, and my mental concentration allowed me to focus, however disoriented I was. I learned lots of valuable lessons in the Santanonis that weekend, beyond the example of what can happen without enough to eat and drink. It was humbling to face this incident at a time in my hiking career when I thought I was indestructible. These are probably lessons for others to ponder as well, which may be why the editor wanted me to share this uncomfortable experience with others. ᕦ

Alan M. Via: I was outings chair for the Albany Chapter of ADK for fourteen years, and have been ADK's insurance chair and risk manager for over twenty-two years, awarded the Distinguished Volunteer Award in 2006. I'm a multiple-round 46er, #1426W, and 3500er, completing the Catskill Hundred Highest in 2008 with my Labrador, Bookah. I've been married to my supportive wife, Barbara, for thirty-seven years, and we have two wonderful children.

64

MOUNT MARSHALL IN JANUARY

SO NEAR AND YET SO FAR

Louis R. Silver

To keep in shape, Seth, Freido, and I had been riding bikes at night in January using bike lamps on an unlit road. As much social gatherings as exercise, after the excursions we'd talk of many things over a beer. Freido and Seth are both big hikers; Freido has even hiked in the Italian Alps. He's a twenty-year veteran of the Adirondack High Peaks, with more interest in "being there" than "peak-bagging." I talked about some less popular peaks that I climbed to become a 46er. Freido seemed particularly interested; I was interested in stories of their winter hikes and overnight stays.

"We gotta do a winter climb" was heard around the table. I decided to do what I do best—delegate. Between the first and second Bass Ale, I told Seth he was in charge of picking a date. Much to my surprise, three days later Seth asked what time were we leaving tomorrow for the Adirondacks? Seth was foregoing opera tickets and his sons' college lacrosse game. I told him I could go. Freido decided we were doing Marshall—being the most experienced, he got to choose the mountain.

Our first mistake was not starting until 2:00 PM on Friday. All of us were involved in construction, and getting away early wasn't easy. We stopped at Rock & Snow in New Paltz to properly equip me, and $700 later I had plastic boots with molded insulated liners, high-tech lightweight snowshoes and insulated stretchie pants (thin, comfortable, and amazingly warm).

We arrived at the Upper Works trailhead at 8:00 PM. It was mid-January 2006 and 12°. I was so excited with my new Scarpa Alpha plastic boots—I pictured those guys climbing Everest with plastic boots and crampons, and now I was one of them. We hoisted fifty-pound packs and hiked 4.5 miles to Flowed Lands. Walking in from Upper Works was a phenomenon I have only experienced once before. The stars visible on a clear, moonless night here are tenfold that seen from the city or suburbs, where ambient light blots out less brilliant stars. Bright stars become quasars, and faint stars become shining stars. The sky is a 360° tapestry of light. We gazed up in awestruck amazement many times. I recommend a night walk if one should be lucky enough and conditions right to experience this magnificent, clear, sharp, blue-black background with diamonds cast on black velvet in copious quantities by the hand of God. The first half hour of hiking was worth the whole trip.

The Hudson River is in its infancy as it courses along the trail. The width of this formidable river is measured here only in feet, and it went mostly unnoticed during our night walk. We didn't notice Calamity Brook or the marker commemorating the death of a man for whom the calamity is named. But the sky—oh, the sky!

Arriving at 11:30 we found no room at the inn at the first lean-to. The sleeping bag-clad occupants barely moved so as not to have to make room for these late visitors. After checking the three lean-tos, we wandered out onto the frozen snow-covered lake, headlamps shining. The fourth lean-to overlooking the lake was also occupied with similarly non-responsive hikers. We backtracked 0.2 miles to the trail and headed toward Lake Colden, where there is a ranger station if all else failed. Forty-five minutes later we arrived at vacant accommodations. I never thought the site of an empty, three-sided, unheated, dark, log box sitting in the snow would look as good as it did that night at 12:30 AM.

We unrolled sleeping pads, unfurled bags and made ready to bed down. Seth and Freido didn't like the looks of my bag, temperature-wise, so Freido lent me an extra bag that he carries for when it gets "really cold." "Very cold," according to Freido, were negative-degree temperatures. I was very appreciative. After a ceremonial sip of wine that Seth had brought, we turned in. Seth cautioned us to keep any 2000 vintages (this was one) that we may have at home, because they are a premier year and will age well. He remarked that this one was excellent. I couldn't really savor the vintage, because it was being served about forty degrees too low and my mouth was a bit frozen. Sleeping bag inside sleeping bag worked well, but occasional small breaches in the upper mummy portion of my down tomb kept my shoulders and neck pretty chilly through the 9° night. We put our boot liners and water bottles inside our sleeping bags to keep them from freezing. By one o'clock we were asleep.

We finally crawled out of our sleeping bags at 9:45 AM. It was cold and snowing. We took out camp stoves and made coffee and oatmeal. I had brought a small percolator and made fresh-perked coffee. The little things sometimes are pretty big when you are in the woods. It was the best worst coffee I ever had. Seth and Friedo agreed. I also cooked Asian beef noodles. Meals in the woods don't conform to the strictly prescribed menus that are adhered to back in town. If it's hot and has calories, it can be breakfast. The noodles were pretty good.

We switched to day packs. They carried water, energy bars, a headlamp, two extra pairs of gloves, an extra shirt, a first-aid kit, a GPS, camera, compass, map, extra hat, extra batteries, and another, extra headlamp. Seth also had the remainder of the wine in his pack. I carried a GPS without information punched in, thanks to the rushed nature of the arrangements. That was mistake number two.

We put on our snowshoes and hiked back to the herd path to Marshall. It was well broken—the guys from the lean-to were tramping down many inches of snow. It snowed all day. As we headed up at 11:30 AM, we were very enthused. Once you get going, the cold is a nonissue. The trail mostly followed a wide streambed not overly cluttered with blowdown. We caught up with five well-equipped guys who informed us with a GPS that the summit was a mere 1.6 miles. We would bag this peak! Even with snow and steepness, it shouldn't be more than one and a half to two hours up, figuring an average of slightly less than one mile per hour. I was very excited at just how nice the winter experience was. The pines were draped with powdery pillows of snow. It was dead quiet, and the snow was falling in the most genteel manner as if only to add to our enjoyment of the experience. We tramped up the stream under blowdown and back and forth across the bed, sometimes climbing steep walls.

Our newly met, selfish lean-to companions went on ahead when we waited for Freido to fix a snowshoe. We caught up to them where they were stopped in the middle of the stream. One of them had gone through the ice up to his knee. No injury, but a very wet leg, which in 10° weather is a truly bad idea. The streambed wasn't safe, so we climbed out of the ravine. What an ordeal. Sixty-degree angled banks with snow that was getting very deep, about four feet now. Trees three feet apart with intermingled branches. Progress was slowed by a factor of ten. What took seconds was now taking minutes. Forty-five minutes later we made the semi-circle back to the stream and found we had progressed about three hundred yards. Our neighbors were heading off in a slightly different direction. The five guys from the other party disappeared.

Freido took the lead and followed a faint track. We were making progress again and things were looking great. We hiked for about an hour and met up again with the five. They were slightly ahead, so we gave up the lead. The streambed had ended, and now we were into the upper mountain. The other group reported the summit was ahead at .37 miles. That's when I started to be concerned. We had just spent two and a half hours on a fairly good path, with only one hard bushwhack, but had only gone 1.25 miles! Now we were facing a mega-steep part of the mountain, four feet of snow, and much slower going. Two more men joined us.

The ten of us bushwhacked off the herd path in an attempt to move directly to the summit according to the lead man and his GPS. We were west of the best route, heading up a very steep pitch thickly wooded with small pines. Mostly we were standing in a line and waiting as the lead guy made thirty yards of progress in ten minutes. We were getting cold. The nice balance of evaporating perspiration driven off by body heat created by new motion had ended. Now we were sopped hikers devoid of motion and losing heat quickly. All of a sudden the line started moving and we made some inroads. Two hundred yards gained. Then a dead stop and a wait for the number one guy to dig into the side of the hill with the steel points on his snowshoes and lift himself up by grabbing two trees and then squeezing between them. After thirty minutes Freido stated, "We're never gonna make it this way—we're off the herd path and making no progress. We're getting cold. Let's descend and see if we can find the herd path again. I never should've given up the lead."

I was deflated, but knew he was right. I had climbed about twenty high peaks and had yet to have a failed attempt. Seth had said that he felt Marshall was easy, but that was thirty minutes ago, before we left the streambed where we knew where we were. Now we were in danger of failing. We had ascended to 4,300 feet according to my watch. I never calibrated it at the trailhead, but I knew we were within two to three hundred feet of the top because it has never been off by that much. We were close, but in distance only. On a *time* scale we were nowhere near the summit. The going was slower than ever. If ten yards takes fifteen minutes, then 0.3 mile takes eleven hours!

Freido, Seth, and I descended three hundred feet, picked up what we thought was the correct trail to the east and headed back up. The faint trail had broken tree branches carved out of the wilderness. The only problem was the several feet of snow. Instead of benefiting from this tunnel through the woods, we were on four to five feet of snow and our heads were up in the trees where no tunnel existed. After thirty minutes, at 3:00 PM, we decided it was over.

With the best of luck we might summit in two hours. That would mean descent in the dark, arrival at our lean-to in mid-evening soaking wet with sweat, facing a zero-degree night. The forecast called for a much colder night. Freido had lent me his extra bag, and either he or I was going to spend a very bad night in a less than proper bedroll. We decided to hike out. I fell at least ten times on the way down, and twice went in up to my crotch into deep snow with snowshoes on. It took minutes to get up both times, struggling out of snow like it was quicksand, using my poles as rails to push down on the snow and gain some height back up onto the path. By 5:15 we had packed up. My hands were very cold. On the ascent, I had changed gloves after my first pair sweated through. I had taken my gloves off while packing, and even that brief time without protection made my fingers ache. I had to put my hands inside my pants for a while to get them back to working condition.

We arrived at the car at 8:00 PM. I was lagging behind the last half mile, fairly fatigued. My 240 pounds was taking its toll. My friends were in much better shape. Seeing the car on the way out was even better then seeing the lean-to on the way in. We all shed sopping shirts and socks and changed into dry clothes—they were zero degrees, but they were dry.

We drove to Schroon Lake for a late dinner and sat by the fire and talked of our errors, but also of the great experience. We agreed that, in our rush to go to the mountains, we had failed to study the map properly. If we had, we would have realized that upon leaving the streambed we needed to head more north and not so much west. In looking at the topo map, we saw that we were trying to make our way up a veritable cliff through the snow and thick hemlocks. I made a personal decision to be absolutely prepared next time and not to assume that one of my colleagues or the member of another party would know the way. We all had made the same assumption.

We arrived home at 2:30 AM. My wife was surprised to see me. I was happy to be in my own bed, instead of out in zero degrees in the middle of nowhere. One of my buddies once said to me that the definition of an adventure is something that is no fun when you are doing it. Not summiting Marshall in January was that, and more than that.

Epilogue: A year later our same intrepid group set off in the snow and cold and stayed in a Flowed Lands lean-to. Freido, Seth and I summitted Marshall in zero-degree weather on a clear January 7, 2007. We started earlier, planned better, took the right trail, and that made all the difference. 🏔

---

*L*ouis R. Silver: *I'm a lifelong resident, with my wife and two children, of Rock-land County, north of New York City—at least four hours from any Adiron-dack High Peak trailhead. I've hiked over two dozen Adirondack high peaks, mostly with my son William. On completion of all 46 high peaks, with any luck, I believe I will have carried more pounds of body weight to the top of those moun-tains than 97 percent of the hiking public.*

65

SURPRISE ON ALLEN MOUNTAIN

AND EN ROUTE

Doreen Heer

My sister Arlene and I had already climbed thirty-one high peaks and were anxious and ready to add Allen Mountain. From everything we had heard or read, Allen would be our biggest challenge yet in the quest for our 46 High Peaks. And Hurricane Floyd had created huge mountains of blowdown that would add to the challenge. We had prepared, pondered, packed, and repacked in anticipation of climbing this remote giant of a mountain.

Our strategy was to carry full packs into the lean-to at Flowed Lands. Bears were wreaking havoc in that area, so we had the place to ourselves. Early the next morning we packed daypacks and headed out, knowing that we had miles to walk just to get to the herd path. Each landmark exuded a "whoo-hoo!" from us. When we reached the gravel pit at the start of the herd path, our anticipation of Floyd's blowdown climbed up a notch. We stood in awe. We climbed on top of giant, log-sized "pick-up sticks," and as we went up, over, around and through, carrying hiking poles became difficult and cumbersome. We stashed the poles and flagged the spot so that we could find our way across this maze on our return. It was impossible to weave under these huge downed trees, so we walked on them and sometimes straddled them like cowgirls. What a blast! We laughed and balanced our way across. We chose a compass bearing based on an Internet account, and emerged from the blowdown at the herd path sooner than expected. Giggling and hugging, off we went, one step closer to Allen.

Climbing the Allen slide was exhilarating. We were excited at being close to the summit. Up, up, and up we climbed, and as we hit the ridge and walked toward the summit, Sis and I let out shrieks of delight. We read entries in the canister—we *just* missed Mark Lowell and Tom Haskins, whose accomplishments we admired. We heard thrashing near the summit, and out of the thicket popped two bloody, scratched, sweaty guys with big grins and outstretched hands. "Arlene, Doreen! Congratulations on getting Allen!" they said. We grinned back, shook their hands … wait … how did they know our names? And how did they get up here? We hadn't seen anyone signed in.

As it turned out, they had looked at trail registers and knew that two hikers were trying for Allen, which they found unusual at that time because of the mas-

sive blowdown. It was Mark Lowell and Tom Haskins, who had waited on the summit to see if we would make it; they were just beginning to bushwhack out when
they heard our yells. They took our picture and then dropped over the side of the
mountain and were gone. Wow. We remain friends to this day.

Now it was time to head back; we wanted to get through the blowdown before
dark. We reached it just before dusk and had to find our flagging. With close
observation we slowly followed our route through and found the hiking poles.
Exhausted, but happy to be out of the blowdown, our minds were ready to accept
the long walk ahead.

I passed a waist-high cut stump on which was a freshly killed rabbit with no
head. It hadn't been there on the way in. Hmmm. What would have bitten off the
head of a rabbit and left the rest? Or was "it" interrupted in the middle of its meal?
It was now dark, with a couple of miles still to go, and I was pooping out. Arlene
could hear my every audible sigh as I trudged along in front of her.

"Hey, Sis," she said, "wouldn't you like a nice glass of red wine when we get
back?" *Great*, I thought, *she knows we didn't have that on our provision list.* We'd
packed together, so I knew there was no wine. Why is she teasing me? "I hiked in a
really good bottle of red wine to celebrate," she said.

I stopped in my tracks. "You did?" We plodded to the lean-to and relived our
huge accomplishment over a bottle of wine. We had done Allen. And we had done
it through the blowdown from Hurricane Floyd.

It was sheer determination and perseverance, sprinkled with lots of humor
and laughter, that allowed my sister and me to reach these goals. It propelled us up
those glorious mountains, creating an adventure and story with every climb. 🏃

~~~~~~

*D*oreen Heer: I was busy raising my four children, so I had no idea how
climbing mountains could change my life. In 1995, at age forty-four, I climbed
Gothics with my sister, and after climbing the 46 High Peaks, #4853W, we climbed
them all in the winter. Now I share the love of nature and hiking with my three
beautiful grandchildren.

66

A MEMORABLE HIGH PEAKS WINTER CIRCUIT

...WHEREIN MOTHER NATURE COOPERATES TO MAKE AN IMPOSSIBLE TRIP MIRACULOUSLY POSSIBLE

Jack Freeman and Donald P. Berens Jr.

A sturdy group of nine from the Rochester Winter Mountaineering Society (RWMS) left on February 18, 1978, for a Presidents' Weekend snowshoe trip to the Adirondack High Peaks. The RWMS began in 1966 when Robert L. Collin, a veteran of the White Mountains, moved from Boston to Rochester. Collin needed winter hiking and camping companions, so he set about recruiting and training his own group for the Adirondacks. The group had no officers and no treasury; a winter trip schedule and a mailing list were all that held the group together. In the early years the schedule listed three or four trips per winter season, all led personally by Collin. By 1978 the schedule listed a trip for every weekend of solar winter.

The nine of us included five Kodak chemists—Jack Freeman, Roger Gillespie, Bill Goebel, John Robertson, and Lou Sorriero—legal eagle Don Berens, and three engineers, Charlie Clough, Bill Crowe, and Bob Fuss. After an overnight in Long Lake, it was 10° and overcast as we snowshoed past the Twin Brook lean-to site and along Upper Twin Brook on the trail into the pass between Cliff and Redfield.[1] Here the real work began. The ridge between the pass and Mt. Redfield had not been practicable since the 1950 hurricane littered this route with blowdown. But this was a winter season of deep snowpack, and conditions along the ridge were ideal—snow covered the blowdown and was well consolidated.

With frequent changes in trailbreakers, we stood atop Redfield at four o'clock. The canister was nowhere in sight, but Berens recalled from a summer visit that he had rested by a chest-high boulder next to which was a tree with the chin-high canister. He spied a low mound of snow that he took for the boulder and, pointing to the top of a nearby tree, said, "Dig here." We uncovered the canister under at least two feet of snow, so the snow depth atop Redfield that day was at least seven feet!

We descended to the east, crossing Moss Pond and up to a flat ridge top, pitching two tents with a view northeast to Skylight. We would have preferred to pitch three tents for a party of nine. Freeman, the organizer, had asked Fuss if he had a suitable tent—but failed to ask Fuss to actually *bring* it! So we stuffed four men in

Freeman's tent and five in Crowe's longer tent; cooking and sleeping conditions were cramped, but we made it work.

Sunday dawned clear and breezy at –6° after a night of light snow. Obtaining Mt. Skylight over easy terrain with well-consolidated snow, we were down to the Four Corners by ten o'clock. We climbed Gray Peak by way of Lake Tear, and then directly to the ice-encrusted summit of Mt. Marcy by 11:45, the latter ascent quite easy with no signs of the cripplebush that plagues summer traverses. We dropped to Four Corners and back toward the Cliff-Redfield pass. Since evening was fast approaching, we hurried to the top of Cliff, but the register canister eluded us.

Sunday evening's supper was a memorable event in the life of the RWMS. Berens prepared a sardine and beefstick stew. He and his messmates were hungry enough to make no vigorous complaint, but at the March 1991 twenty-fifth anniversary RWMS banquet at the Marcy Hotel in Lake Placid, that meal was among the three nominees for the worst RWMS meal ever served on the trail. Other finalists were oysters with Jack Daniels, and spaghetti au rum. We don't recall which meal won the applause/jeer-meter competition, but we suspect that it was Don's beefstick and sardine stew.

Summit, 5,344-Foot Mount Marcy. Photo by Carol White.

Overnight the temperature plummeted again to –6°. Then a sunny Monday had everyone eager to add Allen Mountain, so off we went with full packs, traversing southeast down the south flank of Skylight, crossing Skylight Brook at about 3,700 feet, contouring along the west side of McDonnel Mt., and in belly-deep snow up the northwest ridge of Allen Mt. to its summit at 11:30. Descending westward, frozen Allen Brook and Skylight Brook made convenient snow-covered highways down to the packed lumber roads along the South Branch Opalescent River. We encountered no problems with private leaseholders, nor did we notice any "No Trespass" signs. The frozen Opalescent River was easily crossed back to the yellow trail, and we were out before four o'clock. We had traveled thirty miles on snowshoes in the best conditions in these mountains that any of us can recall.

Berens was given to air drying his sweaty body efficiently without any intervening clothes. Fuss, wishing to preserve the details of this sensible method of personal hygiene, recorded the event on Kodak's best emulsion, but the picture turned out to be of limited use because it could not be displayed in mixed company. ☖

[1]Abandoned in 1980.

Jack Freeman: Upon retirement I worked as conservation associate for the ADK and as volunteer consultant and archivist. I am 46er #1327W, have summitted the high points of the fifty states and the Northeast 113 peaks over 4,000 feet in winter. I am a former personnel director and board member of the Cave Research Foundation, and hold membership in the Association for the Protection of the Adirondacks, the Residents Committee to Protect the Adirondacks, and the Adirondack Nature Conservancy.

For biography of Donald P. Berens Jr., see "Good Grief! Nineteen Years of Halloween Hiking."

67

WHAT YOU WALK UPON GROWS

46ING THE BUDDHIST WAY

Ronnie J. Cusmano

A *Rock and a Boot.* The sun was streaming down through trees at the Ausable Club gate, where I assured the man on duty that I would not stray from my planned route—over Gothics to Saddleback and Basin, retrace to Sawteeth and down. He warned of impending thunderstorms. I felt fortunate; it was Friday, and I'd have the trail mostly to myself.

At the Gothics-Sawteeth col, a light drizzle begins. Gothics is one of my favorite peaks, though I have yet to be there with the sun shining. The rain increases and at the summit, a deluge! All I see is a thick gray mass of swirling clouds and driving rain. Descending the slick rock face, suddenly I'm sliding down the bare rock toward stunted trees. When the slide ends, I notice long scrapes on my right calf and thigh. Shaken but tremendously relieved, staring into the swirling clouds and driving rain, I acknowledge the majesty of the mountains and their supreme indifference. Someone once said, "Y'know, those mountains, they just don't care."

I contemplate turning back. The clouds part ever so gently—an offering, a fleeting moment of something much larger than myself. I continue descending Gothics' cables. The descent off Saddleback's infamous rock face holds me breathless and suspended in the imagination of one false step. The negotiation of life and limb between the fortress of Saddleback and my mortality proves stark and moving. I am granted safe passage for a pleasant stroll to Basin.

The rain has been my companion for three hours. Having welcomed its coolness and refreshing effect on this warm day, I am peacefully enjoying this time. Saddleback invites me again into its magical mountainous majesty, and I find myself between a rock and a no-place as I sit precariously on a small outcrop halfway back up. I see the perfect little foothold and accompanying handhold to the right, if I can only get my left foot over to it. If I miss, I slide for who knows how far. I ease myself off to a small ledge three feet down and five feet below the foothold. I pile up four shoebox-sized rocks. With my step stool waiting, I think of my family and how lucky I am to have them with me now. I mount the step stool and stand there, taking a few deep breaths—I jump up, grab the handhold and hold on. Letting go is not an option any more. One breath, two, a third, and with all my strength I pull myself up. Blindly my foot scans for the foothold. YES! Boot sole, don't fail me now! Up I go.

Loosening my pack, taking a long drink, enjoying being alive, lying there on Saddleback's bare rock face with gentle rain cooling my face, trembling, I know how lucky I am. I will think about that. Up over Gothics—still no view. My favorite peak is still a stranger, still foreboding, still brooding. I love these rainy days. I stand near Sawteeth's summit and regard Gothics, Saddleback, and Basin in a wonderful gray backdrop. They look beautiful. I know them better now, and still know nothing of their true nature. I can only live the experience of their indifference and the joy of our contact, and appreciate the gift they gave to me today.

Some Scratches for Arlo. Day One. Some people think I'm crazy, some are indifferent, and others are impressed when I tell them what I am up to in these mountains. My wife and Arlo are in Maine, so I decide to take my show on the road again. Good luck has found me with my old-time backpacking buddy, "Iron Horse" (appropriately named), and with sun abounding and fair temperatures. We leave the trailhead at 7:00 AM full of expectations and full packs with bear cans in tow like Jacob Marley's money boxes. Oh, the burdens we bear in life.

At the Wright junction, having never been on this range, I'm eager to see what awaits us. I am happily surprised to find the summit wide open and barren and full of panoramic beauty. How much the views are a part of each mountain! On top of Algonquin, it is impossible to separate the two. Rock and air. Two elements of the mountain being linked for all eternity—rock, air, and, at times, me.[1]

On Iroquois, looking back at the range and all the different perspectives, I try to name every peak; then I start naming them after my favorite dead musicians—the Jimi Peak, Duane Allman Peak, the Janis Peak. *What would a mountain sound like*, I wonder, *if you traced its profile on a musical scale?*

Day Two. The beautiful morning sky was full of optimism. From the Opalescent River, we climbed Skylight and Redfield and then experienced Cliff, a friendly mountain that wants to make sure you get to know it intimately and never forget who Cliff is. Cliff likes to prod you, poke you again and again, to remind you where your hat is supposed to be and how much you really liked the shirt you're wearing and your "lightweight daypack" that now has that extra measure of breathability. When I'm on a peak, I like to think of something in my life that deserves to be left on the mountain. It brings peace to know that the mountain now has that little issue, thought, or problem under control and I no longer need to worry about it. Cliff gave me a different experience—I left physical pieces of myself on it—blood, sweat, and tears. A pair of hikers coming up the mountain agreed: "Looks like you've sprung a leak."

Arlo on Cascade. Photo by Ronnie J. Cusmano, a.k.a. Zero-G.

Meandering through swamps over planks, heaving full packs five hundred feet up to Lake Arnold in the midday sun, I think: *If I faint, mosquitoes and leeches will consume me; no one would want to go down to find me.* From the Mt. Colden junction, with daypacks lightly on our shoulders, life flicks a switch—on Colden's north summit I am profoundly captivated by the expansive views. The summit of Colden proudly beckons me, dancing in and out of sight; Avalanche Lake and the Pass are visible far below. I take in the glory of the moment and explore Colden to the southern tip. All is quiet and I see mountains, lakes, blue skies filled with high, billowing, white, fluffy clouds. I hear my son's little voice in my head, "Daddy?" I reply, "Yes, Arlo?" "Did that mountain scratch you again?" "Yes, Arlo." "Are you okay?" "Yes, Arlo, Daddy's okay."

Back at the summit I turn to Iron Horse. "Sometimes when I see things as perfect as this I realize why I keep coming back. When my boys grow up and know their daddy is a 46er, perhaps they'll want to come here too, and maybe they'll think of me and know how much I love them." Sitting quietly at Indian Falls, the water gently flowing down, hammocks strung, the sun is setting behind the MacIntyre Range. It couldn't be more perfect.

Day Three. The climb up Tabletop feels anti-climatic, but now the goal—seven more peaks—is in sight. The sun streams through the trees, and we see an elderly gentleman who is as surprised as we are to see anyone this early in the middle of somewhere feeling like nowhere. As we move closer to civilization, we encounter staggering numbers of day hikers. We have a good laugh, commenting on how nice they smell and imagining what they might be saying about how "nice" we smell.

The Mountain, The Teacher. We mere mortals personify mountains, perhaps because of our struggle of ego versus rock. Allen Mountain left a lasting impression. At 5:15 AM there is a chill in the air and I waste no time in keeping my appointment with Allen. I am surprised by a metal, bouncy suspension bridge that seems oddly out of place in the mountain's material makeup. As I walk, I have thoughts. More truthfully, my thoughts have me. I ask myself serious questions, not so serious questions, inane questions, and downright silly questions. Then the big question— why am I talking to myself so persistently? Allen requires much time for traversing ten miles over undemanding terrain that doesn't require the focus I'm accustomed to, so I talk to myself. My radio is tuned to my favorite song while I have make-believe conversations with my wife, son, friends, the guy who almost ran me off the road, and the milkman who delivered milk when I was a child.

Wow! A floating log bridge! I check the map and the GPS—I haven't gone far. Waypoints come and go; despite the monotony of step after step, I'm making something of the day. Allen, the old sage, the all-knowing presence, insists that I get in touch with myself the way only walking meditation can provide. Another bouncy wooden suspension bridge ... miles of berries ... suddenly, a large wooden sign, shouting in full fury " ← MARCY", followed by a bellowing and forceful wooden sign "ALLEN →". Make no mistakes, the waypoints affirm. The mind quiets as focus increases. The stream and the bandana offer cool respites as I climb steeply over slippery rocks, twisted roots, and through deep, black mud. Allen dominates all thoughts and demands full attention. Not long ago Allen wanted nothing to do with me—Allen wanted me to do with me. Now I belong to Allen, which physically and emotionally consumes me. I approach the summit, and finally Allen presents the "fruits of labor." Like the wizard behind the curtain, Allen exposes its gentle presence, a peaceful summit with shade and cool breezes, modest views and much wisdom. I am invited to lunch and a well-deserved rest.

I start back at eleven o'clock, the steep streamed with its slick rocks offering many opportunities for pause and care. Allen is bidding farewell and conversations pick up where they left off, radio tuned to that familiar song, berries now in a bag, the wooden bridge, the floating bridge, the steel bridge, the trail register. At 3:00 PM my life is better than it was at 5:15 AM—with the wisdom of Allen now permanently etched within.

A Peak at a New Life. Waking to a starry sky at 4:30 AM, my mind strays to the forecast—rain. "Little Boot" readies her daypack. I am excited; today will complete the 46! Myriad birds dance about as if to provide escort along Lake Road. A campsite is draped with clothing set out to dry. My companion tends an injured bird with water and relocates it out of harm's way. Golden rays of sun stream through the trees. Colvin's summit dazzles my senses. Morning light and mountaintops work well together.

Feeling content and peaceful in the seclusion of Blake's summit, I notice my attention turning inward. All the effort put forth to climb these peaks, I live in the question "Why?" Back at Elk Pass, frogs splash in the wetlands. I want nothing more than to enjoy each breath, each step to Nippletop. The climb is joyful and serene, and the summit welcomes us with a cooling breeze and clear views. My acknowledgments and blessings take on new life and flow deeper into the valleys and over the mountaintops.

In concert with air, light, rock, body, speech, and mind, we set off toward Dial. The sky is gray, delivering well-deserved coolness. Each breath is an affirmation. The approach to Dial is effortless and so peaceful. Turning to the summit rock, I "see" a lotus flower. Sitting, I gaze off into air, wind, clouds, mountains, trees, water, earth … and I understand "why." May all sentient beings have happiness and the cause of happiness; may they be free from suffering and the cause of suffering; may they not be separated from the true happiness that is beyond suffering; may they remain in the state of equanimity that is beyond partiality, desire, or aversion; may all the benefits and happiness I receive from this accomplishment be for the benefit of all sentient beings. *Om mani padme hum.* I think of my family and all who helped me. I thank "Little Boot" for supporting me. A celebration, and we leave the friendly summit of Dial, this unexpected jewel of a mountain. A cool rain falls, a cleansing; a new beginning waits. I shall not decide what that new beginning is. A shower, a dinner … I think I'll have that ice cream sundae now. 🚶

[1]Reminiscent of Poet Li Po: "The birds have vanished into the sky, / and now the last cloud drains away. / We sit together, the mountains and me, / until only the mountain remains."

---

*R*onnie J. Cusmano: *A native of New York City, my spiritual path was revealed when the whispers of my ancestors entered my heart whilst "sitting" at Wupatki near Flagstaff, Arizona. In the Hopi reservation I studied the Hopitu—The Peaceable People. I am now a practicing Buddhist, combining meditation and walking; the mountains became one perfect vehicle for finding peace and understanding of the mind in each step. The "path" led me to my wife, Gina, and sons Arlo and Jaco, the most precious gems in my life. I am 46er #5865.*

68

CALAMITY IN OUR TIMES

PLANTING GOOD SEEDS

Dean Macgeorge

I don't drink. I hike, telemark ski, and kayak instead. It used to be the other way around, but I've seen the light and have grown up a bit in the last fifteen years. In this new state I find myself hiking toward Flowed Lands from Upper Works for the first time, to spend two nights at the Calamity Brook lean-to area. I'm working on becoming a 46er and have my eye on Marshall, Redfield and Cliff. Up the trail I meet a father and his son who have been bear hunting unsuccessfully. I've read about bears in this corridor in the Adirondacks and am surprised that they didn't see any. I'm a little relieved, although I'm not quite sure why.

When I arrive at the lean-to, I meet four fellows who just got there, ask them where they're from and what their plans are. They're from Pennsylvania and have come to the Adirondacks for their yearly backpacking trip, which they've been doing for the past ten years. They ask me if I'd like to share the lean-to, and I accept, even though I have a tent. They look like they could be interesting.

Having hiked the 4,000-foot mountains in Vermont and New Hampshire, the Catskills many times, and having been a Scout leader for years, I feel confident of my abilities in the woods. I like to challenge myself by bringing just what is needed—nothing more, nothing less. I call it "being dialed," and so I watch in awe as these guys unpack their gear in the lean-to. Large amounts of heavy food (meats and such) still in the store wrappers, chips, Fritos, salsa, and loads of beer and booze spill from the oversized packs. One guy even has a full-size six-person car camping tent! But no bear canister. I explain about the bears, but they seem unconcerned. Then the bags of marijuana come out, and they soon become even less concerned.

I ask them if they'd like to join me on a hike to Marshall, and three agree. The fourth decides to take a bottle and his bag of pot down to the water's edge in search of God, or so he announces. The others are glad to get a break from the guy, as he'd been struggling with the drink and substance abuse and was looking to get crazy this weekend. Oh boy, I'm going to have to watch this guy.

Halfway up Marshall, the boys ask two guys we meet about views at the summit. Told there were none, they head back. I meet up with folks near the summit and we eat lunch together, basking in the sun with fine views to the south past the summit. We hike into Iroquois Pass and out by Lake Colden, making for a fine loop.

Back at camp I find the six-person tent set up about a foot in front of the lean-to. The boys ask about the hike, and I show them pictures of the view. They are displeased that they had turned around, because all they'd been doing was getting stoned and drunk. Conversation went like this: (first guy) "Let's go down by the water"; (second guy) "Let's smoke a joint first"; (first guy) "I like your attitude!" And so it went.

They are fun to watch, especially when they set up their bear bag four feet off the ground! I loan out a lot of gear, because they had forgotten stuff like forks and knifes, flashlights, cups, aspirin, and such. Three of them stay in the lean-to and one in the tent. One guy gets cold feet in the middle of the night and borrows my down booties. I'm always glad to help others. There is a ruckus by their bear bag, and most of the food is gone when we get up. They are unconcerned. I ask why. They tell me that most of their food was in the lean-to. I explain that they shouldn't be doing that, especially here. They respond with blank stares.

I take off toward Redfield and Cliff. Great hike. Cliff is a blast with all that blowdown. After dinner I suggest that they give me their food and I'll put it in my canister. I say that they should roll a big fat joint, smoke it, and eat everything else. In unison they respond, "We like your attitude!" I am fitting right in!

Talk turns to what had been accomplished that weekend. They are impressed with the fact that I climbed the mountains I'd planned on doing, animals never got to my food, and I was never feeling "out of sorts." I keep my mouth shut, as actions usually speak louder than words. They start to question their accomplishments. They had planned to hike to Avalanche Lake, but did not. There was talk of climbing Mount Colden. Never came off. They become interested in my not drinking and drugging, and I spend the rest of the night answering questions. I explain that Mother Nature couldn't be improved upon with any mood-altering substance. This seems to make the most sense to them. I'd like to think that their next trip will be different and positive. 🏃🏃

*D*ean Macgeorge: I started hiking in the Catskills with my son Chris when he became a Boy Scout. After finishing the Cat 35, I did them again in winter. It was time to give back, and I became a trail maintainer on West Kill Mountain, which I still do today. The White Mountains were my next stop, then the Adirondacks (46er #5716), and the Vermont and Maine 4,000-footers. I taught myself telemark skiing and kayaking, which I enjoy as much as hiking; they add a nice balance.

69

LUCK COUNTS IN THE ADIRONDACKS

WAITING FOR THAT TELLTALE CRACK

Marty Cohen

During a week of Adirondack peak-bagging frenzy, we met our friend Kevin and packed in five miles to near the base of the Seward Range, where we set up camp and climbed Seymour uneventfully. The next morning was foggy, and we quickly lost the path, so we spread out to increase our chances of stumbling on the elusive mud track. From fifty yards away Wanda yelled, "I'm on the herd path!" Then Kevin yelled, "I'm on the herd path." I was tracking an established mud channel and yelled, "I'm on the herd path!" We decided to rely on the compass and persevered through challenging territory to Seward and through wet fog to Donaldson and Emmons along unambiguous herd paths. Descending Seward, we vowed not to lose the herd path, which we quickly did, and again resorted to the compass to find our camp, successfully and before dark! We'd just finished dinner when a deluge fell, driving us into our tents.

The next morning we headed out. Coming in, we'd crossed a brook with no difficulty, but after the deluge the streams were high and bridge logs were soaking wet. Wanda crossed first. My foot slipped in between two of the saplings halfway across, and my body, under the control of my sixty-pound pack, canted to the left and I tumbled sideways off the bridge into the stream—with my left leg still wedged in between two logs! As I was toppling over in slow motion, the thought ran through my brain that I was about to suffer my first broken bone. Wanda and Kevin were waiting for the telltale crack. Miraculously, as I fell into the stream, landing on my backpack, my knee had folded perfectly around the outermost log so that, although I was lying in the stream on my pack with my left leg yet entrapped between the logs a couple of feet above me, all my bones were intact!

Kevin edged onto the bridge where he said, quite formally, "Can I be of any assistance?"

I replied, far less formally, "Get me out of here!"

He pulled me up, pack and all, impressing me that slim Kevin had the strength to elevate my 180 pounds with its 60-pound backpack. I didn't break my leg—but should have. 🚶

Bear bag near Ward Brook lean-to. Photo by David White.

*M*arty Cohen: In my forties I became hooked on long-distance running, then drifted into cross-country skiing and hiking. I am 46er #4191. Later I became involved with trail maintenance and taking city children hiking, which expanded to teaching kids to play clarinet and saxophone. My wife, Wanda, a regular Adirondacks trail maintainer and 46er director, and I are hosts at the ADK Loj campground.

70

A MAN-KILLER HIKE?

THIS ONE SHOWS "WHAT A MAN IS MADE OF"

Ray Bell

In 1973, with twelve of the 46 in my peak-bagging portfolio, I decided I wanted to be a 46er! My friend Jim Heron had done them all many times and had a reputation for assisting anyone in their quest. I said that I could go only once a month, being a father of two. We planned short hikes, like Cascade and Porter, when daylight was limited and long hikes, like Allen, in June. As I approached thirty peaks Jim said, "I found an interesting hike I'd like to try." It would be very difficult and we'd stay at the Adirondak Loj for an early start—which for Jim was 9:00 AM! I'd learned that, if I walked four miles every night for a month, I could do Jim's man-killer hikes. Before the hike I walked five miles in an hour one night, after a month's conditioning.

The weather was clear that June day—no rain and a temperature in the sixties, perfect hiking weather. We carried a light pack—poncho, a couple of sandwiches, water, no purifier or pills for the additional water we'd be taking from brooks and springs, a light jacket, and a hat. Years later I would never have left so unprepared, but I was young, foolish, and under the wing of Jim, whom I trusted entirely. We quickly climbed Mount Marcy on the Mount Van Hoevenberg Trail, descended to the gap between Marcy and Gray, and started the 300-foot climb up Gray. This was tough, but the month of conditioning was paying off and we soon started down to Lake Tear of the Clouds, the source of the Hudson River. Next was 600 feet up Mt. Skylight, its summit adorned by a huge rock cairn from which is a magnificent view.

"Where the heck is Redfield?" I asked. Jim pointed to a mountain in the distance. "It's a three-mile bushwhack to Redfield," he told me. How did I ever agree to this? And we still had Cliff after Redfield. The bushwhack was mostly downhill in an open forest with Moss Pond visible through the trees and virtually no blowdown. But all good things come to an end—I can *still* feel myself pulling on those trees and branches, pushing against them with my boots, crawling on my stomach over rocks and downed trees up that last three hundred feet. The black flies, with us all day, began to bite, and I can still feel those biting flies! At the limited summit view, I remember saying, "Jim, let's go! I can't get up, but these flies will lift me."

At the lean-to at the base of Cliff, it quickly became totally dark, so all we had to do was ascend 500 feet to Lake Arnold and walk seven or eight miles back with flashlights. I was so tired that all I remember is a sign that said, "Trail Closed." But I got a second wind! Passing a Boy Scout campsite at midnight where the leader told us that we shouldn't be out at night because we could get hurt, we never even slowed down. I remember walking as fast and feeling as good as I had in the morning. The total distance of the hike was twenty-two miles with an elevation gain of about 6,000 feet. Sometimes the biggest ascent in the Adirondacks is the 200 feet back up to the parking lot! That night we hiked it like it was level ground, finally finishing at 3:00 AM. I was asleep before we reached Route 73, and didn't wake up until we made a breakfast stop. My house was locked and I had no key, so I crawled into the camper and slept until noon. I was forty-five years old; Jim was fifty-nine. A heavy smoker, he died the following year from lung cancer. He had been a POW in Germany, and maybe that, plus getting free cigarettes during World War II, got him started smoking. He tried to quit, but couldn't. I'll never forget the hikes we shared and the stories he told. His wife told me that he liked to take people out on long hikes to see what they were made of. He never told me what he thought I was made of, but he was a good friend. 🚶

*R*ay Bell: *Two fathers climbed Mount Washington with their boys; the joy of leaning into a 60-*MPH* wind and being held up by it was a new, ecstatic experience. They went the wrong way, and Dad later hitchhiked to the car. At age fifty, hiking the 46, I realized what my father went through—how lucky I was to have such a wonderful dad. I completed the 46 in 1980 (#1653), the 111 4,000-footers in the Northeast in 1991, and the Appalachian Trail in 2003.*

71

A THREE-SEASON HIKE IN JUNE

WHAT IF ADAM'S GROUP HAD TURNED BACK?

Adam S. Morrell

My friends Seth and Kit and I hiked to Slide Brook lean-to in order to climb the Dix Range in June 2006. With sunny skies and temperatures in the seventies, we set up camp at the lean-to, made a fire, and enjoyed ourselves before the long hike.

At 6:00 AM we set off for Macomb and the temperature plummeted as we climbed the slide. It was 44° with wind chills in the low 30s, and it started raining. At the top of the slide we had the best views of inside a cloud that anyone could ask for! At the boulder field near South Dix/Carson it began snowing and when we stopped, we found ourselves shivering. At the summit of Grace/East Dix, ice pellets hit us in the face in a 30-MPH wind—potential for hypothermia. By 4:30, climbing 800 feet to the Beckhorn, we were whipped!

Here it started to get interesting. On Friday while we were eating dinner, two guys and a girl came in, all twenty years old. It was their first time in the Adirondacks, and they planned on spending ten days in the backcountry. On the Beckhorn, we heard cries for help and saw a head appear from below. It was one of the guys we'd met. He had the girl's pack with him and was heading down to get his pack. The girl was in bad shape and freezing to death. We told him there was no way she was going to make it to the Boquet River lean-to before dark in her condition. Seth and Kit took turns carrying her pack down the mountain, while I helped her down. The worst blowdown was on the descent from the Beckhorn.

The two guys disappeared when they figured we would help the girl; I was angry that they had ditched her. An hour later we saw them, waiting, then they took off again as if just insuring she was in good hands. It was as though she was a burden to them. After two hours of the three of us taking turns with her pack, I caught up with them, told them the girl was feeling better and that we were going to press on without them. I told one of the guys not to let her out of his sight; he agreed and said that leaving her behind was a stupid thing to do. We were relieved to learn later that they made it back safely. The trail back was a river, with areas of standing water two feet deep. We finally made it back just after 9:00 PM.

This was the first time that I experienced three-season hiking in June—summer sun, spring rain, winter snowflakes and freezing rain ice pellets. Unreal! We

Seth on Macomb Slide. Photo by Adam S. Morrell.

ran into Wende Grubbs Hokirk and her husband, Larry, who had adopted the herd path to Macomb and were going in to do a blowdown sweep. Wende is in the book *Women with Altitude*, so it was really cool meeting her. One thing I learned from this trip is that the Adirondacks are not forgiving if you are ill-prepared. 🏃

A dam S. Morrell: My journey began with my parents taking me to the Adirondacks every summer. My first backpacking experience in college was to Marcy Dam to climb Phelps. I was hooked and completed the 46 (#6111) on Giant on the 70th anniversary of 46er historian Grace Hudowalski's finish. My understanding wife and I have a five-year-old daughter, and one day I hope she'll hike with her daddy.

Part III:

ADVENTURES IN THE GREATER ADIRONDACKS

I saw the silhouette of the culprit approaching from the lake, crawling on all fours toward the lean-to. Fear embraced me as I stared into the eyes of a black bear, huge by any standard. Should I run? Not quite paralyzed from overwhelming fear, I scuttled into my sleeping bag to feign sleep, trembling and with perspiration soaking the bag and me. ... An eternity passed; bravely I poked my head from beneath my sleeping bag and peered into the darkness, wondering why the fire pit appeared to be so close. Alas, it was the bear, obviously unafraid of my presence. The last sound I heard before fainting was the bear sniffing my sleeping bag

Paul A. Sirtoli, "Adventuresome Appetites"

Dominic Luckhurst. Photo by Neil Luckhurst.

72

WHY DO WE HIKE?

WILDERNESS: MORE A STATE OF MIND AND SPIRIT THAN A PLACE

Bruce C. Wadsworth

I have hiked some 4,000 miles in the last twenty years, sharing trails with friends in all seasons, enduring both the nasty bite of the black fly and the searing bite of the winter wind above tree line. The question, "Why do we hike?" brings on a rush of memories that makes my answer one that is more felt than spoken.

Twenty years ago, heading back to Heart Lake after spending an unplanned wet night in the col between Street and Nye, my family met a lone hiker heading into the woods. I'll never forget him. He said, "I love this rain—it drives everybody out of the woods. I have them all to myself." With a big grin he bounced off along the trail toward Scott Clearing.

Unexpected things happen on hikes. From a ledge on Brown Mountain in the Tongue Mountain Range, my young son and I gazed down on Lake George. Not wanting to frighten him, I nevertheless felt he should be cautioned that rattlesnakes were on this ridge.

"Pete, you have to watch where you step—sometimes snakes are found up here."

"I know, Dad, there's one over here."

In a rock crevice, where it couldn't coil to strike, a timber rattler was quietly trying to crawl to safety, more frightened of Peter than Peter was of it. The unexpected and unplanned make up a great portion of why we leave the comforts of home to swat deer flies on Blue Ridge, wade chest-deep across the Miami River, climb an ice-swept ridge, or maybe just pick up a day pack and mosey along a trail to a nearby pond to look at the shore flowers. They invigorate the mind.

Setting up camp beside Fall Stream near Piseco, my wife and I noticed another couple. The husband quietly sat by the cook fire while his wife hustled about collecting firewood, doing all the chores. It seemed peculiar, but the man had a contemplative look on his face and the wife, though obviously tired, happily carried out her tasks. I alternated between envying the man his astounding good luck to have such a wife and annoyance at his inactivity. After dinner we introduced ourselves and learned that the husband was blind. Besides hiking the Northville-Placid Trail, they winter-camped, hiked in desert country, and canoe-camped. The following morning they set off at a good pace, the woman's long, flowing shirttail tightly gripped by her husband as they disappeared up the long grade to Spruce Lake. Our own problems didn't seem too big that day. We felt we knew why they hiked, but we still don't fully grasp the extent of their great courage.

To experience change in your daily routine, to let the nerve endings rest awhile, to learn how to live from other human beings—that's all part of it. Climbing off Basin on our way to Saddleback, we met doctors Howard and Elizabeth Jaffe studying a fault zone. Recognizing us and knowing of my interest in geology, Howard exclaimed, "This is the most exciting place in the Adirondacks!" He began explaining thrust faults, Grenville Orogeny, and many fascinating pieces of geological information. It was 1984, and I remembered reading his 1941 *Adirondac* article on Adirondack geology. That's a long time to study a problem. The mountains do not give up their secrets easily, nor do they reveal

View of Lake George from the Tongue Range. Photo by Bill Ingersoll.

them to the impatient. It is in knowing you are getting closer to the answer each time you head into the hills that makes you keep accepting the challenge. We each have our private challenges, and it's the way we meet them that is important. It is the journey, rather than whether the goal is reached, that gives meaning to life. To persevere against unforgiving mountains makes persevering in everyday life much easier.

In 1977 my daughter and I stopped hiking rather early on a very hot day. After lunch we gazed at the Sawtooth Mountains from Moose Pond lean-to for a long time, with little inclination to do more than melt into the setting. Suddenly, the largest snowshoe hare I've ever seen fearlessly hopped into view from behind the lean-to. Its fierce glare made me realize it was either a close relative of the General in *Watership Down* or the imperial beast itself. Eleven years later my wife and I completed a difficult bushwhack to the summit of Rocky Mountain in the Catskills. A snowshoe hare hopped over to us to observe the strange interlopers. In each case there was no fear of us; we felt part of nature, rather than intruders. Animals, trees, sky, brooks, and everything else in wilderness can somehow become part of you when you accept them unconditionally. Once you realize this, hiking becomes a release that nurtures self-growth, a stimulus that resurrects your spirit, and an enjoyment that is both timely and timeless.

We glided along the dim shoreline of Long Lake through early morning fog. Only dripping beads of water as we lifted paddles from the water made the slightest sound. Faint traces of rain brushed my face. Silent mallards edged out of view back into the haze, permitting only momentary glimpses of ghostly forms. The air was still, and my mind wandered to another morning years ago. I'd slipped out of my sleeping bag without waking anyone to tread quietly to the end of a rocky peninsula jutting out into Pharaoh Lake. The coolness, fog, and silence encapsulated me in such a reverie that I might have been alone on some distant galaxy. In solitude you can detach yourself from the unimportant to arrive at clarity of thought that absorbs every event into your being—not as isolated stimuli, but as a cohesive whole that an uncluttered mind can instantly assimilate.

Is it the silence of the forest that we escape to, in order to renew ourselves? It was Bob Marshall who said, "For me and for thousands with similar inclinations, the most important passion of life is the overpowering desire to escape periodically from the clutches of a mechanistic civilization. To us the enjoyment of solitude, complete independence, and the beauty of undefiled panoramas is absolutely essential to happiness." Wilderness is more a state of mind than a physical place; hiking is as much an inward journey as an outward one. That is why, in different ways, the person who walks for ten minutes along a path by a gurgling brook can be renewed as much as the technical climber who reaches the top of Wallface's cliffs. Is it an escape, or a returning home? 🏃🏃

From the Adirondack Mountain Club newsletter, Winter 1991–1992. Reprinted with permission.

*B*ruce C. Wadsworth: *I was an Eagle Scout, a graduate of the BSA National Aquatic School, a waterfront director in scout camps, an instructor in the Voyager Program, and a winter camping instructor with the Boy Scouts. I worked with the Indian Guide Program in the YMCA. I am a 46er, #1340, an active outdoor hiker, skier, and paddler. I chaired several ADK committees and authored ADK's* Day Hikes for All Seasons: An Adirondack Sampler; An Adirondack Sampler II: Backpacking Trips; Guide to the Northville Placid Trail; Guide to Adirondack Trails: Central Region; Guide to Catskill Trails; *and* With Wilderness at Heart, A Short History of the Adirondack Mountain Club.

ADVENTURESOME APPETITES

WILD EXPERIENCES

Paul A. Sirtoli

Adirondack Highs. I can't pinpoint when my interest in the Adirondacks became a very strong attraction. My wife, Joanne, will sometimes say the Adirondacks are my first love, a relationship richly steeped in personal history, friends and memories, and with the promise of more to come. The lure of the Adirondack wilderness tugs at my soul; perhaps it is a pantheistic calling to find balance in my life. Maybe the remote mountain or the isolated pond or the tranquil brook is my personal hideaway to de-stress from the daily routine of being a teacher, father, and husband. I have explored many nooks and crannies in the park solo, and with friends and family, and each excursion carves a meaningful notch in my heart.

Cooney Lake, a.k.a. Lost Pond, off the Northville-Placid Trail, will always be near and dear to my heart until my last breath. That little circular pond provided hours and lessons in patience for my sons while we fished for brook trout. I can envision the warm breeze and azure sky as we floated round and round in the john boat that I found hidden near the shoreline. Remembering the glee and excitement in Aaron or Jordan when that sudden tug of the line jolted us from our reverie, and the commotion that followed to net that huge fish, still brings a tear to my eye. Each tug of the line prompted the kids to plead, "A little while longer, Dad?" Those fishing trips have led us to other Adirondack adventures that the boys and I will always treasure. They, in turn, have become masters in making their own adventures.

Bear Encounter. One memorable rainy night at the Cedar Lake lean-to along the Northville-Placid Trail, lingering sounds from a wet forest canopy found me nervously shining my light toward the lakefront for animal intruders. I was particularly wary of animals that night because I had absentmindedly neglected to pack a rope to hang my food bag. This lean-to had a voluminous trash dump nearby. Faint critter trails spiraled away from this heap of refuse. Not to be outsmarted by mice and chipmunks, I hung the food bag from a rafter in the lean-to, next to my backpack. Although somewhat concerned, I squelched the rising knot of trepidation inside me and prepared for the overnight respite. Having no one to converse with and with a steady rain pounding the region, I settled into my sleeping bag.

Weariness eventually overcame me and I drifted into a fitful repose, wondering what animal would dare enter the lean-to to filch the food.

A loud snap from inside the lean-to startled me from my reverie. Alarmed, I scanned the area with my flashlight, noting that my food bag was gone! Suspecting hiking thieves, I hastily dressed and scouted the muddy trail. Although it had stopped raining, water droplets from the trees were pounding the earth, muffling any other sounds that there might be. I returned to the lean-to, sat against the back wall facing the lake, and with broom in hand waited for the thief's return. I saw the silhouette of the culprit approaching from the lake, crawling on all fours toward the lean-to. Fear embraced me as I stared into the eyes of a black bear, huge by any standard. *Should I run?* Not quite paralyzed from overwhelming fear, I scuttled into my sleeping bag to feign sleep, trembling and with perspiration soaking the bag and me. Heavy rain droplets from trees pounded the roof and muffled any sound that might be coming from the bear, so I never knew his exact whereabouts. An eternity passed; bravely I poked my head from beneath my sleeping bag and peered into the darkness, wondering why the fire pit appeared to be so close. Alas, it was the bear, obviously unafraid of my presence. The last sound I heard before fainting was the bear sniffing my sleeping bag!

I awoke very early, fearful that the bear might still be lingering. Not only had he snatched my food bag, but he'd also emptied my pack and scattered its contents. Not eager to get up and possibly stumble across a sleeping bear, I remained in the damp sleeping bag until daybreak. A careful inspection of the area turned up all my scattered equipment. Other than a scratch or a tooth mark, however, everything (including myself!) remained unscathed. Now for the long twenty-five-mile hike out with little food! It took me two days to hike to my car. As a result of that encounter, to this day I have second thoughts about solo camping, and even solo hiking.

I have since learned that it is to your advantage to know your adversary. Black bears are curious but timid, and will try to avoid humans. Be noisy when setting up camp, as bears will generally steer a course away from you. They are unpredictable and may attack if startled or provoked. They are sexually active in June and are more incautious then. Their stomach always comes first, especially if sweet food is available! Don't bring any food or sweets into your sleeping area, and especially not into your sleeping bag. Cook well downwind from your sleeping quarters, clean all cookware thoroughly, and don't sleep in the clothes you wore when cooking. Bears are nocturnal, so look for them in the evenings.

Current regulations in the Adirondack High Peaks require carrying a bear canister, which can be rented or purchased. If you are without a bear canister, left-over food and rubbish should be wrapped in a plastic bag and placed in a food bag hung fifteen feet above the ground from a solid limb of a tree well downwind

from the sleeping area. It may be wise to also leave clothes you wore while cooking with the food bag. If a bear approaches, don't panic and run; slowly back off to
avoid threatening the bear. Bears can run twenty-five miles per hour, though not
for a long distance, and they are excellent climbers. Be especially careful if cubs
are around, as the mother will be protective of them. Let the cubs do their own
thing without your interference. Provoked bears will chop their jaws and exude a
low woofing, growling sound. They have sensitive hearing, and whistle blasts will
usually send them scurrying away. Banging pots and pans may achieve the same
effect. Bears are the essence of wildness. We are the visitors, the intruders. It is for
us to accommodate these magnificent creatures and preserve their right to exist in
a wilderness that is essentially theirs.

Deliverance. A three-day Spruce Lake Mountain bushwhack with Jay O'Hern
and Mike O'Donnell had some sinister aspects. During our last day of hiking,
we were fatigued. Carrying full packs through dense brush, blowdown, and over
streams delayed us considerably. We would not reach the car by nightfall. A roar of
thunder persuaded me that we should find a suitable campsite now and finish the
trek the next day. Jay and Mike wanted to push on to the Spruce Lake lean-to, but
the approaching storm was soon upon us. Sheets of wind-driven rain and ominous
thunderclaps forced us to make camp immediately. I hastily erected my Eureka tent.
Jay and Mike, striving to travel light, had brought only a small tarp. I'm ashamed to
admit that my callous side got the best of me; I wouldn't share my tent with my hiking buddies, choosing to let them get soaked beneath their little tarp for the entire
night. One must be vigilant when common sense does not prevail!

The next day featured a chapter out of the movie *Deliverance*. Several large trees
during the thunderstorm had fallen across the gravel road from the Spruce Lake
trailhead to Perkins Clearing. Being a runner, I volunteered to jog down the road to
find help. I flagged down three scruffy fellows in a dilapidated pickup truck who were
more than eager to help out. All were carrying pistols. Listening to them denounce
the "communistic" DEC (Department of Environmental Conservation) rangers and
the "subversive" Adirondack Mountain Club—with little me squeezed in between
them—made for a disconcerting ride, to say the least. I became really concerned
when they didn't drive to the gravel road where our vehicle was, but instead drove
down a series of dirt roads to an old camp. I was warned that if I knew what was good
for me, I should keep my mouth shut about the location of the camp.

I was relieved to see several children and women there. The men picked up gas
cans and chainsaws, and we drove to the fallen trees. The trees were removed in no
time. With hands on holsters, a monetary reward was suggested. I generally carry
little cash; Jay is good for a few dollars; and then Mike cracks a joke and hands over
a twenty. We're free to go.

Cedar Lake, Northville-Placid Trail. Photo by Bill Ingersoll.

Terror Lake. This remote pond was aptly named as far as Joanne is concerned. Tucked away north of Big Moose Lake, this destination simultaneously evokes love and rage in her.

Jay and I always sought out the most secluded ponds, mountains, or waterfalls to whet our adventuresome appetites. I left home at 6:00 AM to meet Jay, Dave, and another fellow, Joe, for an arduous snowshoe bushwhack to Terror Lake. Plowing through twenty inches of fresh powder and three- and four-foot snowdrifts did not deter us, even though Joe's borrowed snowshoes kept falling off. Friends say that Jay and I are headstrong, because when we embark for a destination, we are determined to get there despite all obstacles. By midnight, giddy with delight, weary and wet, we stood on the shoreline of Terror Lake, which we couldn't see because of snow squalls. I didn't return home until the next morning. Joanne was elated that I was safely back, but so angry she wanted to kill me.

Never Short on Ideas. Given our penchant to explore, Owl Pond presented a unique problem to Jay and me: how to cross the West Branch of the Sacandaga River? Where we wanted to cross was deep and very wide.

I stuffed a deflated rubber raft, plastic paddle, and a hand pump into my large backpack. While crossing, we let the current take us downstream, where we noted a faint trail and decided to investigate. Often when exploring off trail, we will find a treasure. I found a fishing pole this time, complete with reel and line. Anticipation fueled our curiosity and, sure enough, we discovered a partially camouflaged hunters' camp, well-equipped and stocked, including a not-so-hidden, very large dump. Nearby was a nearly brand-new wheelbarrow. Jay, vilifying those who build illegal camps and leave piles of refuse, encouraged me to take the wheelbarrow. Indeed, I was in need of a new one; the problem was getting it out. Never short on ideas, I put the wheelbarrow in the middle of the rubber dinghy. Stuffing the day packs and other items near the wheelbarrow, we squeezed ourselves into the remaining space, feet dangling in the water, and paddled upstream. Water lapped into the raft, but I guess we reached a balance between taking water in and panning water out. I still have that wheelbarrow.

Shiras Pond. This small circular body of water nestled south of Harrington Mountain off Route 8 will always hold special significance in my life. Fishing poles in hand, Dave and I were bushwhacking through dense underbrush and blowdown when, suddenly, a stick slipped beneath my glasses and poked into the corner of my eye. After the initial pain subsided, I could still see well and we continued. Weeks later my vision was blurry and I was seeing sporadic flashes of light; I had a detached retina! After recovery and a miserable summer of inactivity, I am now far more cautious on bushwhacks; I carry a set of goggles, should the need arise.

Why do I keep going back to the Adirondacks, with old and new friends? Isn't it true that if you've seen one pond or mountain, you've seen them all? It is the companionship of my comrades and family that makes each hike different. Each Jay, Dave, Doug, Bill, Aaron, Jordan, brings to those ponds and mountains their own "pizzazz," enriching my Adirondack experience. Every trip is unique, a new etching in my heart. Over the years we have established bonds of friendship through our mutual love for the Adirondacks, and although through age or disability we may have since traveled separate trails, the common thread to our relationship is the trail to that mountain summit, that distant pond. The memories are real; they reunite us. I have told Jay[1] that, should I ever become lost in the Adirondack wilderness, I would want him to lead the search and rescue party. He alone would know how I would think and where I would bushwhack. We established that bond of trust and mutual respect trip by trip, enveloped in the smells, the sights and sounds of rushing water, falling snow, swaying trees, and bolts of lightning. 🚶

[1]See William J. "Jay" O'Hern's "A Neophyte in Hermit Country."

Paul A. Sirtoli: On or off trail, I enjoy exploring many regions of the Adirondacks by foot, cross-country ski, snowshoe, canoe, or mountain bike, and have written over a dozen articles for the ADK magazine, Adirondac. *I am a 46er, #2211, and member of the Iroquois Chapter of the Adirondack Mountain Club, where I serve as trips chairman. Joanne and I and our three children live in Central New York.*

74

A FALL FROM GRACE

JUST ONE STEP FROM THE SUMMIT

Melinda Broman

In December 1997 my friend Lynne and I hiked up Crane Mountain. It was a mild day, mostly cloudy, but the clouds parted and brilliant sun shone through as we stepped out on an open, rocky place and sat down to enjoy the view. We had snacks and congratulated ourselves on the relatively easy climbing in one-to-two-foot-deep snow. We had had to break trail through an icy crust, but above 2,900 feet the snow was soft and deeper and easier on snowshoes. We both had snowshoes with Tucker bindings.

We ascended a twenty-five-foot ladder to the summit. The ladder was encrusted with snow, but it was easy to get footing. At the top, I regarded with dismay the area onto which I must now step—a maneuver to the left onto a ledge with small footholds. There was little ice or snow, however. I decided not to think about it, but to just move ahead quickly. I lost my footing, and my body hurtled straight down the icy precipice. At the bottom I turned over and skidded down another steep incline, headfirst. Finally I stopped. Though badly shaken, I was intact.

My companion was bending over me. I asked for my ski poles. I was disappointed that I would not walk out onto the summit, but that was replaced by other concerns when I realized that I could not walk at all. A sharp pain gripped my right foot. Lynne helped me up; I was dismayed to find that I could not even stand on the foot.

At three o'clock, having given me spare clothing, Lynne descended 1.8 miles to the trailhead to get help. The first rescuer arrived at 5:30, shortly after dark; more soon arrived, and I became the subject of a massive rescue. A fire engine, ambulance, helicopter, physician, forest rangers, firemen, and search and rescue personnel came to my aid from all quarters of the Adirondack region. I was laid in front of a roaring fire near where I had fallen, and kept warm by blankets and outer garments. My foot was examined by a wilderness doctor, who inserted a Heparin lock in my wrist to prepare for emergency administration of fluids and pain medication. Men stood around the fire and communicated with men at the bottom about my ultimate evacuation from the mountain.

I was overwhelmed by the sheer size of the rescue effort—there were twenty-two men on the mountain ministering to me. Was I, with my useless ankle, worth the magnitude of this response? Push me over the side of the mountain, I thought despondently. But the men did not seem to mind; in fact, they seemed to enjoy themselves. They checked my status and told stories and jokes to pass the time. I was given glucose and propped up on a tree to urinate.

"Have you ever had so many men paying attention to you?" they asked, and I said, "Only the contractors who renovated my house." They laughed and reported to the ranger below that I was in good spirits. I put my sweater back on and insisted on turning it right side out. "You are a perfectionist, aren't you?" the man said. I was embarrassed; he was right.

Forest rangers arrived with a Stokes litter. I was lifted onto it and covered with an orange sleeping bag. The hood was laced up, and my arms were strapped to my body. "I'm claustrophobic," I protested, but I surrendered control calmly. I was a human mummy as they carried me down the steep mountain trail. Men in front and men in back shouted information and instructions, using head-lamps to illuminate the path. On steep places they belayed the stretcher with ropes from trees.

We arrived at a trail junction where more men stood around a roaring fire. They were debating whether to prepare an overnight camp at Crane Mountain Pond, a half mile on the cutoff to the west, so that my evacuation could be more safely completed the next morning. More radio communications transpired, and it was decided to complete the evacuation that night. Men lifted me again and continued the belay down the mountain.

"Aren't you sorry you won't be spending the night with us?" they joked. I lay looking up, feeling calm and watching the black sky dotted with stars and the huge pines frosted with snow glide by. *So beautiful here at night*, I thought.

We reached the trailhead at midnight. With so many lights and people and Lynne bending over me, I wanted to cry. We walk up mountains to feel in charge of our lives, of our physical selves. Yet here I was, as helpless as an infant, as humbled by the limitations of my body and mind as one could be.

It will be a long trip back from there to get to a place of forgiveness for fall-ing from grace, after so many years of a perfect body and an unblemished record of forays in the wilderness. To err is human and to forgive is divine, and I am still seeking divine forgiveness for my humanity. I had lots of time for this, because I did not walk on my injured foot for six weeks.

My rescuers, of course, I cannot thank enough for their good humor through it all. "You work so well together," I tried to compliment them. "Like ants," came the reply. "One of us is nothing much, but a whole colony is amazing to watch." Then there are the rescuers I never met, the folks in the house at the bottom of Crane Mountain who opened their door when a stranger came crying for help that Saturday evening. They emptied out their refrigerator and cupboards for the rescuers, and allowed their garage to be used as a command station by the forest rangers. The little boy in the house waited up until I came off the mountain. They wanted to know what it was like for me up there. So, here it is:

Although I could cite practical factors that might have played a part in my accident, I stress the psychological factors. The Adirondack Mountain Club's book *Winterwise* notes that accidents usually happen because of a combination of factors. I was hiking with a less experienced companion who was, against her wildest expectation, pressed into service as my rescuer. Fortunately, her experience has not dampened her enthusiasm for winter hiking, and she is looking forward to going back again—not on the same trail, however! Having a less experienced person along should be cause for greater caution. It constitutes a set of details to think about. We were not well equipped, having neither crampons nor an ice axe to negotiate the terrain; I had not considered the necessity of these items beforehand. These factors, together with the allure of the summit, set the stage for a terrible error of judgment. Although many who read these pages know about these hazards, I cannot stress enough the need to monitor one's psychological and practical situation at every point. If I'd admitted that several factors weighed against me, I might have turned around, stepped down the ladder, and safely walked down the mountain instead of taking an unacceptable risk. ⚇

Originally published in the January/February 1999 Adirondac, *the magazine of the Adirondack Mountain Club, Inc. (ADK). This abridged version is reprinted with permission of ADK, www.adk.org.*

Melinda Broman: *I've hiked in many parts of the United States and in other countries. The Adirondack region is by far my favorite place for outdoor recreation for the beauty and diversity of its topography and natural habitats; I have a second home in one of its quirky hamlets on Great Sacandaga Lake. I was president of the Knickerbocker Chapter of the Adirondack Mountain Club, recently merged with the New York Chapter. I have written several articles for* Adirondac *magazine.*

75

THE PITCHER PLANT

THE LURE OF THE WILD

Bill Ingersoll

Lexie was down at the lake's edge, engaged in her all-time favorite hobby of hunting frogs. Her tail wags with uninhibited enthusiasm whenever she corners one, but now she was pointing it upward in tense anticipation as she searched through the brush. We'd been camping here, and the frogs were well acquainted with her. Those that could get away had done so, and Lexie's efforts had not been fruitful. She knew that I'd been packing, so it was no surprise when I called her back. She knew the routine—it was time to go hiking! This is another favorite pastime of hers, so she came right along. I donned the pack, tightened the hip strap, and took one last look around. The fire ring was in much better shape than when I found it. Beyond the shoreline trees, West Lake stretched off a mile deeper into the wilderness, its surface languidly lapping up the sunlight. Slender rushes stood like sparse bristles out of the shallow water; yesterday I stood twenty feet from shore with dry knees. The graceful balsam trees that formed our campsite's cathedral ceiling rustled in a slight breeze. I would have liked to linger longer, but it was time to venture off past Brooktrout Lake to my car on Indian Lake Road.

I noted that we had more daylight than required for the six-mile walk back north. There would be time for a detour—my plan from the start. The trail was a familiar one, but the deep woods on either side were mostly *terra incognita*. Today we would dispel some of the mystery by venturing off the trail into those unknown woods. It was a short walk from West Lake to Brooktrout Lake, and in fifteen minutes we reached the log lean-to there. The shelter was empty with no one around, although a square dome tent was set up down by the water. Like most lean-tos, it suffered from too much trampling, with bare ground all around and blackened, unusable cooking utensils hanging on the outside walls. By most societal standards this would qualify as "rustic," but to me it was an outpost of the civilization I had come here to forget.

It was much too early for a break, but curiosity drove me to see if there were interesting stories in the journal. The people who were camping here returned—a middle-aged couple back from a trip to West Lake. Their conversation ended when they saw us. They were friendly, but their responses to my comments about good weather and the advantages of being in the woods—straight out of the wilderness small-talk handbook—were short; they weren't interested in company. The husband was talking while the wife pawed at the ground with her feet in distracted impatience. Lexie ignored these signs as she attempted to know these people to her own satisfaction. I sympathized with their thirst for privacy, which I would respect by getting on my way; but they should have realized that solitude was contradictory with their taste in campsites. Lean-tos are the newsstands and cyber cafés of backcountry life! Any hiker on this trail would without fail pause here—including me, who values solitude as much as anyone. To some, wilderness is enjoyable only to the extent that a day's hike ends at a place with a roof, a floor, and a place to go to the bathroom. I had long ago progressed beyond that stage, and the wilderness that I sought lay in the thousands of acres of open space surrounding us in every direction. The log walls of a lean-to were a barrier to be avoided—a barrier to the forest connection I sought and would soon find.

We parted company, and Lexie trotted deftly up the rocky trail while I plodded in bipedal awkwardness from one rock to the next. The height-of-land was a soupy affair—a lukewarm stew of moss, surplus rainwater, and trail mud—and the descent was a combination of both rock and soup. Lexie occasionally sent a curious glance my way—what was taking me so long? Toward the bottom of the hill, the woods filled with large spruce with the sound of rushing water rising like a continuous round of applause. We arrived at the largest stream on the Brooktrout trail and the most vexing to many because there is no bridge, although the stream is neither very wide nor deep. I stepped across on rocks and hardly got my soles wet, then stopped for water and a quick break. Lexie was up the trail sitting picturesquely in an angled beam of sunlight between young spruce trees, watching me for the cue to start moving, but I was about to throw her a curve because this was where we were going to leave the trail.

I rechecked my map to make sure I knew what we were about to attempt. It showed the dotted black line of the trail crossing the solid blue line of the stream less than half a mile below the place where another blue line—the outlet of Deep Lake—came in. You can get to Deep Lake by a trail that comes in from the opposite end, which in turn leads back to the Brooktrout trail. By bushwhacking up the stream and around the lake to that trail, we'd be in trackless woods for perhaps a paltry mile and a half. I'd been to Deep Lake four years ago when I had established my own no-trace campsite (where, unlike that lean-to, I was sure no one had camped before) and spent my free time ranging out into the surrounding wilderness, following the upper portion of this stream all the way to Twin Lakes. That trip had been in September, and what had impressed me most were the leaves of the red maple trees at the height of their crimson coloring. At Deep Lake there was nothing but sensual pleasure, and I was eager to see it again.

Lexie was momentarily confused when I left the trail and headed through woods beside the stream, but she was game for anything. We weaved through the woods along the north bank, which I soon found had its disadvantages. A storm had been hard on these woods, and I was frequently required to adjust course or squeeze through awkwardly tight spaces. Lexie demonstrated that following the streambed was easier, where we could step from rock to rock and avoid the brush. By comparing the topography with the lines on my map, I quickly saw that the trail crossed the creek farther downstream than the map showed, instantly adding a modest but measurable distance to our bushwhack. The stream passed through an interesting canyon with an overhanging rock ledge on the north bank and then mossy rock walls on the south bank. Fortunately most rocks were dry and stable, offering good footing. The streambed was not without impediments, however. Stepping over one fallen tree, I started to stand on a balsam log just below it. The log rolled out from under me before I could rebalance my weight on something else. *Watch it*, I reminded myself. This was *not* a good place to twist

Deep Lake. Photo by Bill Ingersoll.

an ankle! Progress was much slower than I expected—a half hour had passed, and I'd expected by now to be bushwhacking around the lake. A knoll appeared above the north bank and through the trees I saw sky, indicating open space on the far side. This is the siren call for all impatient bushwhackers, whether they are heading toward a mountain summit or toward a secluded lake. The light might mean that Deep Lake was over that knoll.

We left the friendly openness of the stream and waded into a balsam forest with a man-deep understory of young balsams. This emerald sea extended in every direction. I fought my way to the top of the knoll only to find a small swamp on the other side, with no lake in sight. The understory sea rolled over the hillsides like massive swells, and the canopy of mature balsam firs blotted out the sun and made the sky seem green. Young trees grew so thickly that there was scarcely space for a backpacker and a dog to stand and breathe. Pushing our way deeper into this was out of the question; the streambed was the only relief from this claustrophobic nightmare. I would have hated this place were it not so essentially wild and beautiful. At last the streambed led us to Deep Lake's outlet, which was hidden in an extension of the same boreal forest. Lexie made her way easily up the cascading outlet to the lake, but I had to fight for every step. This was the spot I *knew* was going to be unpleasant, but only briefly—the woods would open up as we made our way around the lake.

Either my memory was faulty or things had changed dramatically in four years. Long after I expected the understory to clear, we were still mired in thick spruce and fir. Glimpses of the lake were frustrating, showing how little progress we were making. The north end of the lake with its trail was only a quarter mile away, but it might as well have been six miles away for all the good it was doing us! It was getting late, and if we didn't get to the trail soon, we'd be in this trackless wilderness in the fading light of dusk. It didn't matter whether we stayed near the lake or sought higher ground; it was all one impenetrable matrix of balsam and spruce. The spruce boughs were the worst, because of their Velcro-like tendencies. Spruce twigs latched themselves onto my pack and clothing, and I had to pick needles out of my collar and hair.

It was not just the thick brush, either—what it concealed was just as unforgiving. I couldn't see fallen trees that lay prostrate across our route until I rubbed against the fungus-covered bark, nor could I see various little ledges with short but precipitous drop-offs until I came unexpectedly upon the very edge. The brush parted only where small tributaries flowed toward the lake, and at least one of these had been somewhat enlarged by beavers, forcing us to seek yet another detour. Lexie had long since stopped trying to lead; she now followed close at my heels, depending on me to get her out of this. She could fit through the tight spaces a little better than I could, but I was taller and could see farther ahead. I knew my memory was not at fault, because on my first trip I had bushwhacked all the way around this lake. If it had been this bad, I never would have come back. The only way to extract ourselves from this trap—like coming up temporarily in water for a gulp of air—was to find an opening on the shoreline and stare across the open space of the lake. The water was dark and still, and nothing moved across its surface. On nearly all sides the forest came right down to the water's edge.

I thought about how a man had disappeared into the woods a few miles north of here. They had found his car and his campsite in the Moose River Plains, but they never found his body or any other sign of him despite an extensive search. It seemed improbable that a man could be so irrevocably lost without it being premeditated. The Adirondacks are a benign wilderness, not very fond of the taste of human flesh. People thought he must have skipped the country, and was lost only if you consider it "lost" to be in the Bahamas with your mistress. But now I imagined him wandering into a place exactly like this, into the emerald sea; he had fallen and been overwhelmed. He had been drawn in and couldn't get out. They would never find the body.

Nor would they find ours. If something happened to immobilize me in a place like this, the only certainty was that salvation would be slow in coming. I had neglected to mention before I left home the possibility that I might take this side trip. As far as anyone knew, I was on the Brooktrout trail. The last people to see us were the couple at the lean-to, who would not be able to provide much information. By choosing to walk in the streambed, we had left no tracks. Lexie would be good company, but she would not be a help, because she would be reluctant to leave me. The forest was doing nothing to harm us; it was merely what Charles Dudley Warner called the "gigantic indifference." Our biggest threat came from ourselves. We might injure ourselves in fear, in desperation. We slip, break an ankle, become immobilized, and the forest closes in, enveloping us. It swallows us, digests us, and creates new trees from the nutrients it dissolves from our bodies. But the forest doesn't trip us or break our ankle or immobilize us. We do that to ourselves by our own carelessness.

I once looked inside the pitcher of a pitcher plant, saw a tiny bug floating dead in the ounce of water inside, and wondered how a living thing that flew freely through that wide opening could not fly freely back out. An insect flies into a pitcher plant because it thinks it will find something it needs there. The pitcher plant does nothing actively to capture a bug. Its slight nectarous smell and garish coloring embodies the essence of what a tiny fly would consider beauty. The only mechanisms the plant has for keeping the bug there are the fine, downward-pointing hairs that line the insides of the veined leaves. The bug enters the beautiful, water-filled chamber of enclosed leaves on its own accord, and once inside it either can or cannot find its way back out. If it can, it will likely be drawn back soon by the same charms, to place itself in the same danger once again. If it can't, it will drown and the plant will supplement its diet with whatever nutrients it can dissolve from the body. From the point of view of a dispassionate observer, it may appear that the fly went willingly to its doom.

We pushed forward along the path of least resistance toward the north end of the lake and its promise of an exit. The understory opened up—it could not go on forever—and in the end the only real inconvenience was that there was now no time for supper. It was seven o'clock—three hours had passed since we had left the Brooktrout trail, three times as long as the trip should have taken. Lexie ate, but all I had left were camp dinners with no time to cook; three miles of trail lay ahead of us. I checked off landmarks we passed—Wolf Creek, Falls Pond turnoff, the beaver meadow. The sun's last light disappeared behind distant hills and left us in dim woods. Reaching the car at 8:15, I was finally free to conclude that it had been a good trip. I would mostly remember sitting by my campfire last night at West Lake, where the graceful balsam trees had been lacy silhouettes above us reaching into the night sky, posing no threat to anyone. This was, after all, a benign wilderness—the essence of what I consider beautiful. ⚇

Bill Ingersoll: I have hiked and backpacked throughout the United States, but I feel most at home in the grand forests of the Adirondacks. I am the publisher and coauthor of Barbara McMartin's Discover the Adirondacks *guidebook series, and the author of* Snowshoe Routes: Adirondacks and Catskills. *I'm an active member of the Adirondack Mountain Club, serving at the state and local levels. I reside in Barneveld, New York.*

76

THE NORTHVILLE-PLACID TRAIL

SOLO THROUGH-TRIP IN WET CONDITIONS

Dorothy Myer

One fall I had some very interesting experiences during ten days on the Northville-Placid Trail. Because this trail keeps to the lowlands, it sounds fairly easy, one reason I chose it for a solo trip. It was raining the first morning, but I was eager to get started. Little did I know that this rain would seldom stop. I faced a variety of challenges different from those in the mountains. The pack itself was the first challenge. Eleven days' food and supplies seems to weigh ten times as much as three days' food and supplies. I'd advise any-one doing the same hike to arrange a food pickup along the way. For the first two days, I hardly dared to put my pack down except on a rock or log; it was too heavy to lift all the way up from the ground! This nearly resulted in a minor disaster—I left my pack on a log, and it tumbled down into two inches of water on the trail. Luckily, a plastic bag inside my stuff bag kept my sleeping bag dry.

I'd been warned that the trail was very wet. At the start there was plenty of puncheon and other trail supports, but farther in these were in bad repair, and finally there was nothing. The fact that it had been raining for two weeks didn't help! About 11:00 AM I came to the first of many nearly uncrossable streams. The guidebook said to cross on stones, but the stones were under a foot of fast-flowing water. I checked upstream and downstream for a place to cross, and then tried throwing in more stones. Finally I found a strong walking stick and waded across, boots and all; I thought my boots couldn't get much wetter anyway. At the first step, I knew I was wrong. My boots could get *much* wetter! For most of the rest of the trip, I wore plastic bags between my boots and my socks, and always had socks hanging on the back of the pack hoping they would dry—but they never did.

Each brook crossing seemed to require a different solution. Some I waded across, with or without boots—once even barefoot on a beaver dam! Other times I walked upstream or downstream and eventually found a better crossing. Once I walked upstream and found an old but perfectly usable bridge with no blazes or signs and only a faint path leading to it. After many crossings and nearly one hun-dred miles, I finally fell in when I least expected it. I slipped off a two-foot-wide log and was in water up to my waist. After the first shock I realized I wasn't hurt, climbed back on the log, and crossed.

I passed many lovely lakes and interesting beaver ponds. There were huge beaver houses, and the trail often crossed beaver dams. The leaves were at their peak, and their colors were often reflected in the ponds, even in this dull weather. The most spectacular sight was Blue Mountain reflected in Lake Durand. The colors brightened everything, so the weather didn't feel quite so gloomy.

On that first day I also reached the second type of common problem along this trek—a large marsh. The trail slips in to many herd paths, all seeking a way around the marsh. I followed some of them and made more of my own, and was soon up to my knees in mud and water. Finally I got across and found the trail again. I went thirteen miles that day—only about half as long as some of my longest hikes, but nearly as hard. Someone told me later that you should always add 20 percent to your mileage on the Northville-Placid Trail to make up for going around marshes and finding brook crossings.

It was still raining the second day, and I came to a lean-to about noon. I had planned to use my tent that night, but decided that by having one very short day and then one very long one, I could use lean-tos both nights. So I spent the afternoon in my sleeping bag reading, eating gorp, and playing with the resident chipmunks. There were two chipmunks there, and one was incredibly brave. I saw them peeking around the edge of the lean-to and left them a little pile of food that they quickly got. The brave one soon started coming right up to me for more food. If I didn't throw it fast enough, he'd nibble the end of my finger (but never bite into it). If he didn't see my hand reaching out with food, he'd climb up on my lap to find out why. He was not only brave, but smart. I'd leave a little pile of food and go back to reading; when he came for the food, I'd throw him more. Once, I became too engrossed in my reading and didn't hear him; he went right by the pile of food, climbed up on my sleeping bag to make sure I knew he was there, then went back and picked up the pile of food.

The third day I hiked through Piseco. The trail north of the village followed old logging roads—and so did all the rain of the last few weeks. Some trails have wet spots; this was just one big wet spot. When I wasn't crossing boggy places, I was hiking up a stream. It was discouraging, but it led to a lean-to on lovely Spruce Lake. In spite of the discouraging times, there were also magical times of walking in carpets of red and gold leaves so thick that I could hardly tell ground from water until I stepped in it, times of listening to owls at night, watching geese overhead or a fisher play on a log, times of good hiking.

The big problem the next day started with a simple statement in the guidebook: "Cross the end of a vlei." A vlei is a marshy area, very common here. What the guidebook neglected to say was that the end of the vlei was the beginning of a roaring river. The water suddenly rushed downhill over boulders and formed great rapids. Where the marsh became river was a single, slippery, slanting log with one end under water—the remnants of a bridge. I thought briefly of straddling the log and crossing, but I'd be soaked to the waist and if I slipped I might be washed down the rapids. I had several topo maps, so I got them out and discovered where I was—Sampson's Bog. It might take days of extremely difficult going to get around it. Impossible. In the other direction the river enlarged and joined West Canada Creek. Not very promising either, but the better of the two options. Expecting a long walk, I started through the bushes along the riverbank. Luck was with me! About 1,000 feet downstream was a good sound log across the stream. I crossed and headed back upstream, feeling triumphant.

That afternoon I met other hikers for the first time, two men going in the opposite direction. Even though one of them wore Bean boots, they were as wet as I. A yellow side trail was supposed to lead to a lean-to in half a mile. In five hundred feet it led to the middle of a beaver pond. With difficulty I bushwhacked around it, but couldn't pick up the trail on the other side, so I missed what was supposed to be an excellent campsite. At 5:30 I still had at least two miles to go to another lean-to, but it turned out to be the best place I camped. Cedar Lakes #2 is on a little hill on the shore with good views up and down beautiful Cedar Lake. I fell asleep to the sound of an owl and woke to the sound of a loon.

I planned to have a short day and get my clothes washed and dried, but it was the first beautiful hiking day, so I continued on. The afternoon included 6.6 miles of hiking on country roads. Hiking on the road made my feet sore. Late in the afternoon, with sore feet and a pack full of wet and dirty clothes, I came to where the trail left the road and saw a sign: "Housekeeping Cabins." I rented a nice four-room log cabin with hot water!

The next morning I was going to Tirrell Pond, clean and with dry clothes for the first time since I started this hike. I was looking forward to Tirrell Pond because I had had a wonderful time there before; what I remembered most was a loon so loud and clear he must have been almost on shore. That evening I was relaxing in Tirrell Pond lean-to and suddenly there was a horrible roar. I half expected to see motorcyclists. A seaplane flew over—a disappointment, seaplanes instead of loons.

The next day I climbed the only real hill on the Northville-Placid Trail. Descending, I met a girl going in the opposite direction, and we chatted for quite a while. I crossed the Long Lake Highway and found long stretches of reasonably dry trail between the marshes—and nearly all the brooks had bridges! I met more hikers in my first hour there than I had in the whole preceding week.

A fisher was running along a log and he gradually worked his way closer to the trail, searching under logs with his pointed nose. I stood still, and he came very close before his bright little eyes saw me and he scampered away. He was very furry and had a cute face with pointed nose, very bright black eyes, and little round ears. He was dark, though not as dark as some fishers I've seen, and almost gray around his shoulders. He was rather like a miniature fox, but with short legs and round ears. I hadn't seen a single porcupine; in Vermont I would have seen several by now. It's amazing how the fisher can kill porcupines and keep their population down.

At the Seward lean-to I was lulled to sleep by the Cold River flowing along and going over the falls; the trail follows the river for some distance. I met a friendly ranger who later gave me a ride from the trail's end to Lake Placid.

The last night I shared a lean-to with two young men—the only night that I shared a lean-to. After a diversion up to beautiful Wanika Falls, another scenic 6.5 miles of trail ended in Lake Placid. ⚱

Originally published in the October 1980 Adirondac, *the magazine of the Adirondack Mountain Club, Inc. (ADK). This abridged version is reprinted with permission of ADK. www.adk.org.*

*D*orothy Myer: *With the University of Vermont Outing Club, I climbed Mt. Marcy and started serious winter hiking. I later joined the Green Mountain Club and became the second woman to climb the Winter 46 in 1978, #914W, and the first woman to climb in winter the 111 High Peaks of the Northeast, in 1985. I've remained active through my seventies in the Green Mountain Club, as membership chair of the Burlington Section, outings chair, president, and trailwork volunteer. It is important to pass on outdoors interests and skills to young people. I've led Girl Scout troops for many years and volunteered at Girl Scout and Audubon camps. I completed the Long Trail in Vermont and the Appalachian Trail in 2003.*

77

FORTY YEARS OF ADIRONDACK HIKING

DISCOVERING THE ADIRONDACKS
AND THE FIRE TOWER MOUNTAINS

Faith W. Eckler

In 1968 I discovered the Adirondacks. My husband and I and three daughters had been hiking the trails of Harriman State Park and the Wyanokies. It was time to move up to the big ones. On our first trip with friends we stayed at Johns Brook Lodge; some of us climbed Big Slide, while others climbed Marcy. I was hooked, and over the next ten years on our annual trips to the Adirondacks I climbed many more of the 4,000-footers. I never aspired to be a peak bagger and am not even sure I approve of the concept. I think that peak baggers tend to value the achievement more highly than the joy of the climb or the beauty of the view. In the extreme case the peak bagger dashes up one mountain only to dash straight down again to climb the next peak. I prefer to linger, eat my lunch, enjoy the view, and save the next peak for another adventure.

My husband has a collecting urge, however, so we began to collect fire towers. In the1960s, New York State had 108 manned fire towers, with 58 in the Adirondack Park. The state encouraged people to visit, and the fire warden gave you a signed card attesting that you had visited. On one memorable day in 1970, we added four Adirondack fire towers to our collection—Makomis, Belfry, Hurricane, and Poke-O-Moonshine. By the end of the day, we had hiked six and a half miles and climbed 3,400 feet!

The state decided to abandon many towers and replace the wardens with aerial surveillance. After 1971 we encountered few occupied towers, so it was a pleasant surprise to find two manned towers in 1984. A genial ex-Marine was stationed at Wakely fire tower and, because of its remote location, he received few visitors and welcomed us heartily. He proudly told us that his, at ninety feet high, was the tallest tower still in use in New York State. He was about to leave, so we walked part way down the mountain together. In his pack, an open Adirondack guide basket, he was carrying a wounded blackbird whose broken leg he had splinted weeks earlier. The bird had become his pet and had made three trips up and down the mountain with him. The warden hoped that he could return it to the wild.

The next day we visited Blue Mountain fire tower, which was also manned. Here the warden had planted a garden around his cabin, growing carrots, radishes,

Fox at Bald Mountain fire tower. Photo by David White.

and other vegetables. Blue Mountain was a popular destination, and the warden here had lots of company.

We found the fire wardens to be a happy and friendly bunch, although there was one we suspected of being drunk. Indeed, it must have been a temptation to relieve one's lonely life with a bottle. Wardens were full of mountain lore and delighted in regaling the nervous hiker with stories of their most recent bear sighting. We visited fifteen Adirondack fire towers in all, some several times; I was sorry to see them abandoned. A fire tower provided a 360° view, and the map table equipped with pointer enabled you to orient yourself and identify all the peaks. Frequently the warden suggested routes that were not obvious from the ground.

A dozen or so Adirondack fire towers have been nominated to the National Register of Historic Places and are adopted and being restored. Hikers were encouraged to try areas less traveled than the High Peaks, so in the 1980s we climbed Snowy, Hadley, Bald, Cathead, Crane, and other fire tower mountains. By the 1990s we were hiking the southern Adirondacks, and there we encountered the infamous Adirondack mud!

As we near four score years of age, we no longer essay the heights and have traded their spectacular views for the cry of a loon over Murphy Lake or the purple fringed orchid near Brownell Camp. We've enjoyed taking our grandchildren to Kane Mountain fire tower or to Good Luck Cliffs, and with luck we'll have great-grandchildren to introduce to the joys of Adirondack hiking. 🌲

Faith W. Eckler: I am a wife, mother, grandmother, and freelance writer who came relatively late to real hiking in the United States and abroad. An inveterate record-keeper, for many years I hiked more than three hundred miles a year, all day hikes. Other interests include genealogy, gardening, and local history.

78

ON A CLEAR DAY YOU CAN SEE NEW HAMPSHIRE

WITH TWO BOYS AND DAD, YOU SEE MUCH MORE

Roger Menges

Snowy Mountain, west of Indian Lake, at 3,899 feet is the highest mountain in the southern Adirondacks. The trail to the summit lookout begins 6.5 miles south of Indian Lake village on Route 30 and is 3.75 miles long—about right for an afternoon jaunt. I go outside and ask my ten- and nine-year-old sons Kent and Todd if they want to go. Yes, they do, and their half-built fort is forgotten.

We hike through a forest of beech, yellow birch, sugar maple, and other deciduous trees. Striped maple forms much of the understory. This tree seldom grows more than fifteen feet tall, but its lack of stature is more than offset by its handsome bark—smooth bright green with vertical white stripes. Kent says it looks good enough to eat, and I reply, "Yes, that's how it got one of its names. Moose eat it, which is why it is sometimes called moosewood. Another name for it is goosefoot maple. See? The leaf looks a lot like a goose's foot." Kent soon meets another plant with an appropriate name. Chasing a chipmunk, he trips and takes a header—it's not a root that tripped him, but hobblebush. This viburnum with large, heart-shaped leaves has arching branches that often root at the tip; fastened at both ends, they form loops that can snare the foot of an unwary hiker.

At a stream a couple is drawing pictures with pointed sticks on artist's fungus, a kind of bracket fungus that grows like a shelf on the trunks and stumps of trees. The upper side is hard and dark, the underside softer and pure white. When a pointed stick is drawn across the soft white surface, the injured tissue turns brown, the effect being like a soft brown pencil on paper. Kent and Todd are fascinated. From here their main goal is to find a nice piece of artist's fungus. I see an opportunity to slip in an ecology lesson with the fungus as an example, and point out that although fungus is a plant without a stem, leaves, or roots, it gets along nicely. A bracket fungus gets its food from the tree on which it grows. What we see is not the main part of the fungus, but a reproductive body. This produces spores from which new fungus plants grow. Underneath the bark is the main body of the fungus, a mass of threadlike enzymes that break down the wood and slowly rot the tree. Though fungi kill trees, I explain, they are a necessary part of nature's scheme as they rot away fallen limbs and other debris, converting dead wood into humus that fertilizes the forest floor. Without the fungi, forests would accumulate huge brush piles until fire struck and burned it all away. "Any questions?"

Kent looks at Todd. "What are you going to draw on your fungus?" End of ecology lesson for today.

A young fellow descending says, "Oh brother, that last mile is really steep." Am I imagining it, or is he casting a doubtful look at me? As if to offer me incentive to struggle through that last, steep mile, he adds, "But the view up there is terrific—you can see all the way to the White Mountains of New Hampshire!" They must be one hundred and twenty miles away as the crow flies. Excited, we move faster. Among the wildflowers in early fall is an impressive display of touch-me-nots. We have much fun with them later in the season when seed-pods replace the flowers. The pods "explode," shooting seeds out as far as four feet. As pods dry out, tensions build in their walls until they become like tightly wound springs. If not touched, they soon pop by themselves. Because the seeds are scattered, rather than dropped, young plants that sprout from them have room to grow without overcrowding; the scattering also makes the seeds less conspicuous and so less likely to be eaten by hungry birds. Their stems are said to be edible in the spring and early summer. The watery liquid that comes out when the plants are crushed in the hand is supposed to be an effective treatment for poison ivy.

The smooth, light gray bark on handsome beech trees is unfortunately a temptation to insensitive exhibitionists—initials are carved into tree after tree. A scout troop of twenty boys and three leaders stampedes past. The trail tilts upward more steeply—breathing turns into puffing. Beads of sweat become rivulets that run into the eyes. Legs begin to wobble; time for a brief rest. The picture of me on a mountain peak is replaced by another scene—me in an easy chair sipping a long, cold drink. A voice breaks into my reverie: "It's not much farther now," says a young fellow, "but it's beginning to get hazy." Kent and Todd are way ahead; this hike is a turning point. For years you interrupt your hikes with frequent stops to let your small children rest. You look forward to when they'll be strong enough to keep up with you. The day arrives—but instead of just keeping up, they are leaving you behind.

A scramble up rock on all fours and suddenly I'm on a ledge in full sunlight, with a sheer drop of several hundred feet. Indian Lake stretches out, and mountain follows mountain like waves rolling toward shore. The High Peaks cut the skyline into a jagged profile, the cone of Mount Marcy pushing above the rest. Giant Mountain's slides stand out like a gray streak in dark hair. To the east are Vermont's Green Mountains, followed by the White Mountains of New Hampshire. A path leads to the fire tower; trails take us to many viewpoints. We sprawl out on a ledge, nibble a candy bar and savor the view.

Shadows are lengthening; it's time to start back—always a letdown. On the way the boys find two good specimens of artist's fungi. How can I describe the beautiful pictures that were drawn on them? I can't, because there are no pictures to describe—the two pieces of fungi lay forgotten outside our back door. The fort, however, is progressing nicely. 🏃

Originally published in the August 1975 Adirondac, *the magazine of the Adirondack Mountain Club, Inc. This abridged version is reprinted with permission of ADK, www.adk.org.*

*K*ent Menges: Reading the story above that my father, Roger, wrote brings back memories. My family moved to the Adirondacks when I was six. My father always liked the outdoors, and it was important to him to be able to raise his children in that environment. My father's guidance taught me many things that I've been able to pass on to my children.

79

LOST IN WINTER

CHILLING OUT

Jane R. Marcus

On Martin Luther King weekend in the mid-1990s, five friends and I decided to go cross-country skiing in the Adirondacks. A mid-January thaw had set in, and by Sunday we couldn't ski, so the folks at the ski touring center at Garnet Hill suggested a hike. We could follow a path up a small mountain nearby and descend the same way, or from the top of the mountain we could bushwhack to another mountain and come down another path.

At the top, some wanted to head back down and some wanted to bush-whack—the latter won. We stopped for a snack and decided that, since it was getting late and we hadn't yet found the other path, we should head back the way we came. We tried to retrace, but couldn't find the way we had just come. The woods in winter are not like woods in summer; the ground everywhere is matted down, so it looks like a path that you have just walked through, no matter where you look. We tried to get our bearings by the sun, but it was overcast; we tried to discern where the sky was lighter. One of us climbed a tree to see if they could see Garnet Hill, but no luck.

We ultimately decided that, yes, we were lost and we must stop walking around or we would never be found. It was getting dark, drizzling lightly, and we were making no progress. We were near a stream, and moved away from it so we could hear or be heard by rescuers. We decided to build a shelter and went off in pairs to collect things. We took evergreen branches and rested them against a stand of trees, and made a floor of branches and leaves over which we threw a scarf. The shelter took on a sort of igloo shape. It was relatively cozy, all things considered, and leaked minimally.

When we spoke in a group, everyone was positive and upbeat, voicing assurance that we would be rescued by morning for sure. The Garnet Hill folks would see that we had not checked out and come looking for us. But when we went off in pairs, we were not optimistic; it was only Sunday, and we weren't supposed to check out until Monday afternoon. We weren't expected back at work until Tuesday, and no one would be concerned if we didn't show up at work until Wednesday at the earliest, would they?

We periodically called for help. We thought that the most effective method was to stand in a circle facing out and *scream* for help simultaneously. After doing that for a while, we would retreat to our shelter. The only food we had were light snacks we'd brought for our "short walk in the woods." When night came we got quite cold as temperatures dropped and our clothes were damp from the drizzle. Making matters worse was the fact that we all had dressed for a short walk in the woods, with many of us wearing jeans and sweaters. To keep warm all six of us lay down together, spooning and alternating who was on the outside and thus the coldest. One of us had recently come back from a trip to Vietnam and, thankfully, she regaled us with stories of her adventures. Her tales were a godsend, keeping us distracted and holding creeping panic at bay.

Every half hour we climbed out, formed our circle, and yelled. When no reply came, we'd crawl back in, spoon, and search for distraction. Someone would posit reasons why we were likely to be rescued, with the rest of us silently thinking the opposite. This went on for hours. When we yelled, we would hear voices in the distance and would yell even louder, but there was no reply. At 10:30 PM we crawled out, formed our miserable circle, and called again. Still nothing. Then, in the distance, we saw a tiny point of light and heard voices. Oh, did we scream, and the light grew, as did other voices—and we were rescued.

When we hadn't returned to get our cars, folks had become concerned and alerted the authorities, who sent out a rescue team. They led us out of the woods in about twenty minutes. The rescuers said two things of note. First, even though they knew the woods very well, they would not have been able to lead us out without a compass. Second, and most chilling, was that it was a good thing it wasn't the previous weekend, when they had been sent out to rescue a hunter who had frozen to death. 🚶🚶

Jane R. Marcus: While this hike in the Adirondacks was not my first, in retrospect it may have marked the beginning of a hiking history that often includes an unexpected adventure. My husband, children—sometimes with waning enthusiasm—and I still enjoy a walk in the woods. I guess it's the unexpected adventure that often makes it worthwhile.

80

I Won't Tell Anybody If You Don't

Lost

Virginia Durso

I'm *so* happy to be home. It's a beautiful day—sunny, in the seventies. But today I just want to stay indoors, soak my aching muscles in a hot tub, eat and eat, sleep and sleep, and sit at my typewriter and tell you all about it. I'm happy because I slept in my own warm comfortable bed last night. It could easily have been a different story.

Three of us were lost in 234 square miles of the Siamese Ponds Wilderness Area. We had no warm clothing, no food, no map, and no compass. City kids ignorant of the equipment and precautions needed while hiking in the Adirondacks? Nope. Mark and I are Adirondack Mountain Club members. I was formerly a strong hiker, and am now a B or C hiker and old enough to know better. Glen, a friend of Mark's, was the third, and he's a strong hiker who loves to be out in the woods and enjoys an A, B, C, A+ or C– hike.

It was a perfect day, sunny and dry, not too warm. We decided to hike Peaked Mountain, a six-mile hike round-trip, with trail most of the way. From Peaked Mountain Pond you see Peaked Mountain just beyond; ascent would be by herd path and a ridge. This six-mile hike ended up taking us eighteen or nineteen miles and ten hours of almost steady walking at two miles per hour. Deduct an hour for lunch and quick rest stops before swarms of black flies encouraged us to be on our way. Some stops lasted only thirty seconds. We spit out black flies, sniffed black flies, swatted black flies, and cursed black flies. Even our lunch atop Peaked, which should have been a delightful interlude of views, rest, and refreshment, was cut short.

Where did we go wrong? We started out along Thirteenth Lake and gazed into clear water from a rock that would make a good diving rock en route home. We passed painted trillium; I've never seen such a profusion of spring beauty—great masses of pink everywhere. The trail was sparsely marked, but not difficult to follow. All was delightful as far as Peaked Mountain Pond. We bushwhacked up the mountain, taking herd paths where we found them. We climbed the rocks of the summit, enjoying good lookouts; views from the top were superb. Coming down we tried to retrace our steps, but lost them. But down is down, isn't it? We should eventually come to the fair-sized pond, shouldn't we? How could we miss it? We did. Since we had headed slightly east on ascending, we compensated by heading slightly west on descending. But we overcompensated—our second mistake. First mistake—no map or compass! We walked and walked and felt we should be down to the pond by now.

I felt we'd gone too far west; Glen felt we'd gone too far east. Mark was intent upon finding a stream to follow, and eventually we did find one running in the opposite direction from those we'd followed going up to the pond. We were at the far end of the pond, and this stream, if we followed it up, would lead us there. Our spirits revived. We crossed and recrossed it, sinking into muck, brushing away flies. We pushed aside scratchy lichen-covered branches. Finally the end was in sight— the end of the stream, that is. It petered out. Now what? A hill lay ahead. I felt we should continue, but we were too tired to climb if it was not the right direction, and no one could be sure. Mark suggested that we retrace and follow the stream down to where it became fuller because of its confluence with another stream— that must lead to a lake. Even if it was in the opposite direction, we stood a chance of seeing people or a shelter near a lake, and we could hike out along a trail and hitch a ride back.

On and on we went. If we could only gain height for a view, we might orient ourselves, but all we saw were trees and the stream. Yes, the stream was getting fuller. We felt better and plodded on. Ahead was a lake. What's this? The stream was slowing and meandering. We were on a former lake bottom—flat, mucky, and studded with intertwined branches of small dead trees. Impenetrable! We couldn't go ahead. Must we again retrace our steps? Must. We admitted it—we were lost. We were thirsty, tired, and discouraged. We started our long trek back. Soon we would get faster-flowing water to drink. Glen said, "I don't believe this"—his refrain for the rest of the trip. We wanted to rest, but the black flies wouldn't let us.

Soon we were able to drink and cool ourselves. We were making plans to spend the night in the woods. The temperature was expected to go into the low forties; we had no extra clothing. We spoke of building a fire and making smoke signals if we didn't get out the next day. But no one had matches. Besides, who would know we were lost? Not one of us would be missed—we had no appointments and hadn't told anyone where we were going. How embarrassing, anyway, to have to be rescued! We, who should have known better!

We thought we recognized a landmark, and our spirits lifted. We found a beaver pond. Was it the same one we had passed? We were so convinced it was that we fairly ran. After climbing around it, we were disappointed again. Glen thought he saw the top of Peaked Mountain, but we couldn't be sure. Oh, for the sight of people or a sign of people! Litter! A chewing gum wrapper! Silence. Each to his own thoughts. Glen: *I can't believe it.* Me: *We don't have any food—how long can we go without food?* I couldn't believe we would come to the point of starvation, however. Things like that happened only to others, so I started making light of it. *Glen and Mark, no sense in three people dying of starvation. When it comes time, you have my permission to take my life. You're young. I've lived a pretty full life.*

We walked on in silence, with me still contemplating the worst scenario. *Not much fat on me. Hope there's enough muscle. Don't forget the liver is the most nutritious part. And the heart and the kidneys.*

We were climbing large flat rocks in the middle of the stream, which was becoming really beautiful. The thought occurred to me, *They could be held for murder. They could say I died of starvation. No, better that I sign a statement: "Being of sound mind and body, I give permission, etc., having always wanted to die while climbing a mountain, I now wish to hasten that end in order that others may live. Signed ... "*

The sun was setting behind the mountain, and we started looking for a good place to spend the night. We made plans for the next day—go east and not deviate. The forecast was for sun, so we would have our "compass." Relying on our memories of maps and roads, we would eventually hit Route 28. We could have hiked for days before hitting it, however—*northeast* would have been the direction to take. We had twenty minutes before the sun went down, so we started tomorrow's tactic today and walked into our shadows. In ten minutes, I saw a body of water. "Do I see a lake?" Mark and Glen perked up.

Glen said, "Must be Thirteenth Lake." Our legs took on extra energy. Mark limped a little faster. We now had our first goal since the morning. *Maybe people, a trail, a shelter.* We found that we couldn't get to the lake, however, because it was surrounded by a large marsh. *Maybe it's Puffer Pond.* Suddenly, Glen pointed out a canoe. We found a spot nearer the pond to call out and ask what body of water this was. The boy in the canoe said that it was Hour Pond. He pointed to the shore and said, "Ask my father." We saw two tents, two men and a little girl. I plopped myself down near their fire, while the boys asked directions out.

The men told us that we were ten to twelve miles from our car. I couldn't go any farther. The men said that we were only an hour and a half from another parking area, but it was 7:00 PM and we feared that all the day hikers would have left by the time we got there. Glen said that if no one was there, he would hike the extra six miles and bring back our car. He hurried us—we must be out of the woods before dark! We had no flashlights, no time for rest. I struggled to keep him within sight. Mark was now limping badly in the rear. But, great joy, we knew where we were going!

It was the longest hour and a half, but a hopeful one. No one was at the lot, so Glen took his pack off and walked quickly away. It was dark, and Mark and I waited thankfully and patiently. I recalled a sign I'd seen in an orthopedist's office: "Life is either a great adventure or nothing." This was an adventure—one I do not care to repeat. 🏃

Originally published in the October/November 1987 Adirondac *magazine, a publication of the Adirondack Mountain Club, Inc. This abridged version is reprinted with permission of ADK, www.adk.org.*

*V*irginia Durso: *After high school I hated the confinement of work, so in 1938 I joined a water ballet group in Florida and made $7.50 a week! I was a swimmer in Billy Rose's Aquacade at the 1939–1940 World's Fair in New York and met my husband, a trombone player in the show band. I worked as a dancer in nightclubs, then graduated from college with a bachelor of science degree, becoming a food inspector for the New York State Department of Agriculture. Then I discovered the Adirondack Mountain Club and started hiking—until I was eighty-five.*

81

DREAMS AT SUCKER BROOK

THE GREATER WEB OF LIFE

Richard Sederquist

I'm dreaming about a bear trying to get at our food in the nylon sack overhanging the stream. His claws sing out as they cut through the air trying to sever the nylon line. The airy shrill sound of his swinging paw intensifies. Suddenly, I wake up. It's pitch black and dead quiet. My son's hand is on my shoulder. Jeff tells me there was a terrible screeching noise outside the tent.

Although I heard the same sound in my dream, or the sound started my dream, my mind interpreted it as my worst fear. We may have heard the cry of a saw-whet owl, a little guy with a big voice. I remember my good friend Bud, who knows everything about birds of prey, telling me about the saw-whet. In addition to a tooting mating sound, the characteristic call of the saw-whet has been compared to the sound of a metal saw being sharpened on a whet stone, hence the name. Fortunately, that's not as scary as a big black bear.

That happened to us for real when Jeff was fourteen. We had set up camp in a place well known for its bears. Bad decision! We went to sleep to the sounds of banging pots and pans and the screams from other campers as they attempted to discourage the marauders. It was almost humorous. I awoke with a start at 4:00 AM, the moon providing faint illumination. A giant shadow rose up in front of the tent, blocking the light. Then four claws proceeded to shred the bark on the nearest tree as the black bear ascended to cut the line supporting the food sack between two trees. With heart pounding I groped, turned a flashlight on the culprit, and screamed invectives.

Jeff awoke, more befuddled and alarmed than I from my current dream. He joined me in my tirade against a creature that could end our trip, three days wasted. Then, miracle of miracles, the bear spooked and came crashing backward down the tree, blocking the light again. Off he charged, never to be seen again that night. So much for any beauty rest; the night had ended. Morning came and the accounting—bears: seven food sacks missing; humans: three food sacks remaining. One of those was ours. The odds were stacked against us silly humans. Some of the campers went from tent to tent begging for food. How quickly we learn.

Jeff's mood was a little subdued; he kept nervously looking around without saying anything. After another long day the inevitable was descending. Night would arrive in a few hours. Our tent site was far away from the previous site, far from those screaming guys with the pots and pans. How could I relieve Jeff's anxiety? I decided on a half-truth, telling him that bears hate the smell of human urine. Jeff now had the power to cast out his demons. This was better than a garlic-and-crucifix vampire repellent! No bear would dare cross that line. We both slept like babies.

Here we are, twenty years later, camping off the Sucker Brook Trail on a small tributary stream that feeds the larger Sucker Brook in the Indian Lake region of the Adirondack Park. At night next to the stream, you can imagine a conversation. The cascading water sounds something between a "shish" and a party of people talking next door. As you drift off, the sound of the stream comes and goes, turning on and off as you drift back and forth between consciousness and sleep. You can actually tell when you have drifted off and come awake by the sudden "shish" of the stream where there was nothing before.

This morning we climb to the notch above to bushwhack through tangled woods to one of the local trailless summits. We've been working on the hundred highest peaks in New York. After the notch we come on a clearing and an unexpected sound, and are surprised to face a large buck deer in the clearing, which snorts at our approach. Being lulled by the beauty and community of all this, I pick up a twig and toss it at my new friend. He replies with another snort and an advance. We slowly retreat and give the clearing a wide berth. When we return, the buck spooks, breaking branches as he crashes through the woods. Hey, we all spook and change our direction when necessary.

Back at camp we talk about our adventures and the wildlife. Without my knowledge, that morning Jeff had secreted cans of beer in the stream. He slips away as I'm making supper. At twilight we're treated to yet another sight. Silently, gliding down through the trees, a great horned owl lands on a boulder in the middle of the stream. It stays there for twenty seconds or so; then, sensing our presence, it lifts effortlessly and glides downstream. Evening creeps in and leaves us with only the small circle of light from our candle lantern and the sounds of the stream. The guys with the pots and pans are not welcome tonight. The peace is sublime as we lie there listening to the cascades. Tomorrow we'll pack and trudge back for the long ride home, leaving the sounds and dreams of Sucker Brook behind.

We'll return again to these quiet out-of-the-way places. We have many more to visit, many more streams to lull us to sleep. I will lie in bed listening to the stream of my own consciousness, trying to make out the words of the stream's conversations. I will await the bear to steal in and take away my last bit of food. The sounds

Jeff Sederquist near Spectacle Pond. Photo by Richard Sederquist.

of the stream will come and go, turn on and off. That little stream in the woods will still be there, waiting for someone else to stop, and listen, and dream. A saw-whet will cry out and a great horned owl will glide in on silent wings. 👫

Reprinted with permission from the author. Stories appear in Hiking Out: Surviving Depression with Humor and Insight along the Way, *PublishingWorks, Exeter, New Hampshire, 2007.*

*R*ichard Sederquist: *Thirty years ago Ed Swift, friend and aspiring 46er, introduced me to the Adirondacks and became my spiritual guide out of depression. My wife and I completed the New England 4,000-footers; my son Jeff and I completed the New England Hundred Highest, the Catskill 35 in summer and winter, and have almost completed New York's Hundred Highest. That's where I left my blues, floating in deep space. I am 46er #1809.*

82

NORTHVILLE-PLACID TRAIL

TWO WOMEN ON THE TRAIL

Sally Hoy

Most sections of the Northville-Placid Trail can be done in a day hike, spotting cars at road crossings. That is how Barb Harris and I chose to do the 134-mile trail that extends through some of the most remote and pristine parts of the Adirondack Park.

Benson to Whitehouse. This sixteen-mile stretch is dotted with five pretty little lakes—Rock, Meco, Silver, Canary, and Mud. It is fairly flat, soft afoot, and sounds of white-throated sparrow, chickadees, loons, and other birds bring a smile to your face. Smells, too, abound in the forest here—earthiness, balsam and pine, damp leaves. Edible plants can be harvested here—puff balls, teaberry, wood sorrel. What is most memorable about this day is skinny-dipping with the loons in all five of those lakes. Loons like remote places far from humans, and when we joined them, I thought they would depart. Not so! I called to them and they swam closer, curious, particularly on Canary Pond. What a thrill! We did not worry about other hikers; only one came along near the end of the day. We encountered few hikers along the entire trail system, surprising because it is so accessible and a great place to explore. One trip is not enough, for there are many side trails to mountains and other water spots. We have even considered doing the trail in winter.

Whitehouse to Piseco Lake. Barb and I have been friends a long time, and she rarely complains on hikes. But from time to time, her feet give her problems. She has been to many orthopedic specialists, even had very expensive custom-made leather boots made, to no avail. This day she had on brand new boots and her feet were really talking to her by day's end. We even had to walk an extra two miles to the southernmost trailhead because a bridge washed out. One section involves a three-mile road walk off Route 8 by Piseco Community Hall and Oxbow Lake, and I'd insisted that we walk even the sections on county roads in the spirit of hiking the whole trail; perhaps one day these sections will be rerouted through forestland.

We arrived at Hamilton Lake Stream lean-to and had an early lunch so that Barb could shed her pack and rest her feet. I was carrying a present for Barb in my pack, a coconut marked with "Happy 50th Birthday," a milestone due in a few days. While she was at the privy, I put this coconut in a stuff sack in the bottom of her pack. Returning, she flung on her pack and exclaimed, "I feel better. This pack is so much lighter!" I was doubled over laughing and sorry I didn't have anyone to share my tale with. When we reached Route 8, we had the road walk and Barb's feet were unhappy. Feeling guilty, I suggested she wait at the community hall while I walk to the car. When I returned, I thought she would say something about the coconut. No comment.

I expected a call from her about the coconut. No call—she must be upset with me. The day before her birthday, however, she finally calls me and wildly exclaims, "I was repacking for my hike tomorrow, took out my stuff sack and it went 'clunk' on the table. I opened it and there's this coconut!"

"It took you a whole week to find that?" We've laughed about that many times and are now careful of leaving our packs unattended.

Piseco Lake to Wakely Dam. The plan was to hike this section in three days, continue on to Long Lake and hike three days to our final destination, Lake Placid. It didn't happen. The first day was hot and humid, and the infamous black flies attacked our ears and eyes, requiring bug nets. Lunch was pita bread with peanut butter and black fly for added protein. It rained, a welcome relief—black flies go away—so much so that we didn't don raingear, a mistake. This was a minimalist trip—we wore the same things for three days, but packed extra socks, rain jacket, sleeping bag, and food. When we reached the second night's destination, Barb's feet were looking like hamburger and her groin area was chafed. Walking in wet boots was the bane of her existence. She was convinced that she could not get to Wakely Dam the next day.

The Cedar Lakes area was so peaceful, a favorite of ours despite Barb's infirmities. We hung out our clothes to dry, made dinner, and met another family having a campfire. That night we watched an approaching storm and scrambled to get clothes off the line. What a light show! Thunder in the mountains seems to linger longer and bellow deep echoes. Flashes against the inky black night are much like silhouette cutouts of people. High winds could have taken our roof, but didn't. We would find out later that a tornado was in the Indian Lake area. So how did Barb manage to hike out to the Dam? Duct tape! Yes, we found another use for duct tape. As Dr. Seuss might have said:

> She had duct tape on her feet.
> She had duct tape on her seat.
> She had duct tape near her groin.
> She had duct tape that was sweet.

When we arrived at Wakely Dam, our campsite was in a shambles from the previous night's strong winds. We assessed Barb's blisters and chafing, and prudently cancelled the rest of the trip.

Long Lake to Lake Placid. I caught the Charlotte Ferry across Lake Champlain to Essex, New York, at 10:30 PM and drove to Lake Placid to pick up Barb at the end of the NP Trail. We spotted her car and drove to the Long Lake trailhead. It was after midnight, and we decided to sleep in the parking lot. I worried about getting run over, so we moved the car. A nearby streetlight shone brightly, so we tried sleeping in the car's shadow. Forget it. Morning wasn't far off, though, and a quick breakfast got us moving.

On Long Lake there are lean-tos I didn't know existed. Our first lean-to stop was too wet and muddy. Another mile up the lake, at Rodney Point, was a Boy Scout troop of fifteen! After tromping in our boots all day, neither of us wanted to return to the previous site, however. The scouts told us of another lean-to in half a mile that was occupied by one man. This lean-to was downhill from the trail on a lovely site above the lake.

We startled a muscular man who had a very large backpack resting against the lean-to. He stood very erect, but what caught our eyes immediately was the sight of his holstered gun around his hip. We said hello and quickly went off to a spring to pump water, primarily for the purpose of holding a powwow. "What do you think?" Barb asked.

Cold River, Northville-Placid Trail. Photo by Bill Ingersoll.

"Hey, the Boy Scouts are just down the path. Don't you think they'd come running if they heard gunshots?"

The man was a bit weird. We would discover that he was out for only one night and yet carried two of everything, "in case things failed," he said. That's two stoves, two headlamps, two rounds of ammo, two Therm-a-rest pads. But he was gracious enough to hang our bear bag. I was reminded of the time when four of us gals in New Hampshire passed an Appalachian Trail through-hiker sidearmed with a machete—we kept a wide berth. Characters of threatening appearance are seldom encountered on the trails, however.

In the morning we pressed on to Plumley's Point, a pretty little spot where Grace Hudowalski would carry birthday cakes fifteen miles to the "Mayor of Cold River," the celebrated hermit Noah John Rondeau. We snacked and pushed on to the Cold River area past Shattuck Clearing. This trail had been rerouted around blowdown and wet, Adirondack mud, so it was confusing. Across a suspension bridge over the Cold River, we bedded down in a lovely lean-to by the water's edge; moonlight glistened on the water as night brought in the dew.

Our next day's travel took us past Seward lean-to, a gorgeous place for swimming, with a natural chute near Miller's Falls. We visited the remnants of Noah John's hermitage, pretended to have tea with the "Mayor," and imagined what it must have been like to live there.

The first time I heard Barb screech about creatures was when she spent the night in my daughter's room with a cage of mice. Each lean-to had relatives of Mickey and Minnie who were active at night, scurrying across our packs looking for morsels. If you don't leave all compartments open on your pack, it may be full of holes in the morning! At the last lean-to we stayed, Barb was determined not to be near the critters, so under a starlit sky we slept in our bivy sacks on the beach at Duck Hole—a marvelous experience. 🏃

Sally Hoy: Outdoor experiences with my family gave me a deep appreciation of nature that I've passed on to my three children. Daughter Kate and I hiked the 46 together, she finishing at age thirteen; I went on to climb them in winter, #2924W. We continued climbing the Northeast 111. These experiences inspire us to be active in preserving what we hold dear. I served as chair of ADK's Glens Falls/Saratoga Chapter, am currently a director of the 46ers, and serve on the 46er Conservation Trust Committee.

83

MISADVENTURES ON CRANBERRY LAKE

ADK FALL OUTING IN THE REMOTE ADIRONDACKS

Kathy Disque

September 30 was a perfect fall day, clear and cool. For the Grass Pond Mountain hike our group of twelve met at the Ranger School in Wanakena and boarded a fifteen-passenger party boat for the ride across Cranberry Lake to the trailhead. As we crossed the lake in the 30° morning, the sun was reflected through the rising mist.

Our leader, Jamie, is an instructor at the Ranger School and knows these woods. We were lucky to have three other Wanakena residents with us. We were dropped off at the trailhead to Grass Pond, a 4.2-mile canoe carry from Cranberry Lake to Lows Lake. A short hike brought us to Chair Rock Creek; we could hear the water rushing as we approached. Heavy rains had turned Chair Rock Creek into a raging river. After leaders scouted up and downstream, they determined there was no safe way to cross the creek. We went with plan "B" and hiked to Darning Needle Pond; that hike follows Chair Rock Creek, but does not cross it. Everyone was just glad to be out enjoying a beautiful fall day.

We were hiking in the Five Ponds Wilderness, an area stretching from the north shore of Stillwater Reservoir north to Cranberry Lake and east to Lows Lake, one of the most remote parts of the Adirondacks. We discovered that the tributaries into Chair Rock Creek were also raging torrents; our hike was turning into an Outward Bound team-building exercise as we tried to figure out how to get our group with various skill levels safely across. We used downed logs from the forest floor to build makeshift bridges. With teamwork and wet feet, we reached Darning Needle Pond, ate lunch, and split into two groups; one headed back to the Cranberry Lake trailhead, and the other bushwhacked to the next pond.

I watched in awe as "Twinkle Toes June" hopped across rocks without getting any water in her boots, and I then slipped and slid in knee-deep water. The return was easier; the bridges had been built, and once your feet are wet, you don't worry—you just plow through. By 3:00 PM both groups were waiting by Cranberry Lake. A loon floats, keeping us company. Clouds had moved in and it was getting cooler. The boat arrived, and we put on all our layers; it was cold and the wind had picked up.

Halfway back across, the boat sputtered to a stop—out of gas. The only other boat in sight was a canoe. We tried the oars, but the wind was too strong; we had to drop anchor so we didn't get blown onto rocks. We flagged the canoe over and Sherm, a Wanakena local, slid off the party boat into the center of the canoe. They would drop him off at a lean-to that is a two-mile hike to Wanakena, he would hike home, get his boat and return—before dark, we hoped. We now understood how Gilligan felt when his four-hour cruise went awry.

It was cold and we saw rain falling to our north. People huddled under a large tarp trying to keep warm. I had an afghan wrapped around me for warmth, but it didn't help much. A boat appeared, and we lit a flare and signaled with an orange vest tied on a hiking pole. The boat turned toward Wanakena and away from us. We'd now been stranded for an hour, and the rain began.

Two boats appeared. We lit another flare and waved the orange vest. They saw us! We wouldn't have to wait for a freeze and walk out on ice. The two fishermen from Wanakena took charge. Another boat approached—Sherm headed back.

Later, as we approached the mouth of the Oswegatchie River, we saw the Wanakena Rock—a large rock with "Wanakena" painted on it. What a welcome sight! In spite of my "Adirondack Experience," I plan to return. 🏃

Kathy Disque: I have been an active member of the Onondaga Chapter of the Adirondack Mountain Club since 1996, served on the Executive Committee since 1998, and am an advocate of getting people to hike outside the High Peaks. I hike a great deal in the northwestern and west-central Adirondacks; my favorite is the hike to Beaver River on the Norridgewock Trail, which was so overgrown that I organized work groups to improve and maintain this trail.

84

TREADWAY IN OCTOBER

TREADWAY ANYTIME

Paul Dean and Lorraine Chirico Smith

Canoeing up Treadway Mountain? Well, not really, just part way there. Can't decide to canoe or hike? This Treadway "surf and turf" offers both. The twenty-minute paddle across Putnam Pond to the trailhead, besides saving five miles of a nine-mile hike, adds another element to an Adirondack outing. Columbus Day weekend is a perfect choice for this favorite trip in the Pharaoh Lake Wilderness Area. Eight of us canoe-hikers, accompanied by a Brittany spaniel named Annie, put our boats in at the launch site at the Putnam Pond Campground and began the paddle to the trail to Treadway's summit. Colors were at peak—brilliant oranges, reds, whites, and greens reflected in the shimmering blue waters. We hauled the canoes out of the water, dragged them from open view, and were ready for the "turf" half of our "surf and turf" trek.

The trail climbs gently through woods, intersecting with the trail to Grizzle Ocean and Clear Pond. Sunlight filtered through trees that had shed most of their leaves. It was one of those golden days when frequent sounds of contentment seem to echo, "There's nothing else we'd rather be doing."

This is leader Paul Dean's only hike. An Adirondack Mountain Club member for twenty years, he is working on his 46 on one mountain. "Why climb any other?" is his motto. Like bugs? Try Treadway in June. Like winter hikes? Try Treadway in January. Like taking only a half day in the mountains? Try Treadway any time.

The rest of the group included: Paul's wife, Marcia, a 46er the traditional way; Rosemary, who shared tales of her military training and her MREs (meals ready to eat); her twelve-year-old son Jason, whose youthful enthusiasm gave us all a lift; and Bill, our expert photographer. We thoroughly enjoyed each one among us— Joan, the musician, Joe, the retired teacher, and Lorraine, the power plant worker.

The trail climbed gradually for a 900-foot ascent. The mountain is a series of plateaus, some open with large outcrops of rosy quartz strewn about. Abundant blueberry bushes and sumac were bright crimson. A stream showed evidence of beaver activity. Trees thin out as the trail ascends, perhaps because of old burns or the rocky quartz terrain. The summit is U-shaped, with a dip in the ridge. A large trail marker shaped like a cross can be seen on the second summit. The trail drops down through a stand of large evergreens, and then we see the true summit, bare

Summit, Treadway Mountain. Photo by David White.

except for blueberry bushes. The Treadway summit is not one of the most challenging peaks to attain, but it is certainly one of the prettiest.

The marker at the rocky peak reads "End of Trail." We spread out, ate lunch, spent a long time wandering about taking pictures and sharing both our lunches and ourselves. The views showed us Pharaoh Lake and Rock Pond, distant High Peaks and the southern Adirondacks. Jason counted 118 peaks from the almost 360° visibility. Monarch butterflies fluttered around us, spearmint berries grew through cracks, blueberries were very sweet, and abundant huckleberries were past peak but fun to eat. Jason saw a deer.

This is a wonderful area to explore. Many ponds and small mountains give the day hiker or weeklong camper an abundance of activities from which to choose. The unanimous verdict on our Treadway canoe-hike was: this B-rated trip was an A+! 🏃

Originally published in the September/October 1995 Adirondac *magazine, a publication of the Adirondack Mountain Club, Inc. This abridged version is reprinted with permission of ADK, www.adk.org.*

L orraine Chirico Smith: In midlife I realized that for nature's joy to seep into my being, I had to walk it, hike it, bike it, climb it, swim it, paddle it—make it my own. At fifty I completed the 46 High Peaks, #3967; I climbed in winter the Catskill 35, and hike wherever I travel. I feel compelled to act to protect our precious world. Upon retiring, I started teaching visiting school groups at a New York State Environmental Center. I write about my experiences, communing with others who are on the same Path, to try to express what it is about nature that requires much preparation, much perspiration, and yields so much gratification and exhilaration. So much joy.

85

THE MYSTERIES OF 3,860' BLUE RIDGE

TRAILLESS EXPLORATIONS

Michael Patrick McLean

Have you been up Blue Ridge Mountain? Not the one opposite the Adirondack Museum—Blue Mountain—or the one in the Town of Waverly off Blue Mountain Road—Azure Mountain. It isn't Blue Ridge near Schroon Lake or Blue Ridge East or West south of Blue Mountain Lake. Look southwest of Lewey Mountain or northwest of Pillsbury Mountain, and maybe this largest "blue mountain" in the Adirondacks will reveal its mysteries, but it hides itself well.

I accompanied a Glens Falls–Saratoga Adirondack Mountain Club Chapter hike up Blue Ridge. The goal was the crash site of a 1944 C-46 U.S. Army transport plane along the mountain's eastern flank. We left the Jessup River Road following a well-defined hunters' path and soon came upon the swollen and chilly Miami River. The river bit at us with its coldness, depth, and current, but we braved on. The woods tried to confuse us, but we resisted and soon started hiking steeply upward along Fremont Brook. The sky grew darker, and sprinkles started falling as we came upon an old airplane door. We climbed directly up a steep mountain flank a few hundred feet with increasing snow cover and encountered the main crash. Only the sounds of increasing raindrops and wind were heard as we inspected the eerie, sixty-year-old debris. A memorial and a faded, torn American flag have been placed near a large section of fuselage. Three departed from Syracuse on September 19, 1944, and eleven months later their remains were found on Blue Ridge's steep eastern flank. Fog rolled in and the rain increased, so a summit quest would have to wait.

Two months later my wife, Cindy, and I attempted Blue Ridge again. On a warm, beautiful day we headed in from the Pillsbury Mountain trailhead. An old road goes to a former lumber camp, identified on maps as Lumber Camp 22. We couldn't locate the road, but identified Stony Creek and followed it—an absolute gem, with flowing waterfalls and sunshine falling through the leaves and sparkling in the green pools. The conditions were not a gem, however; rocks were very slippery, blowdown was bad, black flies and deer flies got thicker, and temperatures were too warm.

After two-plus hours of thick going, we ran into an old road, but it was too late to continue. We followed it down off the mountain. The summit of Blue Ridge had gently pushed us aside again. Descending by the road was a piece of cake, and we intersected the trail rather quickly, taking more than an hour off a descent via the creek; we made a mental note of this well-hidden intersection. Deer flies and black flies disappeared, and the going was so much easier on the maintained trail that we decided to run up Pillsbury with the remaining daylight. From the fire tower we noted how Blue Ridge blends in with the surrounding peaks, and we debate how far we had ascended—and vowed to return.

The following month we got an early start on a cloudy, cool day, headed up the Pillsbury Mountain trail to the intersection of the old road to Lumber Camp 22. We followed it to an old clearing where the camp obviously had been—we found an old refrigerator, old metal stove, glass bottles, odd bulky metal items that must have been used for logging, and lots of other trinkets. The mountain tried to distract us. We realized that we had spent over an hour exploring the area.

We bushwhacked uphill along Stony Brook for another half mile and came across a beautiful, several-acre, grassland/former beaver pond at 3,200 feet. The sun had come out, and we sat in tall grass with a great view of the true summit. I took out my fancy new GPS that I'd hand programmed with the coordinates of the summit, and it pointed us in a direction that was not at all toward the summit; the mountain had tried to turn us back again. Confused, we referred to the map, our compass, and our visual sense. Trusting our instincts, we shut off the GPS and set a 350° compass reading. An hour of quite open going and the occasional steep pitch got us to the wooded summit, where four pieces of faded survey tape greeted us. We sat in dry needles and listened to the wind whisper through the spruce and balsam, and then, amazingly, heard a very close call of a loon. He must be lost, too. We wondered how many others had been here and also discovered but a few of the mysteries and wonders of Blue Ridge Mountain. 🏃🏃

For biography of Michael Patrick McLean, see "A Sawtooth #1 Odyssey."

86

REFLECTIONS ON RAQUETTE LAKE

GROWING STRONGER IN MORE WAYS THAN ONE

Snapper Petta

I first traveled on Raquette Lake as a teen during the summer of 1969. Because of a death in a coworker's family, I was an emergency hire for my camp's Adirondack canoe trip program. I would return six years later to begin a relationship that opened new avenues for growth in my life. My initial glimpse of Pine Knot Point came as I walked across a frozen waterway I'd paddled six years earlier. It was a less than hospitable welcome—the air temperature hovered near zero, while cold arctic wind whipped our faces. I was going to Camp Huntington as part of SUNY Cortland's Recreation Department winter camp, to improve on my winter backcountry skills—and learn we did! We oriented ourselves via map and compass over the frozen vastness of Raquette Lake, and snowshoed and cross-country skied through snow-blanketed woods.

We learned far more than the activities would imply. First, we learned what it meant to work together. A gathering of individuals evolved into a cohesive unit that worked cooperatively to meet objectives, ranging from an orderly serving of meals, to plotting a route to lead us out of a confused state somewhere on Woods Point, to getting our equipment across the snow and ice for a night's encampment on Big Island. We learned that, to meet daily challenges, we needed to pool our resources and, when a decision was reached, we depended on each other to complete our task.

I learned a lot about myself. In my outdoor adventures I'd always thought of myself as a leader, someone who could make big decisions and then allow others to follow. It was an important discovery for me to realize that I didn't have to be at the forefront of all decision making; that it was possible to trust in the sound judgment of others, especially my peers. I'm convinced that this newfound trust and respect in the abilities of others led to my becoming a more valuable group member and, when necessary, a stronger group leader.

I looked forward with anticipation to a return trip to Camp Huntington as a student in the department's summer program. What a misnomer! "Summer" camp, for my class, began the third week in May. Summer conjures up images of warm, lazy days spent lying in the sun, but in May the lake water was just above freezing (the ice had only been off the lake for a few weeks), nights were cool, and when the sun was out no one wanted to lie under its warming rays. The reason? No one could strike up an amicable relationship with the region's seasonal host—the black fly. Still, the two weeks that lay ahead turned out to be an experience of a lifetime.

At the orientation meeting I still remember listening spellbound and intrigued while director, George Fuge, filled our ears with the history of Pine Knot Point and its famous residents and guests. Fuge introduced us to Adirondack literature and said that we were welcome to borrow volumes on Adirondack lore. A new world was opened to me. My snoring prevented bunkmates from getting their beauty sleep, so a bargain was struck—I'd give them an hour of sleep before turning out my own light. From then on, my nights were shared with Adirondack luminaries like William West Durant, the developer of Adirondack architecture and the original owner of Pine Knot Point, Seneca Ray Stoddard, the most famous of the early regional photographers, and Noah John Rondeau, hermit and mayor of Cold River (population, one). The region's history and its colorful cast of characters unfolded before my eager eyes as I pored through books.

Backcountry trips usually present people with challenges. Our group of ten possessed energy, enthusiasm, and commitment, and these qualities held us in good stead as our trip unfolded. We decided on a route that hadn't been attempted before—the traditional Tupper Lake to Raquette Lake journey with a side trip into Blue Mountain Lake, including day hikes to fire towers atop Kempshall and Blue Mountain. We were challenging ourselves to paddle, portage, and hike over one hundred miles into prevailing winds and against the water's flow, in six days; similar trips covered a third less distance and hiked to only one summit.

The first day brought its share of tribulations. Canoe partners were changed to enable our group to stay together; navigators adjusted to looking at inverted maps (traveling from north to south); everyone had to attune their muscles to paddling upstream against a healthy spring flow. Ten tired, black fly-bitten people camped at the lean-to where Stony Creek empties into the Raquette River, and the potential was there for our goals and dreams to come tumbling down; we were discouraged with our progress, tired from paddling upstream, and needed a morale-booster. I still marvel at how we didn't fall apart, but reached deeply into our personal reservoirs for strength.

Rather than griping, we banded together as a unit. We collected wintergreen, crushed the leaves, and boiled them in water. The oils released from the leafy mash floated to the surface, were skimmed off, and rubbed into aching muscles. We worked toward the benefit of everyone, instead of against our common cause—a scene we repeated many times as each day's challenges attempted to trip us up. We grew stronger as a family might. The rhythm of paddling into the wind and waves, the chore of crossing portage after muddy portage, the challenge of climbing mountains, and the daily job of setting up camp became easier as we worked with, and leaned upon, each other. We discovered that we could accomplish far more as a group than our individual efforts might attain. After our 105-mile journey we were no longer surprised at what we could accomplish. We knew that we had grown both physically and spiritually as individuals because of our joint energy and efforts. We had coalesced into a tight knit "family." Though unrelated by blood, we would always be joined together through spirit.

Years later, I am fortunate to be able to witness Cortland students as they grow and mature in the Raquette Lake program. As a member of the program staff, I've witnessed time after time the transformation that takes place in young people, from an individual concerned only with their own thoughts and problems to a contributing member of the trip group; it happens all the time. While today's canoes may be lighter, tents more spacious and packs better fitting, the personal discoveries, realizations, personal growth, and feeling of satisfaction at trip's end continue to play an important part in the lives of our students. 🏃

Snapper Petta: My dad introduced me to the out-of-doors, fishing and tramping the old woodlands of Long Island. Working in scout camps furthered my outdoor interests, and today I'm Director of Outdoor Programs for SUNY Oneonta. I've introduced my daughters and now my grandson to all that nature offers. I owned and operated my own guiding service throughout the 1990s and have served on both regional and state boards for various outdoor-oriented organizations.

87

FIRETOWER

A POEM

Will Nixon

Never mind your replacement, the airplane.
You've pulled lightning from the sky,
tickled your legs blue with St. Elmo's fire.
You've bathed in cold fog, shed icicles
like thousands of earrings. You've whistled
through hurricanes, watched meteors
scratch the black dome in every direction
without leaving a trace. You've ignored
wars. You couldn't name a president.
You've chaperoned two generations of trees.
You've tolerated thousands of visitors
climbing the zig-zag of your spine
to stand inside your empty square head
& believe they see what gods see.

For biography of Will Nixon, see "The High Peaks Bear, a Love Story."

Glossary

bivouac: Camping in the open with no shelter, or an improvised shelter.

bushwhacking: Off-trail hiking with map and compass.

cairn: A pile of stones that marks a summit or route.

col: A pass or low point between two adjacent peaks.

dike: A band of different-colored rock, usually with straight, well-defined sides, formed when igneous rock is intruded into existing rock.

gorp: "Good old raisins and peanuts," known as "gorp," is a homemade snack that hikers pack for quick energy. There are many variations on the ingredients.

herd path: Rough path without markers or maintenance, created by climbers.

hitch-ups: The elaborate boardwalks and trail work fastened to the cliffs and rocks to create a trail next to Avalanche Lake.

lean-to: A three-sided shelter with an overhanging roof and one open side.

post-hole: To sink deeply into snow with each step, requiring snowshoes.

slab: To traverse around a mountainside, along a river bank or other sloped area where footing is more difficult.

spruce hole: Often invisible large hole in the snow created by many feet of snow blanketing small spruce, whose branches create spaces below the snow surface.

snow: Eskimos have at least twenty words for different kinds of snow. Winter mountain climbers fully appreciate how each type is worthy of a separate word. Here are three of them:

Qaninerraq: Freshly fallen, soft snow. (Makes steep ascents difficult.)

Nepcalluk: Wet, sticky snow. (Sticks and adds weight to snowshoes.)

Meciqaq: Water-soaked snow. (Gathers in passes during thaws.)

SUGGESTIONS FOR FURTHER READING

Adirondack Mountain Club. Guides to Adirondack and Catskill trails, Forest Preserve Series: 8 volumes. Lake George, New York.

Brown, Phil, ed. *Bob Marshall in the Adirondacks.* Saranac Lake, New York: Lost
Pond Press, 2006.

Burnside, James R. *Exploring the 46 Adirondack High Peaks.* Schenectady, New
York: High Peaks Press, 1996.

Carson, Russell M.L. *Peaks and People of the Adirondacks.* Lake George, New York:
Adirondack Mountain Club, 1973.

Dunn, John M. *Winterwise: A Backpacker's Guide.* Lake George, New York: Adirondack Mountain Club, 1988.

Dunn, Russell. *Adirondack Waterfall Guide.* Hensonville, New York: Black Dome
Press, 2004.

Freeman, Jack. *Views from on High: Fire Tower Trails in the Adirondacks and
Catskills.* Lake George, New York: Adirondack Mountain Club, 2001.

Goodwin, Tony. *Ski and Snowshoe Trails in the Adirondacks.* Adirondack Mountain
Club, 2003.

Ingersoll, Bill. *Discover the Adirondacks* series. Barneveld, New York: Wild River
Press. Eleven four-season, multiuse Adirondack guidebooks.

Mesinger, Stuart F. *No Place I'd Rather Be.* Lake George, New York: Adirondack
Mountain Club, 2006.

Morrissey, Spencer. *The Other 54.* Lake Placid, New York: Dacksdescents Publish-
ing, 2007.

Rivezzi, Rose and Trithart, David. *Kids on the Trail.* Lake George, New York: Adirondack Mountain Club, 1997.

Slack, Nancy and Bell, Allison. *Adirondack Alpine Summits: An Ecological Field
Guide.* Lake George, New York: Adirondack Mountain Club, 2006.

Tefft, Tim, ed. *Of the Summits, of the Forests.* Morrisonville, New York: Adirondack
Forty-Sixers, 2001.

Wadsworth, Bruce. *An Adirondack Sampler: Day Hikes for All Seasons.* Lake George,
New York: Adirondack Mountain Club, 1996.

———. *An Adirondack Sampler: Backpacking Trips for All Seasons.* Lake George,
New York: Adirondack Mountain Club, 1996.

Weber, Sandra. *Mount Marcy: The High Peak of New York.* Fleischmanns, New York:
Purple Mountain Press, 2001.

White, Carol Stone. *Women with Altitude: Challenging the Adirondack High Peaks
in Winter.* Utica, New York: North Country Books, 2005.

Winkler, John. *A Bushwhacker's View of the Adirondacks.* Utica, New York: North
Country Books, 1995.

ABOUT THE EDITOR

Carol Stone White compiled and edited *Catskill Peak Experiences: Mountaineering Tales of Endurance, Survival, Exploration and Adventure from the Catskill 3500 Club*, published by Black Dome Press in 2008, and *Women with Altitude: Challenging the Adirondack High Peaks in Winter,* published by North Country Books in 2005. With her husband, David, she wrote *Catskill Day Hikes for All Seasons*, published by the Adirondack Mountain Club (ADK) in 2002. They are editors of ADK's comprehensive guidebook, *Catskill Trails*, Volume 8 of the Forest Preserve Series, for which they measured 345 miles of trails by surveying wheel.

Carol received the Susan B. Anthony Legacy Award in 2007 at the University of Rochester with polar explorer Ann Bancroft and long-distance cold-water swimmer Lynne Cox. They spoke on the theme "Daring the Impossible: Strong Women Take on the World," on how they draw attention to causes larger than their own ambitions.

The Whites are regular and winter Forty-Sixers, those who have climbed the 46 High Peaks of the Adirondacks, and Carol served from 2003–2007 on

Summit of Pyramid Peak. Gothics south face in background. Photo by David White.

the Forty-Sixers Executive Committee. They are members of the Adirondack Mountain Club and Dave is an ADK director. The Whites are regular and winter members of the Catskill 3500 Club, whose members have climbed the 35 peaks exceeding 3,500 feet in the Catskill Forest Preserve. Dave is membership chairman of that club, and Carol is conservation chair. They participate in trail maintenance and lead club hikes. In 2000 they became Northeastern USA 111ers, climbers of peaks that exceed 4,000 feet in New York and New England, and in 2006 they completed climbs in winter of the 48 White Mountains of New Hampshire. They have climbed eight of the 14,000-foot peaks in Colorado.

David is retired president of Community Computer Systems, and Carol's work was in politics and public policy. She was chairman of a village planning board for six years, followed by election as village trustee, serving as water commissioner. She was president of a Housing and Urban Development project to work with Boards of Realtors to ensure the fair marketing of housing. She was president of a city food bank, edited an inner-city periodical and fundraised for A Better Chance, a program promoting educational opportunity for inner-city youth. Carol was president of a regional committee to elect Hillary to the U.S. Senate, and as a congressional coordinator for Common Cause and president of a League of Women Voters chapter, wrote weekly columns on campaign finance reform, congressional reform, and defense issues. She is a tour guide for the Oneida Community Mansion House, markets fair trade handcrafts to benefit low-income artisans in developing countries, and is secretary of the Central New York Astronomy Club. 🐾

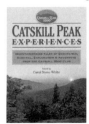
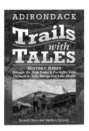
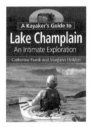
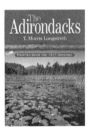
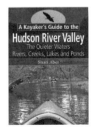
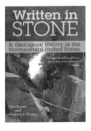

Adirondack Waterfall Guide

New York's Cool Cascades

By Russell Dunn, foreword by Bill Ingersoll. Paper, 4.5" × 7.5", 248 pages, 50 maps, 40 illustrations. ISBNs 9781883789374 / 1883789370 **$14.95**

● *Many of the falls are well known, but this is an especially good guide to cataracts that hikers might otherwise miss.* **Adirondack Life**

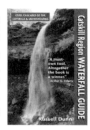

Catskill Region Waterfall Guide

Cool Cascades of the Catskills & Shawangunks

By Russell Dunn, foreword by Edward G. Henry, Refuge Manager, US Fish & Wildlife Service. Paper, 4.5" × 7.5", 248 pages, maps, illustrations. ISBNs 9781883789435 / 1883789435 **$14.95**

● *This book is highly recommended for its unique combination of appealing writing, strong research, intriguing destinations, and interesting history.* **Kaatskill Life**

Mohawk Region Waterfall Guide

From the Capital District to Cooperstown & Syracuse: The Mohawk and Schoharie Valleys, Helderbergs, and Leatherstocking Country

By Russell Dunn, foreword by Dr. Daniel A Driscoll, Chair of Land Preservation & Stewardship, Mohawk-Hudson Land Conservancy. Paper, 4.5" × 7.5", 336 pages, 90 illustrations & maps. ISBNs 9781883789541 / 1883789540 **$15.95**

Berkshire Region Waterfall Guide

Cool Cascades of the Berkshire & Taconic Mountains

By Russell Dunn. Paper, 4.5" × 7.5", 288 pages, 17 maps, 60 illustrations. ISBNs 9781883789602 / 1883789605 **$15.95**

Hudson Valley Waterfall Guide

From Saratoga and the Capital Region to the Highlands and Palisades

By Russell Dunn, foreword by Ned Sullivan, president, Scenic Hudson. Paper, 4.5" × 7.5"", 352 pages, maps & illustrations. ISBNs 9781883789473 / 1883789478 **$17.95**

● *Will very likely open eyes to a world of the outdoors that would have passed us by otherwise.* **Fred LeBrun, Times Union**

Trails with Tales

History Hikes through the Capital Region, Saratoga, Berkshires, Catskills & Hudson Valley

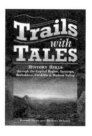

By Russell Dunn and Barbara Delaney, foreword by Karl Beard, National Park Service. Paper, 6" × 9", 304 pages, illustrations, 80 photos, 13 maps. ISBNs 9781883789480 / 1883789486 **$17.95**

● *This is a refreshing twist on the traditional guidebook.* **Adirondac**

OUTDOOR TITLES FROM BLACK DOME PRESS

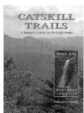

Catskill Trails Book One

A RANGER'S GUIDE TO THE HIGH PEAKS
Book One: The Northern Catskills

By Edward G. Henry. Paper, 5" × 7", 184 pages, photos, maps, keys to hikes. ISBNs 9781883789220 / 1883789222 **$14.95**

● *Mr. Henry has tried to get us to slow down, smell the flowers, and appreciate those "empty" miles between the trailhead and destination.* **TrailWalker**

Catskill Trails Book Two

A RANGER'S GUIDE TO THE HIGH PEAKS Book Two: The Central Catskills

By Edward G. Henry. Paper, 5" × 7", 184 pages, trail maps, photos, keys to hikes. ISBNs 9781883789237 / 1883789230 **$14.95**

So as you prepare for this season's Catskill hiking, I would add an eleventh to Edward Henry's ten Hiking Rules and Guidelines: pack and use Catskill Trails. **New York State Conservationist**

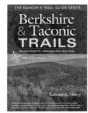

Berkshire & Taconic Trails

Massachusetts, Vermont and New York: The Ranger's Trail Guide Series

By Edward G. Henry. Paper, 5" × 7", 192 pages, maps, photographs, GPS coordinates. ISBNs 9781883789565 / 1883789567 **$14.95**

● *Serves as the perfect companion for Berkshire residents attempting to trek some of the most daunting but rewarding hikes in all of New England.* **Berkshire Record**

Gunks Trails

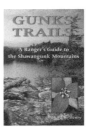

A RANGER'S GUIDE TO THE SHAWANGUNK MOUNTAINS

By Edward G. Henry. Paper, 5" × 7", 208 pages, photos, maps, key to hikes. ISBNs 9781883789381 /1883789389 **$14.95**

● *Occasionally ... a book comes our way that is different from our usual fare, yet so excellent that we would be remiss not to draw your attention to it.* **New York History**

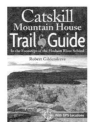

Catskill Mountain House Trail Guide

In the Footsteps of the Hudson River School

By Robert A. Gildersleeve, foreword by Dr. Robert Titus, professor of geology. Paper, 6" × 9", 240 pages, maps, illus., GPS locations, rare 19th-century maps & descriptions! ISBNs 9781883789459 / 1883789451 **$16.95**

Another Day, Another Dollar

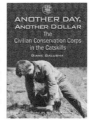

The Civilian Conservation Corps in the Catskills

By Diane Galusha, foreword by Bill McKibben. Paper, 6" × 9", 192 pages, 100 illustrations. ISBNs 9781883789619 / 1883789613 **$16.95**

● *Galusha's book is a delight to read, with a balance of national and local history. ... The research and interviews combine to offer a vivid picture of the CCC.* **Schenectady Daily Gazette**

WWW.BLACKDOMEPRESS.COM   800-513-9013

OUTDOOR TITLES FROM BLACK DOME PRESS

The Catskills

By T. Morris Longstreth. Paper, 5.5" × 8", 336 pages, 33 photographs, map.
ISBNs 9781883789367 / 1883789362 **$16.95**

● *A delightful telling of the author's 1917 trek through the Catskill Mountains …
filled with observations of nature and human nature that stimulate both
senses and mind.* **TrailWalker**

John Burroughs

An American Naturalist

By Edward J. Renehan, Jr. Paper, 6" × 9", 368 pages, photos.
ISBNs 9781883789169 / 1883789168 **$19.95**

● *In this thoughtful biography we are shown the once sainted "Sage of Slabsides"
as a flesh-and-blood traveler in a now-vanished world.*
The New York Times Sunday Book Review

Rise and Fall of the Taconic Mountains

A Geological History of Eastern New York

By Donald W. Fisher, NYS Paleontologist Emeritus, in collaboration with
Stephen L. Nightingale, foreword by Dr. Robert Fakundiny, NYS Geologist
Emeritus. Paper, 8" × 11", 192 pages, 140 maps, photos & illustrations, full-
color fold-out map of the geological formations of Columbia County.
ISBNs 9781883789527 / 1883789524 **$24.95**

Catskill Park

Inside the Blue Line: The Forest Preserve and Mountain Communities of America's First Wilderness

By Norman J. Van Valkenburgh & Christopher W. Olney. Featuring the
photography of Thomas Teich, foreword by forest historian Dr. Michael Kudish.
Paper, 8.5" × 11", 208 pages, maps, photos & illustrations, 32-page color section!
ISBNs 9781883789428 / 1883789427 **$21.95**

Kaaterskill Clove

Where Nature Met Art

By Raymond Beecher, Greene County Historian. Paper, 8.5" × 10", 224 pages,
maps, photos and illustrations. ISBNs 9781883789411 / 1883789419 **$24.95**

● *In their authoritative and well-researched volume, Van Valkenburgh and
Olney have paid fitting tribute to an irreplaceable part of our national heritage.*
John Adams, National Resources Defense Council

American Wilderness

The Story of the Hudson River School of Painting

By Barbara Babcock Millhouse, foreword by Kevin Avery, The Metropolitan
Museum of Art. Paper, 8.5" × 9.25", 208 pages, 64 illustrations (43 full-color
paintings!). ISBNs 9781883789572 / 1883789575 **$25.95**

● *Books devoted to the Hudson River School today are legion, but none that
I know quite performs the service that this one does, and so entertainingly.*
Kevin J. Avery, The Metropolitan Museum of Art